Principles Trump Diagrams

The Four ICSM Principles

1. Stakeholder value-based guidance.
2. Incremental commitment and accountability.
3. Concurrent multi-discipline engineering
4. Evidence and risk-based decisions.

Risk Meta-Principle of Balance: Balancing the risk of doing too little and the risk of doing too much will generally find a middle course sweet spot that is about the best you can do.

Theory W (Win-Win) Success Theorem: *A system will succeed if and only if it makes winners of its success-critical stakeholders.*

System Success Realization Theorem: *Making winners of your success-critical stakeholders requires:*

1. Identifying all of the success-critical stakeholders.
2. Understanding how each stakeholder wants to win.
3. Having the success-critical stakeholders negotiate among themselves a win-win set of product and process plans.
4. Controlling progress toward the negotiated win-win realization, including adapting it to change.

The Incremental Commitment Spiral Model

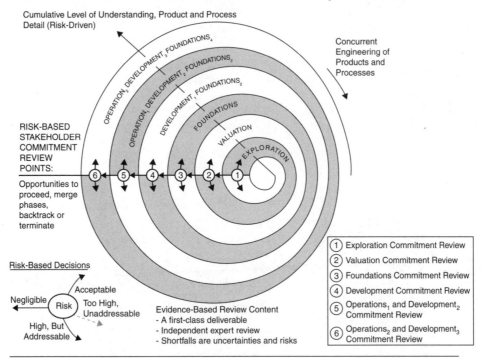

Cumulative Level of Understanding, Product and Process Detail (Risk-Driven)

Concurrent Engineering of Products and Processes

RISK-BASED STAKEHOLDER COMMITMENT REVIEW POINTS:

Opportunities to proceed, merge phases, backtrack or terminate

Risk-Based Decisions

Negligible — Risk — Acceptable / Too High, Unaddressable / High, But Addressable

Evidence-Based Review Content
- A first-class deliverable
- Independent expert review
- Shortfalls are uncertainties and risks

1. Exploration Commitment Review
2. Valuation Commitment Review
3. Foundations Commitment Review
4. Development Commitment Review
5. Operations₁ and Development₂ Commitment Review
6. Operations₂ and Development₃ Commitment Review

Praise for *The Incremental Commitment Spiral Model*

"*The Incremental Commitment Spiral Model* is an extraordinary work. Boehm and his colleagues have succeeded in creating a readable, practical, and eminently usable resource for the practicing systems engineer. . . . ICSM embodies systems thinking and engineering principles and best practices using real-life examples from many different application domains. This is exactly the kind of treatment that an engineer needs to translate the book's considerable wisdom into practical on-the-job solutions."

—George Rebovich, Jr., Director, Systems Engineering Practice Office, The MITRE Corporation

"One might think of this new book as an update of the old (1988) Spiral Model, but it is actually much more than that. It is a ground-breaking treatment that expertly blends together four specific and key principles, risk–opportunity management, the use of existing assets and processes, and lessons learned from both success and failure examples and case studies. This extraordinary treatise will very likely lead to improvements in many of the current software development approaches and achieve the authors' intent 'to better integrate the hardware, software, and human factors aspects of such systems, to provide value to the users as quickly as possible, and to handle the increasingly rapid pace of change.' If one is looking for specific ways to move ahead, use this book and its well-articulated advancements in the state-of-the-art."

—Dr. Howard Eisner, Professor Emeritus and Distinguished Research Professor, George Washington University

"Dr. Boehm and his coauthors have integrated a wealth of field experience in many domains and created a new kind of life cycle, one that you have to construct based on the constraints and objectives of the project. It is based on actively trading off risks and demonstrating progress by showing actual products, not paper substitutes. And the model applies to everything we build, not just software and conceptual systems, but also to hardware, buildings, and garden plots. We have long needed this experience-based critical thinking, this summative and original work, that will help us avoid chronic systems development problems (late, over-budget, doesn't work) and instead build new life cycles matched to the circumstances of the real world."

—Stan Rifkin, Principal, Master Systems

"Barry Boehm and his colleagues have created a practical methodology built upon the one fundamental truth that runs through all competitive strategies: The organization with the clearest view of cold, brutal reality wins. Uniquely, their methodology at every stage incorporates the coldest reality of them all—the customer's willingness to continue paying, given where the project is today and where it is likely ever to be."

—Chet Richards, author of *Certain to Win: The Strategy of John Boyd Applied to Business*

"I really like the concept of the ICSM and have been using some of the principles in my work over the past few years. This book has the potential to be a winner!"

—Hillary Sillito, INCOSE Fellow, Visiting Professor University of Bristol, formerly Thales UK Director of Systems Engineering

"*The Incremental Commitment Spiral Model* deftly combines aspects of the formerly isolated major systems approaches of systems engineering, lean, and agile. It also addresses perhaps the widest span of system sizes and time scales yet. Two kinds of systems enterprises especially need this capability: those at the 'heavy' end where lean and agile have had little impact to date, and those that deal with a wide span of system scales. Both will find in the ICSM's combination of systems approaches a productive and quality advantage that using any one approach in isolation cannot touch."

—James Maxwell Sutton, President, Lean Systems Society and Shingo Prize winner

"The potential impact of this book cannot be overstressed. Software-intensive systems that are not adequately engineered and managed do not adequately evolve over the systems life cycle. The beauty of this book is that it describes an incremental capability decision path for being successful in developing and acquiring complex systems that are effective, resilient, and affordable with respect to meeting stakeholders' needs. I highly recommend this book as a 'must read' for people directly involved in the development, acquisition, and management of software-intensive systems."

—Dr. Kenneth E. Nidiffer, Director of Strategic Plans for Government Programs, Software Engineering Institute, Carnegie Mellon University

"This text provides a significant advance in the continuing work of the authors to evolve the spiral model by integrating it with the incremental definition and the incremental development and evolution life-cycle stages. Case studies illustrate how application of the four principles and the Fundamental Systems Success Theorem provides a framework that advances previous work. Emphasis is placed throughout on risk-based analysis and decision making. The text concludes with guidance for applying ICSM in your organization plus some helpful appendices. We concur with the authors' statement: 'we are confident that this incarnation of the spiral model will be useful for a long time to come.'"

—Dick Fairley, PhD, Software and Systems Engineering Associates (S2EA)

The Incremental Commitment Spiral Model

The Incremental Commitment Spiral Model

Principles and Practices for Successful Systems and Software

BARRY BOEHM

JO ANN LANE

SUPANNIKA KOOLMANOJWONG

RICHARD TURNER

✦ Addison-Wesley

Upper Saddle River, NJ ▪ Boston ▪ Indianapolis ▪ San Francisco
New York ▪ Toronto ▪ Montreal ▪ London ▪ Munich ▪ Paris ▪ Madrid
Capetown ▪ Sydney ▪ Tokyo ▪ Singapore ▪ Mexico City

Many of the designations used by manufacturers and sellers to distinguish their products are claimed as trademarks. Where those designations appear in this book, and the publisher was aware of a trademark claim, the designations have been printed with initial capital letters or in all capitals.

The authors and publisher have taken care in the preparation of this book, but make no expressed or implied warranty of any kind and assume no responsibility for errors or omissions. No liability is assumed for incidental or consequential damages in connection with or arising out of the use of the information or programs contained herein.

For information about buying this title in bulk quantities, or for special sales opportunities (which may include electronic versions; custom cover designs; and content particular to your business, training goals, marketing focus, or branding interests), please contact our corporate sales department at corpsales@pearsoned.com or (800) 382-3419.

For government sales inquiries, please contact governmentsales@pearsoned.com.

For questions about sales outside the U.S., please contact international@pearsoned.com.

Visit us on the Web: informit.com/aw

Library of Congress Cataloging-in-Publication Data

Boehm, Barry W.
  The incremental commitment spiral model : principles and practices for successful systems and software / Barry Boehm, Jo Ann Lane, Supannika Koolmanojwong, Richard Turner.
      pages   cm
  Includes bibliographical references and index.
  ISBN-13: 978-0-321-80822-6 (pbk. : alk. paper)
  ISBN-10: 0-321-80822-3 (pbk. : alk. paper)
  1. Computer software—Development. 2. Continuous improvement process. I. Koolmanojwong, Supannika II. Lane, Jo Ann. III. Turner, Richard, 1954 August 18-. IV. Title.
  QA76.76.D47B635 2014
  005.1—dc23   2014006606

ISBN-13: 978-0-321-80822-6
ISBN-10: 0-321-80822-3
Text printed in the United States on recycled paper at RR Donnelley in Crawfordsville, Indiana.
First printing, May 2014

Contents

Foreword

Developers, thinkers, and writers have wrestled since the 1960s with process models for building software, including my own 1975 simple-minded "Plan to throw one away; you will anyhow." Practitioners in the software development discipline early learned that a patterned development is more likely to succeed than a chaotic one, at any size. Hence, the emergence of process models.

I am firmly convinced that the model set forth in this book is by far the best anyone has developed. First proposed by Boehm in 1988, it was even then the fruit of much thought and a rich trove of practical experience. In the almost 30 years since its introduction, the Incremental Commitment Spiral Model has grown and evolved through actual use in many projects, and through systematic thought. It has been extended from software to systems, and to the larger life cycle.

The most important augmentation of the original spiral model has been the addition of formal, cold-eyed assessments of risk at the various checkpoints. A second important addition is the explicit prescription that the stakeholders regularly and boldly consider abandoning the project. To paraphrase this dictate: "**Plan to consider throwing the project away; you may need to consider that anyhow.**" The Preface lists other ways the model has grown.

The work presented in this book demands and repays careful study. The Introduction sets forth the basic concepts of the model and the experienced-based motivations for each refinement. Since what is treated is not itself a model but a model generator, it can be flexibly adapted for projects large and small, long and short. Such adaptation requires thinking, of course.

The organization of the book into individual, self-contained parts suggests the mode of study. Students with no project experience can manage the Introduction and profit from it. The more sophisticated later parts will come to life for those practitioners who have experienced both successful and unsuccessful projects, and who want to ensure that their subsequent ventures are successful ones. They may want to ponder each part as a chunk, fleshing out and coloring the ideas and recommendations with their own experiences.

—Frederick P. Brooks, Jr.
  author, *The Design of Design*

Preface

This book describes a way to be successful in an increasingly challenging endeavor: developing systems that are effective, resilient, and affordable with respect to meeting stakeholders' needs. Most people would prefer to be part of creating a successful system. Rumor has it, however, that some people would rather deliver an unsuccessful system so that they can continue being paid to make it successful; rumor also doubts those people will read this book.

We have been studying and experimenting with approaches for creating successful systems for many years and have seen constant evolution in system capability, content, and context. The systems we worked on were initially hardware items such as radios, power supplies, airplanes, and rockets. As time went on, the systems became more software intensive. For example, in some classes of airplanes, the functionality performed by software grew from 8% in 1960 to 80% in 2000. Both now and for the foreseeable future, most systems must interact with other independently evolving systems to help provide additional functionality and flexibility. Even more important, precisely because it has often been overlooked, is the increasing role that humans are playing as system elements, as the enterprise is viewed as a holistic interdisciplinary entity. Perhaps the farthest-reaching change is that so many traditional stand-alone hardware devices need to cope not only with software, but also with living in an Internet of Things, preserving cybersecurity, and adjudicating among human users and smart autonomous agents.

The Incremental Commitment Spiral Model (ICSM) is the result of our efforts to better integrate the hardware, software, and human factors aspects of such systems; to provide value to the users as quickly as possible; and to handle the increasingly rapid pace of change. While the ICSM's pedigree lies in Barry's spiral concept first articulated in 1988, this new version draws on more than 20 years of experience helping people deal with the fact that the original version was too easy to misinterpret. The ICSM is both more general and more specific than the original spiral. It covers more of the life cycle, addresses not only software projects but also cyber–physical–human systems and enterprises, and is adaptable to most development endeavors. At the same time, it is much more specific about how to implement the principles and activities.

The ICSM is not a single, one-size-fits-all process. It is actually a process generator that steers your process in different directions, depending on your particular circumstances. In this way, it can help you adapt your life-cycle strategies and processes to your sources of change. It also supports more rapid system development and evolution through concurrent engineering, enabling you to develop and evolve systems more rapidly and to avoid obsolescence.

If things aren't changing much in your domain, and you already have a way to create successful systems, you should keep on using it. But you will be in a shrinking minority as the 21st-century pace of change accelerates. When you find that your processes are out of step with your needs, we believe you will find the ICSM helpful.

Who Can Benefit from Reading This Book?

The book's contents can help you if you face one or more of the following situations:

- Your projects frequently overrun their budgets and schedule.
- Your projects have a lot of late rework or technical debt.
- Your delivered systems are hard to maintain.
- Your organization uses a one-size-fits all process for a variety of systems.
- Your systems need to succeed in situations involving rapid change, emergent requirements, high levels of assurance, or some combination of those.
- Your systems must operate with other complex, networked systems.

Managers and executives stuck in one-size-fits-all decision sequences will find new possibilities and begin to understand their new roles in successful 21st-century development. Practitioners of all development-related disciplines will find a unified way to approach a broad variety of projects, improve their collaboration, respond more agilely to the changing needs of stakeholders, and better quantify and demonstrate progress to managers and executives. Academics will gain a source of information to replace or enhance the way they educate developers and managers, as well as fertile areas for research and study.

As one-step, total-makeover corporate process changes can be risky, this book provides a way for organizations or projects to incrementally experiment with the ICSM's key practices and to evolve toward process models better suited to their needs and competitive environment.

An Electronic Process Guide (EPG), available on the book's companion website (http://csse.usc.edu/ICSM), contains guidelines, subprocesses, and templates that facilitate ICSM adoption. The EPG also supports this volume's use as a textbook for a capstone project course in systems or software engineering. USC has offered such a course since 1995, spanning and evolving across more than 200 real-client projects and 2000 students.

How Is the Book Organized?

The book generally flows from *why*, moves to *what*, and then on to *how*, with a bit of *how much* in between. It begins with a **Prologue**—a cautionary tale drawn from ancient mythology, but highly relevant to 21st-century system developers.

Once suitably enlightened, the reader will find a one-chapter **Introduction** describing our rationale for constructing the ICSM and a *high-level, self-contained overview* of ICSM fundamentals and use. System development stakeholders (e.g., users, developers, acquirers), executives, and managers may obtain a big-picture understanding of the ICSM, and find the summary to be food for thought and action in managing the uncertainties of modern complex product or system development. Readers who would prefer to start by exploring a particular aspect of the ICSM can generally use the Contents list or Index to find and address it in detail, but will often find it useful to refer back to the Introduction for overall context.

Part I provides detailed discussions of the *four key ICSM principles* and explains why they are critical. Each chapter in Part I begins with a failure story and a success story, illustrating the need for and application of the principle, followed by its key underlying practices. Part I completes the *why* part of the book begun in the Prologue and continued in the early part of the Introduction.

Parts II and III explain the *phases and stages* that provide the framework for ICSM's process generation. They introduce the *case study* that we use to illustrate how the stages and phases of the ICSM support success. This case study uses a next-generation medical device—an example of an advanced cyber–physical–human system with the inherent challenges of assuring safety, usability, and interoperability with other devices and systems—to lead the reader (and the medical device team) through the individual stages and phases of the ICSM. Parts II and III contain the majority of the *what* information, and a bit of the *how*.

Part IV completes the *how* and *how much* information. It supports implementation of the ICSM through *phase-combining patterns* and a set of *common cases* encountered in applying the risk-based phase decisions. There is information on adapting the ICSM to a specific project or environment, and an exploration of how its risk-driven, adaptive framework acts as a unifying element to support the effective application of existing practices. Part IV also provides guidance on applying some *key practices* that must be adapted somewhat for ICSM, and ends with an afterword that describes how we intend to evolve the ICSM with help from you, the reader.

The **Appendices** provide additional information on the *tools* developed specifically for ICSM activities, *mappings* of the ICSM to widely used process model and standards, and a comprehensive *bibliography*.

As stated earlier, the **Companion Website** to the book (http://csse.usc.edu/ICSM) provides the *EPG* and other *automated tools*, along with updates, examples, discussions, and *useful classroom materials*. The website is the primary place to find up-to-date information concerning the ICSM and its use, including white papers and guides for ICSM application in particular domains. While most of the material on the site is free, on occasion there may be material for sale. For those cases, the site is linked to and supported by Addison-Wesley and InformIT to provide an easy means to purchase those materials as well as other books of interest to the readers.

Who Helped Us Write the Book?

The organization and content of the ICSM have benefited significantly from our participation in three major efforts to provide improved guidelines for systems and software practice and education:

- The U.S. National Research Council's *Human–System Integration in the System Development Process* study
- The international efforts to define educational and practice guidelines that better integrate software, hardware, and human systems engineering—the *Graduate Software Engineering Reference Curriculum*
- The *Systems Engineering Body of Knowledge* and *Graduate Reference Curriculum for Systems Engineering*

These not only helped improve the ICSM, but also established its compatibility with these reference guidelines, along with co-evolving guidelines such as the IEEE-CS and ISO/IEC's *Software Engineering Body of Knowledge* and *INCOSE Systems Engineering Handbook*.

Funding for much of the initial work on the ICSM was provided through the Systems Engineering Research Center—a U.S. Department of Defense university-affiliated research center. In particular, Kristen Baldwin, Principal Deputy in the Office of the Deputy Assistant Secretary of Defense for Systems Engineering, provided early vision, guidance, and resources to the authors.

The following reviewers provided excellent advice and feedback on early versions of the book: Ove Armbrust, Tom DeMarco, Donald Firesmith, Tom Gilb, Paul Grünbacher, Liguo Huang, DeWitt Latimer IV, Bud Lawson, Jürgen Münch, George Rebovich, Jr., Neil Siegel, Hillary Sillitto, Qing Wang, Da Yang, and Wen Zhang.

The authors have gained numerous insights from collaborations and workshops with our Industrial Affiliate members, including:

Aerospace Corporation: Wanda Austin, Kirstie Bellman, Myron Hecht, Judy Kerner, Eberhardt Rechtin Marilee Wheaton

Agile Alliance: Kent Beck, Alistair Cockburn, Jim Highsmith, Ken Schwaber

AgileTek: John Manzo

AT&T: Larry Bernstein

BAE Systems: Jim Cain, Gan Wang

Bellcore: Stuart Glickman

Boeing: Ray Carnes, Marilynn Goo, Tim Peters, Shawn Rahmani, Bill Schoening, David Sharp

C-Bridge: Charles Leinbach

Cisco: Sunita Chulani, Steve Fraser

CMU-SEI: Roger Bate, Paul Clements, Steve Cross, Bill Curtis, Larry Druffel, John Goodenough, Watts Humphrey, Paul Nielsen

Construx, Inc.: Steve McConnell

Cubic Corporation: Mike Elcan

EDS: Mike Sweeney

Fraunhofer-IESE: Dieter Rombach

Fraunhofer-Maryland: Vic Basili, Forrest Shull, Marvin Zelkowitz

Galorath: Dan Galorath, Denton Tarbet

GE Systems: Paul Rook

General Dynamics: Michael Diaz

Group Systems: Bob Briggs

Hughes: Elliot Axelband

IBM/Rational: Tim Bohn, Grady Booch, Peter Haumer, Ivar Jacobson, Per Kroll, Bruce McIsaac, Philippe Kruchten, Walker Royce

Intelligent Systems: Azad Madni

ISCAS: Mingshu Li, Qing Wang, Ye Yang

ITT/Quanterion: Tom McGibbon

JPL: Jairus Hihn, Kenneth Meyer, Robert Tausworthe

Lockheed Martin: Sandy Friedenthal, John Gaffney, Gary Hafen, Garry Roedler

Master Systems: Stan Rifkin

Microsoft: Apurva Jain

MITRE: Judith Dahmann, George Rebovich

Motorola: Dave Dorenbos, Nancy Eickelmann, Arnold Pittler, Allan Willey

Naval Postgraduate School: Ray Madachy

NICTA: Ross Jeffery

Northrop Grumman/TRW: Frank Belz, George Friedman, Rick Hefner, Steve Jacobs, Alan Levin, Fred Manthey, Maria Penedo, Winston Royce, Rick Selby, Neil Siegel

OGR Systems: Kevin Forsberg

Price Systems: Arlene Minkiewicz, David Seaver

Raytheon: Anthony Peterson, Quentin Redman, John Rieff, Gary Thomas

RCI: Don Reifer

SAIC: Dick Fitzer, Tony Jordano, Beverly Kitaoka, Gabriel Lengua, Dick Stutzke

San Diego State University: Teresa Larsen

Softstar Systems: Dan Ligett

Software Metrics: Betsy Clark, Brad Clark

Stevens Institute: Art Pyster

Teledyne Brown Engineering: Douglas Smith

University of Massachusetts: Lori Clarke, Lee Osterweil

University of Texas: Dewayne Perry

University of Virginia: Kevin Sullivan

Wellpoint: Adam Kohl

Xerox: Peter Hantos, Jason Ho

Finally, the authors are grateful for the support of their partners in life, who put up with working weekends, late nights, unexpected travel, and all of the household inconveniences that writing books entail. To Sharla, Mike, Sohrab, and Jo—our best friends, greatest inspirations, sharpest critics, and truest loves—our heartfelt thanks. We love you.

About the Authors

Barry Boehm developed a conceptual version of the spiral model at TRW in 1978, but only in 1981 was he able to employ it successfully, leading the development of a corporate TRW software development environment. Since the formal publication of this model in 1988, he and his colleagues have devoted extensive efforts to clarifying and evolving it through several intermediate versions into the ICSM. Dr. Boehm is the USC Distinguished Professor of Computer Sciences, Industrial and Systems Engineering, and Astronautics; the TRW Professor of Software Engineering; the Chief Scientist of the DoD–Stevens–USC Systems Engineering Research Center; and the Founding Director of the USC Center for Systems and Software Engineering. He was director of DARPA-ISTO for 1989–1992, at TRW for 1973–1989, at Rand Corporation for 1959–1973, and at General Dynamics for 1955–1959. Dr. Boehm is a Fellow of the primary professional societies in computing (ACM), aerospace (AIAA), electronics (IEEE), systems engineering (INCOSE), and lean and agile development (LSS), and a member of the U.S. National Academy of Engineering.

Jo Ann Lane is currently the systems engineering Co-Director of the University of Southern California Center for Systems and Software Engineering, a member of the Systems Engineering Research Center (SERC) Research Council representing the system of systems research area, and emeritus professor of computer science at San Diego State University. Her current areas of research include system of systems engineering, system affordability, expediting systems engineering, balancing lean and agile techniques with technical debt, and innovation in systems engineering. Previous publications include more than 50 journal articles and conference papers. In addition, Dr. Lane was co-author of the 2008 Department of Defense's *Systems Engineering Guide for Systems of Systems* and a contributor to the *Systems Engineering Body of Knowledge* (SEBoK). Prior to her current work in academia, she was a Vice President in SAIC's Healthcare and Software and Systems Integration groups.

Supannika Koolmanojwong is a faculty member and researcher at the University of Southern California Center for Systems and Software Engineering. Her primary research areas are systems and software process modeling, software process improvement, software process quality assurance, software metrics and measurement, agile and lean software development and expediting systems engineering. She is a certified ScrumMaster and a certified Product Owner. Prior to joining USC, Dr. Koolmanojwong was a software engineer and a RUP/OpenUp Content Developer at IBM RationalSoftware Group.

Richard Turner has more than 30 years of experience in systems, software, and acquisition engineering. He is currently a Distinguished Service Professor at the Stevens Institute of Technology in Hoboken, New Jersey, and a Principal Investigator with the Systems Engineering Research Center. Although on the author team for CMMI, Dr. Turner is now active in the agile, lean, and Kanban communities. He is currently studying agility and lean approaches as a means to solve large-systems issues. Dr. Turner is a member of the Executive Committee of the NDIA/AFEI Agile for Defense Adoption Proponent Team, is a member of the INCOSE Agile SE Working Group, and was an author of the groundbreaking IEEE Computer Society/ PMI Software Extension for the Guide to the PMBOK that spans the gap between traditional and agile approaches. He is a Fellow of the Lean Systems Society, a Golden Core awardee of the IEEE Computer Society, and co-author of three other books: *Balancing Agility and Discipline: A Guide for the Perplexed*, co-written with Barry Boehm; *CMMI Survival Guide: Just Enough Process Improvement*, co-authored with Suzanne Garcia; and *CMMI Distilled*.

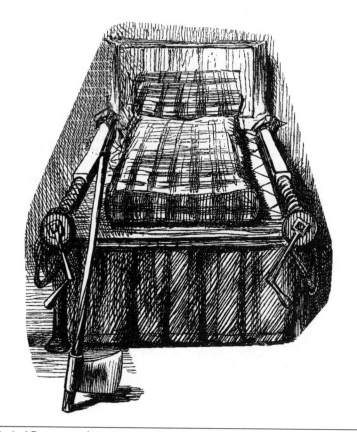

The Mythical Bed of Procrustes (with Tailoring Tools)

Prologue

A Cautionary Tale: The Bed of Procrustes

In the ancient world of the Greeks, there were gods and goddesses, demi-gods and heroes. The normal Greeks were quite entertained by the antics of these divine and semi-divine creatures, and followed them in their spare time (when they weren't creating democracy, mathematics, astronomy, history, and all manner of interesting things we occasionally use and appreciate today). There is a wealth of literature on the gods and goddesses, but we are interested in only one minor miscreant, who provides a wonderful metaphor for one of the main reasons this book was written.

His name was Procrustes, and he was a son of Poseidon, the god of the sea, among other things. Procrustes, although trained as a smith, made his living as an innkeeper cum bandit, having a nice hostelry on one of the mountains that happened to be on the way between two fairly important towns in ancient Greece. Of course, Procrustes wasn't your usual, run-of-the-mill bandit. Think of him as an early incarnation of a cross between Lizzy Borden and Norman Bates. While not someone you would want your sister to marry, he was creative in the way he relieved unlucky travelers of their goods. This creativity buys him a bit of mythological slack, as well as provides our metaphor.

Procrustes liked things to fit nicely into specified buckets—very much like many of the program managers and executives we have met along the way. He had an iron bed that he believed was the perfect length. In fact, he thought it should fit everyone. Procrustes did not have a therapist, so we'll probably never know the reason he was so enamored by the bed. Instead, we'll simply assume there are deep-seated reasons for his fixation, feel sorry for his affliction, and get on with the story.

His hostelry offered a night's rest for those who traveled the road across Mount Korydallos on the way between Athens and Eleusis. The stories are not clear as to how Procrustes selected his victims, but he would invite them in, show them his cherished bed, and offer it to them for the night, claiming, not unlike modern mattress salespeople, that it was magical and would perfectly fit whoever slept in it.

As statisticians and human factors experts will tell you, humans, even in the time of the ancient Greeks, generally varied in height and weight according to a normal distribution. And, of course, the iron bed was not created to adjust easily for such a distribution. In fact, it was a very precise length and width. It should be clear that the odds of having a person perfectly fit this bed, while not impossible, were probabilistically small. Ignoring the odds, or perhaps depending on them, Procrustes was nearly always presented with a person who did not fit the bed.*

Procrustes would bind the person to the bed, quickly realize that the guest did not fit it perfectly, reach for his smith's tools, and then carefully tailor the person to fit it—less magically, and more messily. If the unfortunate guest was too tall or too wide, he would simply lop off the offending parts. If too short or too narrow, then he would forcefully stretch the individual out until he fit. Needless to say, this generally proved fatal to the guest. Having assured himself of the perfection of the bed, and shaking his head at the imperfection of this particular human, Procrustes would gather the now-deceased's valuables into his hoard and begin the task of cleaning the room for his next guest.

Procrustes, whose name, ironically or mythically, meant "he who stretches," continued this endeavor until he mistakenly invited the hero Theseus to stay the night. Theseus turned the tables (or the bed, as it were) on Procrustes and did some tailoring of his own. While the disposition of Procrustes's famous bed is not reported, the concept of "one size fits all" has found its way down through the centuries.

The Point of the Story

Many organizations today find that their previous world of relatively stable businesses, products, processes, personnel, and technology is changing at an increasingly rapid pace. They find their investments in one-size-fits-all corporate and development processes are functioning like a Procrustean bed when applied to engineer and develop an increasing diversity of system types. They encounter problems with emergent and rapidly changing requirements and different balances of needs for agility, assurance, or both. The need for personnel with different skills, motivations, and lifestyles surfaces. Their rapidly evolving information and communication infrastructures are increasingly penetrating physical systems via three-dimensional printing and Internets of Things.

---

* In fact, some writers suggest that there were two beds, giving Procrustes even better odds.

Unfortunately, trying to escape from their Procrustean bed is difficult. There are conflicts between their impatient, change-oriented technical people and their settled, THWADI ("That's How We've Always Done It") administrators, each of whom has little understanding of the others' world. Employees working in single domains where one size is enough feel that *their* solutions ought to work for everybody else. It is even challenging to identify criteria for selecting alternative processes. The organization may have tried changing everyone to a new method and found that it is yet just another Procrustean bed.

We have gone through these difficulties ourselves during our periods in industry, government, and academia: trying to undo overenthusiastic corporate commitments made using the waterfall model; trying to get flexible acquisition standards approved by inflexible standards administrators; and trying to evolve best practices to teach students and have them apply in real-client project courses. The Incremental Commitment Spiral Model is the best approach we have found so far, and our applications of it across a wide range of project sizes and domains have worked out better than the project stakeholders' previous experiences. As we learn more, this model continues to evolve. We have also found that it is better to adopt its changes to organizations' current practices incrementally, and have identified practices that can be adopted incrementally, based on understanding organizations' strongest needs and opportunities.

We are not alone recognizing the problems. Other initiatives are making progress in moving people and organizations away from their previous one-size-fits-all processes. Several of our University of Southern California (USC) industrial affiliates have developed criteria for selecting alternative process models. Per Kroll and Philippe Kruchten's book, *The Rational Unified Process Made Easy*, separates its guidance into four tracks: Projects Deimos, Ganymede, Mars, and Jupiter. Frank Kendall's reorganization of the previously Procrustean U.S. Department of Defense Instruction 5000.02 into six different system acquisition swim lanes is another major step forward. We hope that this book and its website can benefit your organization and enable it to avoid having future projects stretched or lopped to fit Procrustean beds.

0

Introduction

"I strongly believe the way forward is to embrace and develop the Spiral Model. I suggest punctuating the spiral with explicit contracting points, augmented with clear specification of what can be contracted, with what certainties, and with what explicit distribution of risk."

—Frederick Brooks, *The Design of Design*, 2010, p. 58

"Progress, far from consisting in change, depends on retentiveness. When change is absolute there remains no being to improve and no direction is set for possible improvement: and when experience is not retained, as among savages, infancy is perpetual. Those who cannot remember the past are condemned to repeat it. In the first stage of life the mind is frivolous and easily distracted, it misses progress by failing in consecutiveness and persistence. This is the condition of children and barbarians, in which instinct has learned nothing from experience."

—George Santayana (1863–1952), *The Life of Reason*, Volume 1, 1905

In Chapter 0 (we consider this to be the fundamental ground floor of the book, creating a common understanding across the various audiences), we provide a rationale for the Incremental Commitment Spiral Model (ICSM) approach and an overview of its structure and use. Executives and managers can read this chapter to understand how ICSM supports the enterprise and to gain a sense of the changes that might be necessary to use it most effectively. All readers will find sufficient information to continue reading the remainder of the book. Readers who would prefer to start by exploring a particular aspect of the ICSM can generally use the Contents list or the index to find and address that topic in detail, but will often find it useful to refer back to the Introduction for overall context.

0.1 A World of Change

"The world is changed." These first four words heard in Peter Jackson's film of Tolkien's *The Fellowship of the Ring* are simple, yet they create a sense of uneasiness, of imbalance, of uncertainty. For the last few decades, system developers, acquirers, operators, and users have had that same sense of foreboding and disease. We hear incessantly about the acceleration of technology change and

the rapid evolution of markets, threats, corporate needs, and consumer desires. We grapple with the increase in the complexity and the interdependency of the solutions we, our competitors, and others create. We feel the stress this applies to our system development and deployment approaches, our management techniques, and our bottom lines. As authors and teachers, we also notice our course materials and papers on future trends become obsolete much more rapidly [1].

On a more positive note, rapid and diversified change creates opportunities for future success, as shown by emerging high-value companies like Amazon, Google, Facebook, Tesla, and Space X. It's hard to do this, especially if you and your organization have invested a lot of your career in learning one-size-fits-all technical and management approaches that don't support extensive change and diversity. The traditional development processes tend to turn already harried developers and managers into unwitting 21st-century Procrustes—continually chopping off pieces to force-fit the work to the process. We hope that this book will prove to be a literary Theseus, putting Procrustes out of business permanently.*

Wayne Gretzky, who is generally acknowledged as the greatest hockey player of all time, ascribes a good deal of his success to the ability to anticipate where the hockey puck was going, and to skate to where he could capitalize on that knowledge. We believe that anticipating where technologies, competitors, organizations, and the marketplace are going is increasingly critical to successful systems and software engineering. In contrast, organizations that spend their time asking, "How could we have done our last project better?" are actually skating to where the puck has been. Clearly, such "reflection in action" is good [2], but in a world of rapid change, reflection in action needs to be balanced with anticipation.

The Incremental Commitment Spiral Model integrates reflection, anticipation, and agility to take advantage of evolving knowledge through a risk-based, principle-driven approach to system development. We are still firm believers that there are no panaceas, silver bullets, or one-size-fits-all solutions. We are confident, though, that the ICSM offers a coherent and useful way to approach systems development in a world that has not only changed, but will also continue to change throughout every system's life cycle.

We also think that our evolutionary experience in developing the ICSM has been helpful, as we've seen quite a few organizations try to instantly transform themselves into something completely different, painfully fail, and drop back into their old practices. So at the end of this Chapter 0, we have identified some incremental-commitment (surprise!) approaches for approaching full adoption of the ICSM, which we hope will make it easier for your organization to evolve into more change-adaptive processes.

---

*If you didn't read the Prologue: In Greek mythology, Procrustes was a son of Poseidon who set up a hostel on a mountain. For his own enjoyment, his "guests" were forced to fit into one of two beds by Procrustes literally hammering them into shape by either lopping off limbs or other parts that didn't quite fit or stretching them out on a rack-like device. Theseus ended this early incarnation of Hitchcock's Norman Bates by forcing Procrustes to abide by his own fatal rules.

On the surface, much of the ICSM may seem familiar. This is due to a fundamental understanding of the principles that inform so many old, new, and future practices. The ICSM encourages and enables predicting future needs from current knowledge—the core of the scientific method—and applies that knowledge to whatever "best practices" arise within the continuously changing system development landscape. Given the innovative talents of the development workforce, new methods and practices will continue to appear as our organizations learn and grow as enterprises.

The spiral model [3] was the first of the life-cycle generators that attempted this kind of classification—a meta-approach to organizing, managing, and evolving both the systems under development and the processes and practices that apply to the development. Other models have since appeared, some for individual projects (like Scrum, the PMBoK, and the Rational Unified Process) and others at the enterprise level (like PMI's Organizational Project Management and Portfolio standards, Leffingwell's Scaled Agile Framework [SAFe], the Dynamic System Delivery Method [DSDM], and the Information Technology Infrastructure Library).

The ICSM refines the original spiral model, providing a more complete framework and better guidance for use. The revised model can be informative and useful in almost every type of development activity—whether a small agile software development activity for the web, a process architecture for an enterprise, or a guide to the evolution of a complex, multiple-stakeholder system of systems. Having matured the ICSM over more than 20 years, we are confident that this incarnation of the spiral model will be useful for a long time to come. ICSM principles help us understand the relationship between practices, old or new, and the core concerns of system development. As the old song says, "The fundamental things apply, as time goes by [4]."

0.2 Creating Successful 21st-Century Systems

As systems have become larger and more complex, our development processes have evolved, but often failed to keep up. Too many times, the planned system never results in a usable product or the product is obsolete by the time it is ready for use. We are frustrated when others' applications (e.g., mobile device apps) seem to appear overnight with very light, agile processes. We are also aware of agile and lean failures.[†] In essence, we seek to answer the following questions:

- How can we more quickly get projects on a path to success?
- When are significant up-front investments still necessary for success?

---

† The 2013 National Defense Industrial Association Systems Engineering Conference cited a number of agile failures, many due to overzealous trainers and consultants and overstated expectations. The mixture of successes and failures illustrates that the epigraph quote from Santayana is only half-right: Those who cannot remember the past cannot repeat its successes either.

- How can we provide value to the intended users and stakeholders quickly, no matter how large or complex the system is, and then allow the system to evolve at a pace close to the rate of change in stakeholder needs?

- Can we learn from recent lean and agile successes and failures, and find ways to scale up the successes?

The Incremental Commitment Spiral Model provides ways to answer such questions, while cautioning that there are no one-size-fits-all, silver-bullet solutions. To better understand the context and motivation for the ICSM, we first step back and look at what it means to be successful in system development endeavors. We then identify key sources of needed change in the approach to system development and evolution over time.

0.2.1 What Is Success?

To define success for engineered systems, we rely on *Webster's* definition of engineering as "the application of science and mathematics by which the properties of matter and the sources of energy in nature are made useful to people [5]." Earlier definitions of engineering, still in use, focus on the hard sciences such as physics and chemistry as those to be applied. But the phrase "useful to people" implies that additional sciences, such as economics and the social sciences, need to be understood and applied as part of engineering.

The definition of systems engineering developed by INCOSE and adopted by the Systems Engineering Body of Knowledge (SEBoK) is "An interdisciplinary approach and means to enable the realization of successful systems [6]." Based on its contracting-for-hardware origins, the traditional definition of success has been interpreted as "satisfying the specified requirements at a minimum cost." This is a workable definition of success if the requirements are properly specified and continue to be what the stakeholders most need. But if the requirements are wrong (or are frozen in place while stakeholders' needs change), the traditional definition of "success" becomes "delivering the wrong system at a minimum cost."

Numerous examples of successful and unsuccessful systems exist (we've been involved in quite a few of both). These experiences, along with the previously mentioned definitions and participation in the integrated, cross-discipline, systems engineering initiatives cited in the Acknowledgments, have led to a more workable definition of success as expressed in the following Fundamental System Success Theorem:

> *A system will succeed if and only if it makes winners of its success-critical stakeholders* [7].

An informal proof follows. It should be noted that human value-based theorems and proofs are less formal than those in such areas as mathematics and physics.

Proof of "if":

1. Everyone significant is a winner.
2. Nobody significant is left to complain.

Proof of "only if":

1. Nobody wants to lose.
2. Prospective losers will refuse to participate or will counterattack.
3. The usual result is lose-lose.

The Fundamental System Success Theorem does not tell us how to realize and maintain a win-win state. This requires the System Success Realization Theorem:

Making winners of your success-critical stakeholders requires:

1. *Identifying all of the success-critical stakeholders.*
2. *Understanding how each stakeholder wants to win.*
3. *Having the success-critical stakeholders negotiate among themselves a win-win set of product and process plans.*
4. *Controlling progress toward the negotiated win-win realization, including adapting it to change.*

These four sufficient conditions for success provide a value-based systems and software engineering process framework for realizing a successful system. This framework and the underlying success theorems undergird the Incremental Commitment Spiral Model, and are elaborated in Chapter 1.

0.2.2 Why Is Success More and More Difficult to Achieve?

Systems engineering and development processes and principles were created 40 to 50 years ago. At that time their users could generally make the following assumptions about the system:

1. The system would operate as a stand-alone device.
2. Its requirements could be specified up front.
3. Its behavior would seldom change.
4. It could be designed top-down, starting from a clean blackboard or sheet of paper.

Today, these assumptions are becoming less valid. This section identifies six system-related trends that require changes if we are to develop successful systems now and in the future:

1. Increasingly complex, global systems of systems
2. Broadening of the focus of "systems" to cyber–physical–human systems
3. Emergent requirements
4. Rapid, accelerating change
5. Expanding high assurance of qualities
6. More and more non-developmental items (NDIs) and legacy systems

0.2.2.1 Increasingly Complex, Global Systems of Systems Drive the Need for Scalability and Interoperability

Had John Donne lived in the 21st century, he may well have wisely admonished, "No system is an island, entire of itself; every system is a piece of the cybersphere, a part of the main."[†] The Internet, the World Wide Web, and ubiquitous, inexpensive communication devices are knitting almost everything and everyone together into an Internet of Things [8]. Developers of 21st-century systems will need to consider not only how they fit within their own enterprise, but often how they fit within multiple networks of independently evolving, co-dependent systems in a variety of cultures.

A lot of work needs to be done to establish robust success patterns for global collaborative processes. Key challenges in this area include the following:

- Cross-cultural bridging
- Establishment of a common shared vision and trust
- Contracting mechanisms and incentives
- Handovers and change synchronization in multi-time-zone development
- Culture-sensitive collaboration-oriented groupware

Most software packages are oriented around individual use and require research and experimentation to become collaborative. There have been successes within individual companies, and in ventures where corporate global collaboration capabilities have made collaborative work largely location independent.

Current systems and software development processes are often recipes for stand-alone "stovepipe" systems with high risks of inadequate interoperability with other stovepipe systems. Experience has shown that collections of stovepipe

---

† Donne, John. "Meditation 17," from *Devotions Upon Emergent Occasions*, 1624.

systems cause unacceptable delays in service, uncoordinated and conflicting plans, ineffective or dangerous decisions, and inability to cope with rapid change. The ICSM's commitment milestones require evidence that the system be scalable enough to operate with its intended full-up environment, and be interoperable with its co-dependent systems.

0.2.2.2 Broadened Focus on Cyber–Physical–Human Systems Drives the Need for Early Risk Analysis

The initial focus of systems engineering on physical devices and of software engineering on computer programs led to "hardware-first" and "software-first" processes that overly constrained the solution space for systems from enabling their hardware, software, and human elements to interoperate smoothly. The broadened focus on integrated, concurrently engineered cyber–physical–human systems heralded by societal systems [9], soft systems methodology [10], systems architecting [11], and human–systems integration [12, 13, 14] has identified further sources of uncertainty and risk in systems definition. This is particularly true for emerging systems such as self-driving cars, smart highways, smart hospitals, smart cities, and automated stock trading. These systems will require some balance of automated and human decision making to ensure their safe and fair operation. Convincing evidence of this need can be found every quarter in the "Risks to the Public" section of the ACM publication *Software Engineering Notes*, which usually chronicles more than a dozen significant failures caused by shortfalls in systems and software engineering.

0.2.2.3 Emergent Requirements Drive the Need for Prototyping and Evolutionary Development

Asking prospective users of a cyber–physical–human system how they would like their user interface to look and behave usually results in a response such as "I'm not sure, but I'll know it when I see it" (IKIWISI). The most appropriate user interfaces and collaboration modes for a complex human-intensive system are not specifiable in advance, but rather emerge with usage. Forcing users to specify them precisely in advance of development generally leads to poor business or mission performance and expensive late rework and delays. The ICSM provides support for incremental and concurrent definition of system requirements and solutions, including competitive prototyping approaches.

0.2.2.4 Rapid Change Drives the Need for Agility and Evolutionary Development

As discussed at the beginning of this chapter, almost everything is changing, and changing at warp speed. Trying to stay competitive in such a world requires new levels of agility and shorter times between new releases of products and

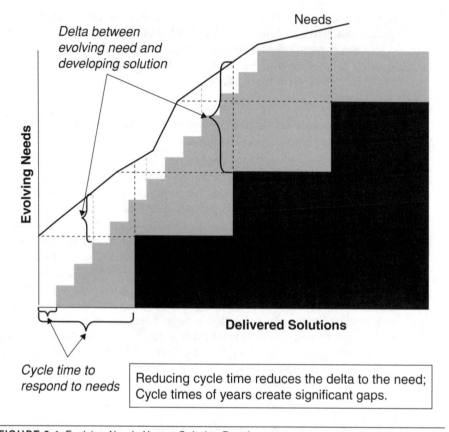

Delta between evolving need and developing solution

Needs

Evolving Needs

Delivered Solutions

Cycle time to respond to needs

Reducing cycle time reduces the delta to the need; Cycle times of years create significant gaps.

FIGURE 0-1 Evolving Needs Versus Solution Development

services. Figure 0-1 shows that changing needs can rapidly outstrip development of solutions. The longer the development increments, the greater the delta between what is delivered and what is needed, and the more likely that some development is not meeting any current need.

On a cost-competitive contract, the bidder has no incentive to provide more than is specified. In turn, specifying requirements using a current point-in-time snapshot generally leads to a point-solution architecture that is hard to adapt to new developments. Each of the many subsequent changes then leads to considerable and nonproductive rework of documents, software, or, in the worst case, hardware, and renegotiation of contracts.

0.2.2.5 High Assurance of System Quality Drives the Need for Balance and Satisficing

At the same time that systems engineering and development need to become more agile, the growing interdependence of systems and people requires systems to have higher assurance levels. Because of their interconnectedness and the trust placed on them by nontechnical users of 21st-century systems, nonfunctional requirements are ever more critical. System qualities such as safety and security are obviously important, but other system attributes are also rising to critical levels, including reliability/availability/maintainability, performance, adaptability, interoperability, usability, and scalability.

Just assuring one of these quality attributes for a complex system of systems (SoS) is difficult. This is hardly surprising given the difficulty of reaching consensus on *anything* among multiple system stakeholders with widely disparate quality priorities. The complex sources of conflict and interplay in tradeoff relationships make multi-attribute satisficing even more challenging. The term "satisficing" means not everybody gets everything they want, but everybody gets an outcome that they are satisfied with. The ICSM's principles of stakeholder satisficing and evidence-based commitment milestones help ensure that key stakeholders' primary quality concerns are addressed.

The ICSM's incremental definition and development stages directly support shorter increments, more agile methods, and evolutionary development. In addition, its principle of evidence- and risk-based decision making provides a way to avoid point solutions. Rather than eliminate requirements that fall below the budget line in a prioritized list, the stakeholders can identify these as likely evolution requirements, and ask for evidence that proposed architectures and solution components will scale up to handle the evolution requirements. The resulting best solution may not cover some unforeseen emergent requirements, but it will most likely produce a better and less expensive life-cycle solution than the usual lowest-cost, technically acceptable development solution based on budget-truncated requirements.

Further, the usual practice of providing systems engineering with single-value key performance parameters often overly constrains the solution space or pushes the solution high up an asymptotic cost curve. An example of this situation is provided in the Unaffordable Requirement story in Chapter 4.

0.2.2.6 Non-developmental Items and Legacy Systems Drive the Need for Simultaneous Top-Down and Bottom-Up Engineering

Non-developmental items (NDIs) include commercial or government off-the-shelf (COTS, GOTS) products, cloud services, open-source software (OSS), and software or systems of unknown provenance (SOUP). Their use can radically reduce the cost and calendar time to deliver a system. Of course, they also imply a more bottom-up design—one based on matching existing functions to need—rather than a purely top-down design from a statement of requirements or a new idea. Even new products, if they are concerned with short market windows, will usually find it preferable to get something out quickly with the use of NDIs. This requires additional effort and skills in analyzing the cost-effectiveness, scalability, and interoperability of the NDIs, and strongly drives the nature of the system's architecture.

Another major constraint on top-down (or greenfield) development is the need to provide continuity of service with respect to the existing legacy systems that the new system is replacing. This often requires the engineering team to reverse-engineer the legacy system to understand how to replace it—or, if the new system needs to be incrementally developed to avoid obsolescence, to ensure that the legacy system can be incrementally replaced. The ICSM supports both NDI-driven development and this brownfield (as opposed to greenfield) development approaches.

0.3 ICSM Distilled

The ICSM is a principles-based, process framework or meta-model that supports the definition of life-cycle processes based on the characteristics, constraints, and risks associated with a given project or program. It incorporates the system success definition described earlier, and so is both technology and stakeholder aware. It handles projects of all sizes, but is particularly applicable to projects requiring multiple life-cycle models for various components:

- New or legacy components
- Software, hardware, or cyber–physical systems
- Unprecedented or common components
- Critical or nice-to-have components

Like the original spiral model, the ICSM is incremental and concurrent in nature, has specific approaches for establishing stakeholders' commitment for those increments before moving forward, and is dependent on evidence- and risk-based decisions.

Given that one-step total corporate makeovers are highly risky, the ICSM does not present itself as an all-or-nothing model (remember Procrustes). Organizations can and do adopt its key practices incrementally; example increments are provided at the end of this chapter.

0.3.1 Principles Trump Diagrams

Most of the problems in using the 1988 spiral model stemmed from users looking at the diagram and constructing processes that had nothing to do with the underlying concepts. This is true of many process models: people just adopt the diagram and neglect the principles that need to be respected. For that reason, it is important to carefully state the ICSM's four underlying principles:

1. **Stakeholder value-based guidance.** If a project fails to include and address the value propositions of its success-critical stakeholders such as end-users, maintainers, interoperators, or suppliers, these stakeholders will frequently feel little commitment to (or even active hostility toward) the project and either underperform, decline to use the results, or block the use of the results.

2. **Incremental commitment and accountability.** Many success-critical stakeholders will object to making total commitments of their scarce

resources to weakly defined ventures, but will incrementally commit to buying better information on them. Once a commitment is made, all stakeholders need to understand that they are accountable for keeping their promises.

3. **Concurrent multidisciplinary engineering.** If definition and development of (a) requirements and solutions; (b) hardware, software, and human factors; or (c) product and processes are done sequentially, the project is likely both to go more slowly and to make early, hard-to-undo commitments that cut off the best options for project success.

4. **Evidence- and risk-based decisions.** If key decisions are made based on assertions, vendor literature, or meeting an arbitrary schedule without access to evidence of feasibility, the project is building up risks. And in the words of Tom Gilb, "If you do not actively attack the risks, the risks will actively attack you." Many of the hazardous spiral look-alikes described over the years [15] conveniently dropped any consideration of risk, and paid the price of an overrun or cancellation later.

These four principles and their influence on the model are discussed in much more detail in Part I.

0.3.2 Metaphors for Applying the ICSM

To illustrate these principles, it is appropriate to follow Kent Beck's eXtreme Programming practice of establishing one or more metaphors for the concept. Here are two different but useful ways of thinking about why risk-driven, concurrent, incremental commitment can bring about successful systems.

Playing the Odds. Our first simple metaphor to help understand the ICSM is to compare it to incremental-commitment gambling games such as poker or blackjack, rather than to single-commitment gambling games such as roulette. Many system development projects operate like roulette, in which a full set of requirements is specified up front, the full set of resources is committed to an essentially fixed-price contract, and one waits to see if the bet was a good one. The ICSM is more like poker or blackjack, in that one places an increasing series of bets to see whether the prospects of a win are good, and decides whether to continue betting based on better information about the prospects of success.

Life Together. Our second metaphor is somewhat more personal. The major ICSM life-cycle phases and milestones work well as common commitment points across a variety of process model variants because they reflect similar commitment points during one's lifetime. Exploration is the equivalent of investing time in going out on dates (yes, the object of desire looks good and seems reasonably intelligent, but so do some others). The Valuation phase leads to the decision point at which you and a partner decide to go steady, investing some of your degrees of freedom in exploring the prospects of a more serious commitment (we're interested enough to forgo other dalliances for a while to see if this could really be "it"). The Foundations phase results in the investment in rings, bringing in other stakeholders, and possibly making domicile arrangements (someone says yes to a "Will you marry me?" question, but it is not yet an "until death do us part" commitment). The firmer commitment happens at the Development Commitment Review (the equivalent of "officially, legally, and in sight of God and everybody" getting married). As in life, if you marry your system architecture and plans in haste, you and your stakeholders will repent at leisure (if, in Internet time, any leisure time is available). Finally, the Operations Commitment Review constitutes an even larger commitment (having your first child, with all the associated commitments of care and feeding of a legacy system).

As with most metaphors, the correspondence of these decision points is not perfect. Nevertheless, the analogies of failure are pertinent: prematurely committing to infeasible requirements and spending lots of resources to create a failed outcome is similar to out-of-sequence life experiences such as dating, creating a child, getting married, and then finding that you can't live with each other.

0.3.3 ICSM Diagrams and Views

Knowing you have been waiting breathlessly to see all the exotic diagrams that are the standard fare in process models, it is now appropriate to introduce the ICSM in all its graphical splendor.

0.3.3.1 The ICSM Spiral View

The view of the ICSM shown in Figure 0-2 is helpful in clarifying that the ICSM is not a single one-size-fits-all process model, but rather a process generation model, in which a project's particular risk patterns and process drivers steer it toward achieving success with respect to its particular objectives, constraints, and priorities. Unlike in the traditional sequential approaches, each spiral concurrently rather than sequentially addresses all of the activities of product development. Every spiral considers:

- Requirements (objectives and constraints)
- Solutions (alternatives)
- Products and processes
- Hardware
- Software
- Human factors aspects
- Business case analysis of alternative product configurations
- Product line investments
- Intentional reflection at all levels

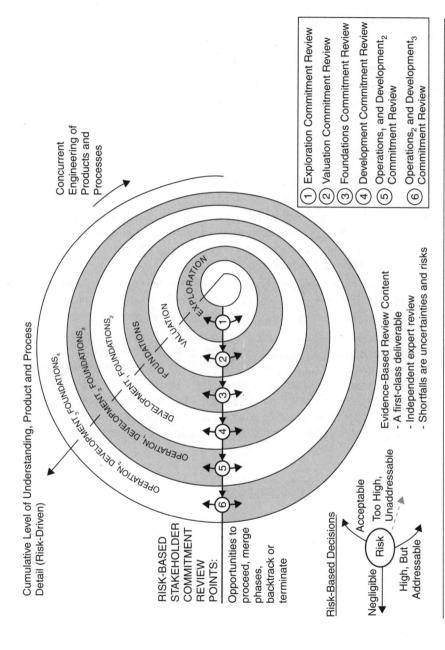

FIGURE 0-2 The Incremental Commitment Spiral Model (Reprinted with permission from *Human-System Integration in the System Development Process*, 2007 by the National Academy of Sciences, Courtesy of the National Academies Press, Washington, D.C.)

All of this concurrency is synchronized and stabilized by the development team producing not only management and engineering artifacts, but also evidence of their combined feasibility. Independent experts assess this evidence at the various stakeholder commitment decision milestones. Any shortfalls in evidence are considered risks, and significant risks should then be addressed by a risk mitigation plan.

Figure 0-3, an expanded view of the numbered decision nodes, shows that each decision has four possible exits. Note that the fourth dotted line, denoting an exit due to unaddressable risks, is not visible on the numbered nodes in the full spiral view; it is pointing in the third dimension (into your paper or screen).

The stakeholders then consider the risks and risk mitigation plans, and decide on a course of action:

- If the *risks are acceptable* and well covered by risk mitigation plans, the project will proceed into the next spiral.
- If the *risks are high but addressable*, the project will remain in the current spiral until the risks are resolved. An example would be working out safety cases for a safety-critical system, or producing acceptable versions of missing risk-mitigation plans.
- If the *risks are negligible*, there is no need to perform separate Valuation and Foundations spirals, and the project could go straight into a combined Valuation/Foundations spiral followed by a Development spiral.
- If the *risks are too high and unaddressable* (for example, if the market window for such a product has already closed), the project should be terminated or rescoped, perhaps to address a different market sector whose market window is clearly still open. Thus, the ICSM provides a set of project off-ramps that make it more acceptable to discontinue the project and save resources for more valuable projects, instead of continuing the project, becoming a Standish Group failure statistic, and perhaps joining the ranks of the unemployed.

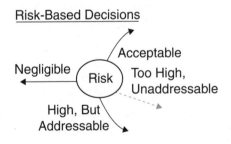

FIGURE 0-3 Decision Points

0.3.3.2 The Phased View

The phased view (Figure 0-4) shows how the overall life-cycle process divides naturally into two major stages. Stage I, Incremental Definition, covers the up-front growth in system understanding, definition, feasibility assurance, and stakeholder commitment. If the Stage I activities do not result in taking an off-ramp, they lead to a larger Stage II commitment to implement a feasible set of specifications and plans for Incremental Development and Operations of the desired system.

The review processes and the use of independent experts at the major phase reviews are based on the highly successful AT&T Architecture Review Board procedures [16]. A Feasibility Evidence Description is the focus of each of the concurrency stabilization reviews. It contains evidence *provided by the developer* and *validated by independent experts* that, if the system is built to the specified architecture, it will:

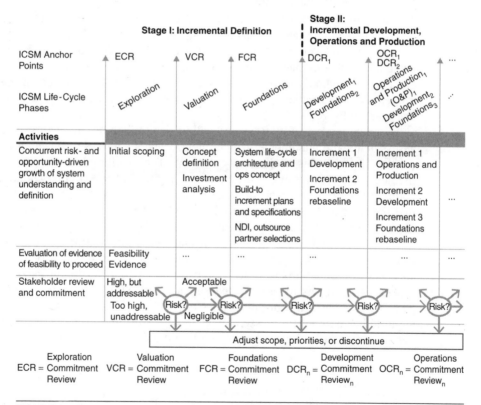

FIGURE 0-4 The Incremental Commitment Model: Phased View (Reprinted with permission from *Human-System Integration in the System Development Process*, 2007 by the National Academy of Sciences, Courtesy of the National Academies Press, Washington, D.C.)

- Satisfy the requirements: capability, interface, level of service, and evolution
- Support the operational concept
- Be buildable within the budgets and schedules in the plan
- Generate a viable return on investment
- Generate satisfactory outcomes for all of the success-critical stakeholders
- Resolve all major risks by treating shortfalls in evidence as risks and covering them through risk management plans
- Serve as basis for stakeholders' commitment to proceed

Stage I: Incremental Definition

The duration of Stage I can be anywhere from one week to five years, depending on factors like the number, capability, and compatibility of the proposed system's components and stakeholders. A small, experienced, developer–customer team, using agile software methods and operating on a mature infrastructure, can form and begin incremental development of a well-defined software project in less than a week. A more complex project[§] requires significant effort and could take up to five years or longer.

Each project's activity trajectory will be determined by the results of the risk assessments and stakeholder commitment decisions at its anchor-point reviews (in the diagram, this is the arrow chosen). The small agile project will follow the negligible-risk arrows at the bottom of Figure 0-4 to skip the Valuation and Foundations phases and begin Stage II after a short exploratory phase confirms that the risks of doing so are indeed negligible. The ultra-large project could, as described in Chapter 3, apply a form of competitive prototyping to fund a number of small competitive concept-definition and validation contracts in the Exploratory phase, a few larger follow-on Valuation contracts, and one or two considerably larger Foundations contracts, choosing at each anchor-point milestone the best-qualified teams to proceed, based on the feasibility and risk evaluations performed at each anchor-point milestone review. In some cases, the reviews might indicate that certain essential technologies or infrastructure incompatibilities need more work before proceeding into the next phase.

[§]An example might be an ultra-large, unprecedented, multi-mission, multi-owner, system of systems that needs to be integrated with numerous independently evolving legacy or external systems. We have provided ICSM elements for the definition and development of such systems, and have at least partially helped improve their outcomes

Stage II: Incremental Development, Production, and Operations

Stage II is planned around the length of the increments to be used in the system's development and evolution. This is a key decision made during the Development Commitment Review. A small agile project can use two- to four week increments. A much larger project could need increments of up to two years to develop and integrate an increment of operational capability. However, the ICSM capability delivery cadence is not necessarily linked to the internal development cadence, and there may be several internal integration cycles within a longer release increment. Some large, inseparable, hardware components might take even longer to develop their initial increments, and would be scheduled to synchronize their capability deliveries with concurrently evolving infrastructure or software increments.

0.3.3.3 The Evolution View

Stage I activities should have assured a common vision, committed stakeholders, and an architecture capable of accommodating foreseeable changes such as user interfaces, external system interoperability requirements, or transaction formats. These enable the features in each Stage II increment to be prioritized and the increment timeboxed.

Timeboxing is also known as time-certain development or Schedule As Independent Variable (SAIV) development, where borderline-priority features are added or dropped to maximize flow while keeping the increment strictly on schedule. As noted earlier in conjunction with Figure 0-1, the shorter the timebox, the faster learning can occur and changes can be handled. However, the user delivery cadence may need to differ from the development cadence in cases where, due to logistics or business process issues, the amount of work to prepare the user for delivery is longer than a development increment.

For critical systems, increments can include a continuous verification and validation team analyzing, reviewing, testing, and integrating the evolving product to increase quality and decrease rework. Consequently, along with timeboxing, methods like value-based testing and test-driven development are easily included. Figure 0-5 provides a graphic depiction of this evolutionary approach.

While the stabilized development team is building the current increment and accommodating foreseeable changes, a separate system engineering team is dealing with sources of unforeseeable change and rebaselining later increments' specifications and plans. Changes might include new COTS releases, previous-increment usage feedback, timeboxed current-increment deferrals to the next increment, new technology opportunities, or changes in mission priorities. Having the development team try to accommodate these changes does not work, because it destabilizes their schedules and disrupts carefully negotiated interface specifications. Toward the end of each increment, the system engineering team also produces for expert review the appropriate specifications, plans, and feasibility evidence

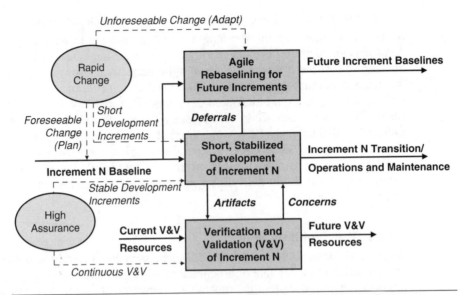

FIGURE 0-5 The Evolution View (Reprinted with permission from *Human-System Integration in the System Development Process*, 2007 by the National Academy of Sciences, Courtesy of the National Academies Press, Washington, D.C.)

necessary to ensure low-risk, stabilized development of the next increment by the build-to-spec team.

0.3.3.4 The Concurrency View

Having addressed the stages, phases, and milestones in the generic ICSM, let's look at the activities. The top row of Activities in Figure 0-4 indicates a number of system aspects are being concurrently engineered at an increasing level of under-standing, definition, and development. The most significant of these aspects are shown in Figure 0-6, an extension of a similar "hump chart" drawn by Philippe Kruchten to illustrate the Rational Unified Process [17].

As with the Kruchten version, this is a conceptual illustration, not a result of some complex, data-driven analysis. The magnitude and shape of the levels of effort are risk driven and will vary from project to project. In particular, they are likely to have micro-level risk/opportunity-driven peaks and valleys, rather than the smooth curves shown for simplicity in the figure. For example, in the Exploration column, although system scoping is the primary objective, doing it well involves a consider-able amount of activity: understanding needs, envisioning opportunities, identifying and reconciling stakeholder goals and objectives, architecting solutions, life-cycle planning, evaluating alternatives, and negotiating stakeholder commitments. As discussed in conjunction with the phased view (Section 0.3.3.2), all of this concur-rency needs to be synchronized and stabilized to avoid chaos. This is done by devel-oping and performing a risk assessment of the Feasibility Evidence Description for the ensemble of concurrently developed elements at each decision milestone.

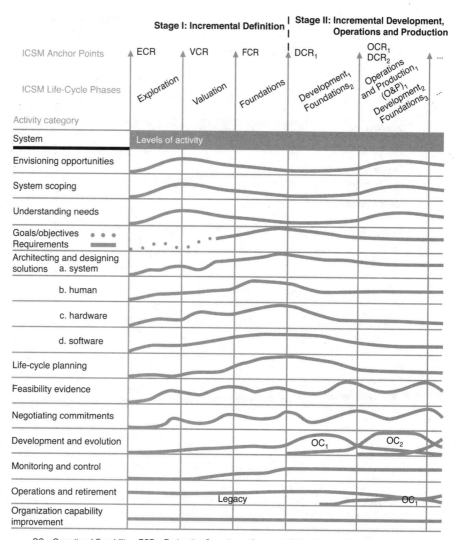

FIGURE 0-6 ICSM Concurrency View (Reprinted with permission from *Human-System Integration in the System Development Process*, 2007 by the National Academy of Sciences, Courtesy of the National Academies Press, Washington, D.C.)

0.4 Using the ICSM

As illustrated in the four example paths through the ICSM in Figure 0-7, the ICSM is not a monolithic one-size-fits-all process model. Like the original spiral model, it is a risk-driven process model generator. However, the ICSM Common Cases make it easier to visualize how different risks create different processes.

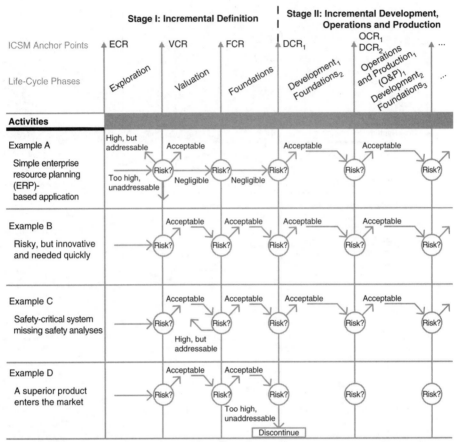

FIGURE 0-7 Different Risk Patterns Yield Different Processes (Reprinted with permission from *Human-System Integration in the System Development Process*, 2007 by the National Academy of Sciences, Courtesy of the National Academies Press, Washington, D.C.)

Example A is a simple business application based on an already-available enterprise resource planning (ERP) package. There is no need for a Valuation or Architecting activity if the ERP package has been purchased and its architecture has already proved cost-effective in supporting more complex applications. Thus, the project can go directly into Stage II, using an agile method such as a combination of Scrum and eXtreme Programming. There is no need for "Big Design Up Front" activities or artifacts because an appropriate architecture is already present in the ERP package. Nor is there a need for heavyweight waterfall or V-model specifications and document reviews. The critical risk identified at the end of the

Exploration phase could be the user acceptance and business process reengineering required for deployment. In this case, that risk would be considered negligible if the system's human interface risks have been sufficiently mitigated via ERP package-based prototyping.

Example B involves a risky but innovative system such as adding a retina scanner to the next model of a cellphone product. In this case, a number of uncertainties and risks/opportunities must be resolved, such as scanner hardware integration and safety of the user. The new capability is needed quickly, however, and there is a fallback option (deferring its introduction to the following model), so proceeding to address the risks and develop the system is acceptable.

Example C is a system that is defined as safety critical. The stakeholders responsible for the safety of the proposed system find at the Foundations Commitment Review that the proposers have provided inadequate safety evidence. It is better to have the proposers develop such evidence through architecture-based safety cases, fault tree analyses, and failure modes and effects analyses before proceeding into the Foundations phase. This is indicated by the arrow back into the Valuation phase.

In Example D, the developers are simply too late to play. It is discovered before the Development phase commences that a superior product has already entered the marketplace, leaving the current product with an infeasible business case. Here, unless the project's scope can be adjusted to create a viable business case, it is best to discontinue the effort. It is worth pointing out that it is not necessary to proceed to the next major milestone before terminating a clearly nonviable project; however, stakeholder concurrence in termination is essential.

0.4.1 ICSM Risk-Driven Common Cases

We have identified a set of seven risk patterns that represent the most often seen paths through the ICSM. We have named these as Common Cases, and provide them with additional elaboration in Chapter 7. The seven common cases are as follows:

- Software application or system
- Software-intensive device
- Hardware platform
- Family of systems or product line
- System of systems or enterprise-wide system
- Brownfield modernization

Table 0-1 briefly describes when to use each common case and some examples of each.

TABLE 0-1 ICSM Common Cases

System (or Subsystem) Is...	Use...	Examples
Software application/system that executes on one or more commercial hardware platforms. It can be a stand-alone software system or a constituent within one or more systems of systems (SoS).	Software application or system	Cellphone app, business application or system, military command and control software system, pharmacy systems, inventory management systems, computer operating system software, database management system
An object, machine, or piece of equipment that is developed for a special purpose and has significant features provided by software	Software-intensive device	Computer peripherals, weapons, entertainment devices, health care devices (including small robotics used in surgeries or to assist injured people), Global Positioning System (GPS) navigation device, manufacturing tools
Vehicle (land, sea, air, or space)	Hardware platform	Small unmanned ground or air vehicle, automobile, military jeep, tank, ship, airplane, space shuttle, space station, Mars rover
Computer	Hardware platform	Supercomputer, mainframe, server, laptop, tablet, cellphone
Part of a set of systems that are either similar to each other or interoperate with each other	Family of systems or product line	Car models that share many core components; interoperating back-office systems such as billing, accounting, customer care, pricing, and sales force automation systems that share a common underlying repository with standard data definitions/formats for the business domain and are provided by a single vendor
A new capability that will be performed by more than one interoperating system	System of system or enterprise-wide systems	Multiple interoperating systems that are owned and managed by different organizations, such as navigation systems that include airborne and land systems that also interoperate with GPS
Refactoring or reimplementation of an older legacy system or set of systems	Brownfield modernization	Incremental replacement of old, fragile business systems with COTS products or technology refresh/upgrade of existing systems

0.5 Incremental ICSM Adoption Approaches

Many system development programs are constrained to support continuity of service with respect to existing legacy systems and business processes. For such programs, it is often not possible to make major process changes all at once. In these cases, incrementally changing processes over time is the only approach available. The ICSM does not have to be adopted at the beginning of a project, although more benefits will accrue when it is. Existing programs can still benefit from the ICSM principles and practices. Problem programs may also find some ICSM practices helpful in recovering viability.

The five practices discussed here can be adopted individually without requiring parts of the others. They are also compatible, so that organizations can choose their own approach to incrementally adopting parts or all of the ICSM. Finally, they are synergetic, in that each supports and enhances the impact of the others.

Practices that make sense to implement incrementally or to existing projects and programs are:

- Adding an evidence-based Feasibility Rationale to the content of current reviews such as system and software requirements and design reviews
- Using a timeboxing process and prioritizing features to be delivered
- Stabilizing development increments by diverting most change traffic to a concurrent systems engineering effort for incorporations into future increment baselines
- Performing continuous versus back-end integration, verification, and validation
- Using risk to determine appropriate common cases of the ICSM to apply to familiar situations

0.6 Examples of ICSM Use

Chapter 5 of the National Research Council's *Human–System Integration* report documents ICSM application to a highly successful commercial medical intravenous infusion pump development [18]. Hospira's Symbiq IV Pump won the 2006 Human Factors and Ergonomics Society's Best New Design Award. That same chapter of the *Human–System Integration* report also includes two other case studies. One shows how the ICSM would help address several challenges in adapting current unmanned aerial systems to work with fewer operators. The other describes the risk-driven incremental commitment approach used in the development of large-scale port security systems.

A well-documented successful government-acquisition project using the ICSP principles was the CCPDS-R project [19]. Its U.S. Air Force customer and contractor reinterpreted the traditional defense regulations, specifications, and standards. It held a Preliminary Design Review, but it was not a PowerPoint show at month 4. Instead, it had a fully validated architecture and demonstration of the working high-risk user interface and networking capabilities at month 14. The resulting system delivery, including more than 1 million lines of software source code, exceeded customer expectations and was delivered within budget and schedule.

Another source of successful projects that applied the ICSM principles is the annual series of Top-5 software-intensive systems projects published in *CrossTalk* [20]. The "Top-5 Quality Software Projects" were chosen annually by panels of leading experts as role models of best practices and successful outcomes. Of the 20 Top-5 projects in 2002 through 2005, 16 explicitly used concurrent engineering; 14 explicitly used risk-driven development; and 15 explicitly used incrementally committed, iterative system evolution. Additional projects gave indications of their partial use. Unfortunately, the project summaries did not include discussion of stakeholder involvement.

Evidence of successful results of ICSM usage on smaller, more agile projects can also be found in the annual series of University of Southern California (USC) e-Services projects [21]. Since 1995, more than 200 user-intensive e-Services applications have used precursor and current versions of the ICSM to achieve a 92% success rate of on-time delivery of stakeholder-satisfactory systems [22]. The model's use on the software portion of the ultra-large Future Combat Systems program enabled the sponsors to much better identify and deal with particularly the software-intensive program risks, and to identify improved courses of action [23].

0.7 How ICSM Might Have Helped a Complex Government Acquisition (healthcare.gov)

As we were finishing the manuscript for this book in December 2013, the roll-out of the healthcare.gov website was a major topic in the news. The results of future investigations and analyses should allow us to determine the specific failures involved in the launch of this website and learn more about avoiding them in the future. However, the initial disclosures illustrate why the ICSM principles and attention to continuing stakeholder commitment are so critical to success. We believe this is a reasonable summary for this introduction and a great starting place for the remainder of the book.

Stakeholder Value-Based Guidance

- System stakeholders were numerous and powerful, and they found it difficult to reconcile win conditions and success models. These stakeholders included various unaligned government parties (legislative, executive, regulatory, and program management), a large contingent of developers, hundreds of insurance providers, and millions of users.

- Stakeholder win conditions were not negotiated, documented, and continuously stabilized to ensure that the system would remain acceptable. Win conditions were not established to encourage the young and healthy to participate in the national health care system—a necessary part of the plan to make it viable for all.

- Explicitly identifying and articulating success models and win conditions creates a shared understanding of values, assumptions, and expectations, reducing the ability to degenerate into blame assignment after the fact.

Incremental Commitment and Accountability

- The overall complexity of the system (more than 5000 pages in the Affordable Care Act and more than 78,000 qualified health plans across the federally serviced states) and the need for simplicity in the user experience were a significant challenge. Within the 5000 pages of the act, the probability of ambiguous language and conflicting requirements was extremely high. A careful analysis of the document and agreement among stakeholders on the interpretation of requirements before committing to architecture, schedules, and contracting seems critical. Documented results of such analysis and agreement on these fundamental issues have not been made public.

- Stakeholders critical to success were not provided with incremental review and commitment opportunities, resulting in the proliferation of errors that could have been resolved earlier.

- Top-level government leadership in the U.S. Department of Health and Human Services (HHS) had no significant experience in overseeing a systems development effort anywhere close to the size and complexity of healthcare.gov and therefore little understanding of commitments.

- The development was set up with an all-or-nothing delivery date, resulting in a very low probability of success given the complexity and visibility of the system.

- Expectations were initially set extremely high and never managed with respect to the reality of the developing system. An obvious example is the early promise to user stakeholders concerning the ability to keep their coverage if they liked it; this promise was not kept.

Concurrent Multidisciplinary Engineering

- Engineering good systems requires both experienced, high-quality developers and experienced, knowledgeable customers. It appears that this was not always the case, as evidenced by the fact that the U.S. government turned to experts in Silicon Valley to fix problems after deployment.

- While concurrency is fundamental to good development and necessary to roll out a large system in a relatively short time frame, it requires adequate planning and the development of a solid foundation to be successful. It appears that careful system architecting, requisite management infrastructure to allow rapid and efficient supply chain communications, and engineering process adaptability were not adequately in place before engaging 55 individual contractors to perform more than $600 million in federally contracted work.

Evidence- and Risk-Based Decisions

- It is doubtful that validated evidence of the system capabilities meeting the anchor-point milestone criteria was presented to any authority by the developers in the last year of development. Such evidence confirms that if the system is built to the specified architecture, it will:

- Satisfy the capability, interface, level of service, and evolution requirements;
- Support the operational concept;
- Be buildable within the budgets and schedules in the plan;
- Generate a viable return on investment;
- Generate satisfactory outcomes for all of the success-critical stakeholders;
- Resolve all major risks; and
- Serve as a basis for stakeholders' commitment to proceed.

- Decisions were made for political reasons rather than technical reasons, and the technical ramifications were not fully understood.

- Schedule was a key driver, yet it appears that there was no prioritization of key requirements and features and inadequate plans to drop requirements or incrementally roll out capability. This resulted in the late drop of the feature that allows users to browse available health care plans without setting up complex accounts in the system. The lack of this feature in the first release appears to have contributed significantly to the difficulties experienced by the earliest users.

- The risks associated with the magnitude and visibility of the healthcare.gov site should have resulted in a careful, collaborative, incremental development strategy that avoided the all-at-once deployment of an immature system.

- Newly published information indicates that the White House and HSS leaders were informed in a March 2013 independent assessment from McKinsey & Co., that the "launch was fraught with risks [24]." Some of the key problems documented in the report (unstable requirements, little time for testing, and little to no time for fixing problems) were never resolved before the rollout.

References

[1] Boehm, B. "Some Future Trends and Implications for Systems and Software Engineering Processes." *Systems Engineering.* 2006;9(1):1–19.

[2] Schon, D. *The Reflective Practitioner*. Basic Books, 1983.

[3] Boehm, B. "A Spiral Model for Software Development and Enhancement." *Computer.* May 1988;61–72.

[4] Hupfeld, Herman. "As Time Goes By." Song from the musical *Everybody's Welcome* (1931), but made famous in the movie *Casablanca* (1942) as the song that Sam plays.

[5] *Webster's Collegiate Dictionary.* Merriam-Webster, 2010.

[6] *INCOSE Systems Engineering Handbook v. 3.1.* INCOSE-TP-2003-002-03.1.

[7] Boehm, Barry, and Ross, Rony. "Theory-W Software Project Management Principles and Examples." *IEEE Transactions on Software Engineering.* 1989;15(7):902–916.

[8] Ashton, Kevin. "That 'Internet of Things' Thing: In the Real World Things Matter More Than Ideas." *RFID Journal.* June 22, 2009.

[9] Warfield, J. N. *Societal Systems: Planning, Policy, and Complexity.* New York: Wiley Interscience, 1976.

[10] Checkland, P. *Systems Thinking, Systems Practice.* Wiley, 1981.

[11] Rechtin, E. *Systems Architecting.* Prentice Hall, 1991.

[12] Boehm, B., and Hansen, W. "Understanding the Spiral Model as a Tool for Evolutionary Acquisition." *CrossTalk.* May 2001.

[13] Booher, H., ed. *Handbook of Human Systems Integration.* Wiley, 2003.

[14] Pew, R., and Mavor, A., eds. *Human–System Integration in the System Development Process: A New Look.* National Academies Press, 2007.

[15] See Boehm and Hansen, May 2001.

[16] Maranzano, J. F., Rozsypal, S. A., Zimmerman, G. H., Warnken, G. W., Wirth, P. E., and Weiss, D. M. "Architecture Reviews: Practice and Experience." *IEEE Software.* March/April 2005;34–43.

[17] Kruchten, P. *The Rational Unified Process.* Addison Wesley, 1999.

[18] See Pew and Mavor, 2007.

[19] Royce, W. E. *Software Project Management.* Addison Wesley, 1998.

[20] *CrossTalk.* "Top Five Quality Software Projects." January 2002, July 2003, July 2004, September 2005. www.stsc.hill.af.mil/crosstalk.

[21] Boehm, B., Egyed, A., Kwan, J., Port, D., Shah, A., and Madachy, R. "Using the Win-Win Spiral Model: A Case Study." *Computer.* July 1998; 33–44.

[22] Koolmanojwong, S., and Boehm, B. "Using Software Project Courses to Integrate Education and Research: An Experience Report." Proceedings of the 2009 22nd Conference on Software Engineering Education and Training, IEEE, pp. 26–33.

[23] Blanchette, S., Crosson, S., and Boehm, B. *Evaluating the Software Design of a Complex System of Systems.* Technical Report CMU/SEI 2009-TR-23, January 2010.

[24] Eilperin, J., and Somashecker, S. "Private Consultants Warned of Risks before HealthCare.gov's Oct. 1 Launch." *The Washington Post,* November 18, 2013.

PHILOSOPHIÆ
NATURALIS
PRINCIPIA
MATHEMATICA.

Autore *JS. NEWTON*, *Trin. Coll. Cantab. Soc.* Matheseos
Professore *Lucasiano*, & Societatis Regalis Sodali.

IMPRIMATUR·
S. P E P Y S, *Reg. Soc.* P R Æ S E S.
Julii 5. 1686.

LONDINI,
Jussu *Societatis Regiæ* ac Typis *Josephi Streater*. Prostant Vena-
les apud *Sam. Smith* ad insignia Principis *Walliæ* in Cœmiterio
D. *Pauli*, aliosq; nonnullos Bibliopolas. *Anno* MDCLXXXVII.

Title page from Isaac Newton's *Principles of Mathematics*, in Latin, first published July 1687.
This book is regarded as one of the most important works in the history of science.

Wellcome Library, London

Part I

The Four ICSM Principles

"Our Age of Anxiety is, in great part, the result of trying to do today's job with yesterday's tools and yesterday's concepts."

—Marshall McLuhan

"Principles trump diagrams."

—Barry Boehm

As humans, we are often tempted to recognize a pattern from a diagram and to infer meaning and context not necessarily intended by the author (a form of syntax and semantics problem common to many graphical representations). This has happened often with the spiral model over the years. People spend more time looking at and interpreting the diagram than they do reading the paper and concepts that are associated with it. In other words, the diagrams are easier to use and require less energy than the study of the accompanying text.

The ICSM diagrams presented in the Introduction provide good perspectives on the ICSM process and hint at how it works in various project situations. However, each diagram is necessarily incomplete, and is thus open to misinterpretations—more than a few of them harmful. To minimize the hazards of misinterpretation, and to provide more comprehensive and applicable guidance, we have provided the four ICSM principles. These, along with a few supporting theories and generalized heuristics, make up the operational definition of the ICSM. They have also been found to help people avoid pitfalls and achieve success.

The four principles are:

1. Stakeholder value-based guidance
2. Incremental commitment and accountability
3. Concurrent multidiscipline engineering
4. Evidence- and risk-based decisions

diagrams misrepresent Concepts. ICSM principles give better look into the Icsm.

This part of the book elaborates on each principle in several ways. First, we share the stories of a failed project that did not apply the principle and a successful project that did. Next, we provide the underlying rationale for the principle. Finally, we discuss key practices for applying the principle, relating these to the ICSM through the stories and other examples.

While each chapter focuses on a single principle, the interaction among the principles is often illustrated—particularly in the stories. As might be expected, the successful-story projects also satisfied the other three principles. In the same way, most of the failure-story projects failed to satisfy more than one of the other principles.

1

The First Principle: Stakeholder Value-Based Guidance

"The principle of Win/Win is fundamental to success in all our interactions ... And it involves process; we cannot achieve Win/Win ends with Win/Lose or Lose/Win means."

—Stephen Covey, *The Seven Habits of Highly Effective People*, Simon and Schuster, 1989

"Systems and software engineering are of the people, by the people, and for the people."

—Freely adapted from Abraham Lincoln's Gettysburg Address, 1863

The principle of "stakeholder value-based guidance" derives from the International Council on Systems Engineering's (INCOSE) definition of systems engineering:

An interdisciplinary approach and means to enable the realization of successful systems.

As discussed in the Introduction, a system will be successful if and only if it makes winners of its success-critical stakeholders. Thus, to create a successful system, you need to identify which stakeholders are success-critical, determine their value propositions or win conditions, and define, design, develop, deploy, and evolve a mutually satisfactory or win-win system with respect to their evolving value propositions.

First, we share the story of a robot project that was a tremendous technical success, but failed to transition into operational use due to unintended but highly disagreeable consequences to one significant stakeholder. We then summarize some of the key lessons learned from the project. We next present the story of a highly successful development of a commercial intravenous medical pump that employed numerous techniques to identify and concurrently satisfy its success-critical stakeholders.

The chapter continues with a discussion of how the theories and their consideration of value undergird the "stakeholder value-based guidance" principle, and provide additional information on their application within the ICSM.

1.1 Failure Story: The Too-Good Road Surface Assessment Robot

The Carnegie Mellon University (CMU) Road Surface Assessment Robot project seemed to have done everything right (Figure 1-1). It delivered a system with radically higher accuracy, efficiency, and labor savings with respect to its manual predecessor system. However, its end product sat unused for 5 years in a storage room [1].

1.1.1 Project Context

Assessing the roughness of roads is important to the contractor delivering a road, since the contractor must fix any deviations to standards for the road's acceptable roughness. Current assessment techniques are manual, expensive, and time consuming. They are necessary, however, because repaving road surfaces with deviations from roughness standards is much more expensive. Any new tools for more efficient and accurate assessment of surface roughness would have a high payoff in time and cost savings.

The client for this particular project was a contracting company that needed to assess the roughness of a specially constructed road. The road was part of a dedicated set of roadways designed to transport standing people at speeds up to

FIGURE 1-1 CMU Surface Assessment Robot [1]

30–40 miles per hour. The client had participated in an engineering design course at CMU that produced an attractive design for a robot to be used as part of the road roughness assessment. Key stakeholders within the client company were its end-user division responsible for road systems, its Research and Development Office responsible for the creation or acquisition of new technology, its current group of manual road surface assessors, and its Quality Assurance organization responsible for monitoring corporate quality in its processes and products. The developer was CMU's Institute for Engineering Complex Systems.

1.1.2 Project Execution

The project was executed over three years. The first year explored alternative operational concepts for a robotic vehicle to identify and mark deviations from roughness standards on the roadway. The business case for the winning design indicated a likely 100:1 time and cost savings for inspection, which would more than repay the investment cost in its use on the specialized roadways. The first year ended with a specification for the system's functional and performance requirements that had been validated by a combination of prototyping, analysis, and review by the client's relevant specialty experts. A potential feature to have the robot's logic determine whether a deviation was critical enough to be marked was rejected, as the quality assurance organization wished to be able to analyze each deviation to determine quality improvement opportunities.

The second year involved selection of outsourced components and detailed build-to specifications for the robot vehicle. The specifications also addressed operations and maintenance procedures for the robot and its components, and assurances that the robot would not cause harm to the roadways. Further prototyping indicated that earlier concerns about sensor accuracy were unlikely to be a problem. The robot vehicle was successfully developed in the third year, and passed an acceptance test on a test track that had representative deviations built into it. It also passed the test of reducing inspection time by a factor of 100.

1.1.3 Final Results

Subsequently, the robot was tried on several miles of the first segment of specially built roadway, which had been produced by the best-qualified subcontractor for roadways. Several high-level managers from the company and the roadway subcontractor were present to observe the initial operation. The system operated entirely according to the specifications, but not according to expectations. Besides performing 100 times faster than the manual system, it reported 100 times as many deviations. A post-analysis by the lead engineer for surface assessment determined that all of the deviations were correctly reported by the system, but more than 99% of them were minor, not ride-quality threatening, and would not have been recorded by a manual inspection.

This outcome created an untenable situation, as the quality assurance organization was obliged to monitor corrective action for each deviation, and rejection of marked deviations could be considered as favoritism to specific subcontractors. The roadway subcontractor felt that its quality reputation was being unfairly degraded. Also, there seemed to be no degrees of freedom to repeat the robot test using comparable quality criteria to the previous manual assessment system. As a result, the best-acceptable management solution was to discontinue the robot project and to continue to use manual surface assessment methods. Fortunately, the sponsoring company appreciated the research value of the initial robot and requested a similar capability that fits its operational win conditions to be developed for future use.

1.1.4 Primary Lessons Learned

The operational concept analyses were good, but the operational scenarios were focused only on the technical performance of the robot vehicle, and not on the effect of off-nominal outcomes on the stakeholders involved. This happens fairly frequently on hardware and software engineering projects, which tend to concentrate on the technical aspects and neglect the sociotechnical aspects. A classic example was Thomas Edison's first patent (#90,646)—an electrical vote-counting device for legislative bodies. Edison learned that faster vote counting on a given bill was incompatible with various legislative strategies such as filibustering and off-line deal-making across multiple special interests and bills, and resolved that he would focus on only inventions for which there was strong public demand.

Another characteristic of sociotechnical systems is that their desired features tend to emerge with use, rather than being requirements that can be specified accurately prior to development. This places a value on designing for flexibility and adaptability, rather than optimizing a point solution on a single quantity and leaving no degrees of freedom to adjust the solution. As also seen in the box describing the experiment on giving developers different criteria to optimize [2], one should beware of the common practice of asking developers to maximize, minimize, or optimize a particular system attribute.

> ### Be Careful What You Ask For—You May Get It
> The Weinberg–Schulman experiment [2] involved five teams that were given the same software assignment: to develop a program for solving simultaneous linear equations using Gaussian elimination. However, each team was given different directions about what to optimize while doing the job. One team was asked to complete the job with the least possible effort, another team was to minimize the number of statements in the program, another was to minimize the amount of memory required by the program, another was to produce the clearest possible program (easy for maintainer-stakeholders to understand

and modify, and for owner-stakeholders to bound their total ownership costs), and the final team was to produce the clearest possible output (easy for end-user stakeholders to understand and use the results).

When the programs were completed and evaluated, the results were remarkable (Table 1-1):

- Each team finished first (or, in one case, second) with respect to the objective it was asked to optimize.

- None of the teams performed consistently well on all of the objectives.

Note in particular the performance of the first team—that is, the team asked to do the job with the least possible effort. Although this team finished first on effort to complete and second in *productivity* (lines of code produced per person-day), it finished next-to-last in the number of statements and amount of memory required to do the job, last in the clarity of their program, and third in the clarity of the output.

These results tend to confirm the following frequently made observations:

- *Software developers have very high achievement motivation.* If you define *good achievement* in terms of what you ask for, the developers will generally work very hard to give you just what you asked for.

- *Different software development objectives* do, indeed, conflict with each other in practice. In particular, as seen from the first team's performance, pure concentration on minimizing the software development effort (e.g., performing on a fixed-price contract) is likely to have bad effects on software life-cycle budgets and schedules and bad implications for effectiveness, because of the penalties paid in other important software dimensions such as program size, output usability and maintenance clarity.

[handwritten margin note: Software devs stick to main reqs.]

TABLE 1-1 Results of Asking Developers to Optimize Different Objectives

Team Objective: Optimize	Resulting Rank of Performance (1 = Best)				
	Effort to Complete	Number of Statements	Memory Required	Program Clarity	Output Clarity
Effort to complete	1	4	4	5	3
Number of statements	2–3	1	2	3	5
Memory required	5	2	1	4	4
Program clarity	4	3	3	2	2
Output clarity	2–3	5	5	1	1

Reprinted with permission from *Human-System Integration in the System Development Process*, 2007 by the National Academy of Sciences, Courtesy of the National Academies Press, Washington, D.C.

1.2 Success Story: The Hospira Next-Generation Intravenous Medical Pump

This section summarizes the systems engineering aspects of the next-generation Symbiq IV (intravenous) medical pump development, which was created by the Abbott Laboratories spinoff company Hospira, Inc., and documented in detail in Chapter 5 of the National Research Council (NRC) report, "Human–System Integration in the System Development Process [3]." The report describes the pump's purpose as being "to deliver liquid medications, nutrients, blood and other solutions at a programmed flow rates, volumes and time intervals via intravenous and other routes to a patient, primarily for hospital use with secondary limited feature use by patients at home."

In creating a next-generation product, Hospira proposed to introduce new IV pump features: multichannel versus single-channel liquid delivery; ability to gang multichannel devices together; associated user-programming capabilities and programmable drug libraries for specifying parallel delivery of liquids; use of color touchscreen devices for safety and ease of use; integration with numerous types of hospital information systems; ease of use for both medical personnel and patients and caregivers at home; handling of potential hardware, software, and human-user faults; compliance with U.S. and international safety standards; use of alternating-current or battery power; and the ability to be cost-competitive and attractive to traditional medical and hospital administration personnel. Many of these desiderata are highly coupled, such as multichannel hardware controls, correctly programmable dosages, concurrent software synchronization, distinctive displays and alarms for multichannel devices, and rigorous medical safety standards.

Views of the resulting Symbiq pump are shown in Figure 1-2. Its systems engineering involved a great deal of concurrent analysis and engineering of hardware, software, human factors, operational, business, and safety aspects. The device has been a commercial success, and it won the 2006 Human Factors and Ergonomics Society's User-Centered Product Design Award and the 2007 Medical Design Excellence Award.

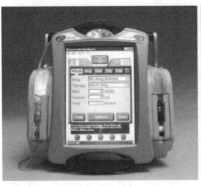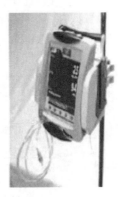

FIGURE 1-2 Symbiq Pump Industrial Design [4]

needed to satisfy many stakeholders

Numerous technical challenges were associated with this project, but the most critical was the need to engineer a product and a life-cycle operational concept that would produce satisfactory outcomes for a variety of stakeholders whose value propositions were often in conflict. Some customers wanted features that would require a complex user interface, while others wanted a simple, easy-to-learn and easy-to-use interface. Some users wanted the most advanced color-touchscreen displays available, while others wanted a simpler, cheaper product that was harder to misuse via inadvertent screen touches. Some organizations felt that a minimal interpretation of the required safety features would be acceptable, while others advocated ultrahigh assurance levels. Some marketing personnel wanted a quick development and fielding of the basic product to capture market share, while maintainers wanted initial built-in life-cycle support, maintenance, and diagnostic capabilities.

In such situations, many organizations focus on making quick requirements decisions and rapidly proceeding into development or outsourcing. However, Hospira's understanding of the uncertainties and risks prompted the company to pursue a risk-driven, incremental-commitment course of buying information to reduce risk. As described in the NRC report, the developers used a version of the Incremental Commitment Spiral Model (ICSM). The following sections describe the project's incremental system definition progress through the ICSM Exploration, Valuation, Foundations, and Development phases. Some evolution of terminology has occurred since the report's publication: the report uses "ICM" instead of "ICSM," and *Architecting = Foundations* "Architecting phase" instead of "Foundations phase." A description of this project has been included as a case study of successful systems engineering in Part 7 of the Systems Engineering Research Center–INCOSE–IEEE Systems Engineering Body of Knowledge (SEBoK) [5]. A summary of the ICSM is also included in the section of Part 3 of the SEBoK on Life-Cycle Models.

1.2.1 Symbiq Exploration Phase Summary

In the Exploration phase, the project carried out numerous stakeholder needs, technical opportunities, and business competition analyses, and determined ranges of preferred options. Stakeholder needs analyses included contextual inquiry via shadowing of nurses using IV pumps and follow-up interviews, along with creating task flow diagrams, use environment analyses, and user profiles analyses. Technical opportunity analyses included initial conceptual designs of multichannel pump configurations, evaluation of commercially available single-color and multicolor display devices and touchscreen capabilities, and software approaches for specifying multichannel delivery options and synchronizing concurrent processes.

Business competition analyses included hiring a management and marketing planning firm to perform next-generation pump major competitor strengths and weaknesses analyses with respect to such capabilities as number of pump channels, therapies, programming options, air-in-line management, battery and alternating-current capabilities, biomedical domain expertise, and alarms.

Several key competitive advantages of a next-generation pump were identified, such as bar-code reading capability, small size and light weight, stand-alone functional channels, an extensive drug library, a high level of reliability, and clear mapping of screen displays and pumping channels.

Market research identified market windows, market segment analyses, pricing alternatives, hospital purchasing decision analyses, and safety aspects. These were iterated with respect to focus groups of key thought leaders in critical care. The results were factored into a product concept plan, cost analysis, and business case analysis. Independent experts reviewed these artifacts as part of the Valuation Commitment Review process. The review identified several risks to be managed, such as safety assurance for the hardware, software, and human usage aspects. A go-ahead decision was made once these risks were covered by risk management plans.

1.2.2 Symbiq Valuation Phase Summary

The Valuation phase focused on the major risks highlighted in the Valuation Commitment Review. These included the multichannel pump options, the types of programmable therapies, the need for tailorable medication libraries, the display screen and user interface options, and the safety considerations. The Valuation phase also elaborated the product concept plan for the most attractive general set of options, including a development plan and operations plan, along with an associated cost analysis, risk analysis, and business case for review at the Foundations Commitment Review.

The multichannel pump options were explored via several hardware industrial design mockups and early usability test of the mockups. These included evaluation of such desired capabilities as semi-automatic cassette loading, special pole-mounting hardware, stacking of channels and total number of channels, and tubing management features. The evaluations led to overall choices of a semi-automatic cassette loading capability with a red–yellow–green LED display to indicate concerns with the loading mechanism and with the pump in general. Field exercises with prototypes of the pole mountings indicated the need for quick-release/activation mechanisms, which were subsequently implemented. Risk analyses of alternative stacking mechanisms and total number of channels established a preference for side-by-side stacking, a decision to develop one-channel and two-channel units, and the need to support a maximum of four channels in a stacked configuration.

The types of programmable therapies considered included continuous delivery for a specified time period; patient weight-based dosing; piggyback or alternating delivery between the two channels; tapered or ramped-rate delivery; intermittent-interval delivery; variable-time delivery; and multistep delivery. These capabilities were evaluated via prototyping of the software on a simulated version of the pump complexes, and iterated until satisfactory versions were found.

Evaluation of the tailorable medication libraries addressed the issue that different hard and soft safety limits were needed for dosages in different parts of a hospital (e.g., emergency room, intensive care, oncology, pediatric care). This established a requirement for hospitals to be able to program their own soft limits (which could be overridden by nurses with permission codes) and hard limits (no overrides permitted). Stakeholder satisfaction with the tailoring features was achieved via prototype exercises and iteration with representative hospital personnel.

A literature review was conducted to determine the relative advantages and disadvantages of leading input and display technologies, including cost and reliability data. After three leading vendors of touchscreen color LCD displays were selected and further investigation of their costs and capabilities was conducted, a business risk analysis focused on the tradeoff between larger displays and customer interest in small-footprint IV pumps. The larger display was selected, based on its better readability and the reduced risk of wrong user entries owing to the larger screen buttons. Extensive usability prototyping and operational concept formulation was done with hardware mockups and embedded software that delivered simulated animated graphic user interface (GUI) displays to a touchscreen interface that was integrated into the hardware case.

The safety risk analysis in the Valuation phase followed ISO 14971:2000 standards for medical device design, focusing on failure modes and effects analyses (FMEAs) based on the early high-level design, such as entry of excessive drug doses or misuse of soft-safety-limit overrides. Subsequent-phase FMEAs would elaborate these analyses, based on the more detailed designs and implementations.

As in the Exploration phase, the results of the Validation phase analyses, plans and budgets for the succeeding phases, the resulting revised business case, evidence of solution feasibility, and remaining risks with their risk management plans were reviewed by independent experts. The Foundations Commitment Review was passed subject to a few risk level and risk management adjustments.

1.2.3 Symbiq Foundations Phase Summary

During the Foundations phase, considerable effort was directed toward addressing the identified risks, such as the need for prototyping of the full range of GUI usage by the full range of targeted users, including doctors and home caregivers and patients; for interoperability of the Symbiq software with the wide variety of available hospital information systems; and for fully detailed FMEAs and other safety analyses. Comparable added effort went into detailed planning for development, production, operations, and support, providing more accurate inputs for business case analyses.

GUI prototyping was geared toward meeting a set of usability objectives, such as the following:

- Ninety percent of experienced nurses will be able to insert the cassette the first time while receiving minimal training. Ninety-nine percent will be able to correct any insertion errors.

- Ninety percent of first-time users with no training would be able to power the pump off when directed.

- Eighty percent of caregiver/patient users would rate the overall ease of use of the IV pump as 3 or higher on a 5-point scale of satisfaction, with 5 being the highest value.

Similar extensive evaluations were done on the efficacy and acceptability of the audio alarms, including use of a patient and intensive care unit simulator that included other medical devices that produced noises and other distractions such as ringing telephones. This helped to adjust the alarms and the understandability of the visual displays.

Software interoperability risk management involved extensive testing of interaction scenarios between the Symbiq software and a representative set of hospital information systems. These tests resulted in several adjustments to the software interoperability architecture. Also, because the product was being developed as a platform for the next generation of infusion pump products, the software design was analyzed for overspecialization to the initial product, resulting in several revisions. Similar analyses and revisions were performed for the hardware design.

As the design was refined into complete build-to specifications for the hardware and the operational software, the safety analyses were elaborated into complete FMEAs of the detailed designs. These picked up several potential safety issues, particularly involving the off-nominal usage scenarios, but overall confirmed a high assurance level for the safety of the product design. However, the safety risk assessment recommended a risk management plan for the Development phase to include continued FMEAs, thorough off-nominal testing of the developing product's hardware and software, and extensive beta-testing of the product at representative hospitals prior to full release.

This plan and the other Development and Operations phase plans, product and process feasibility evidence, and business case analysis updates were reviewed at a Development Commitment Review, which resulted in a commitment to proceed into the Development phase.

1.2.4 Symbiq Development Phase Systems Engineering Summary

The Development phase was primarily concerned with developing and testing the hardware and software to the build-to specifications. Nevertheless, it continued an active systems engineering function to support change management, operations, production, and support planning and preparation, and further safety assurance activities as recommended in the risk management plan for the phase.

For hospital beta-testing, thoroughly bench-tested and working beta versions of the IV pump were deployed in two hospital settings. The hospitals programmed drug libraries for at least two clinical care areas. The devices were used for about 4 weeks. Surveys and interviews were conducted with the users to capture their "real world" experiences with the pump. Data from the pump usage and interaction memory was also analyzed and compared to original doctors' orders. The beta tests revealed a number of opportunities to make improvements, including revision of the more annoying alarm melodies, and revision of the methods for entering units of medication delivery time in hours or minutes.

Usability testing was also conducted on one of the sets of abbreviated instructions called TIPS cards. These cards serve as reminders for how to complete the most critical tasks. Numerous suggestions for improvement in the TIPS cards, as well as the user interface, came from this work, including how to reset the "air-in-line" alarm and how to address the alarm and check all on-screen help text for accuracy.

The previously mentioned usability objectives were used as acceptance criteria for the validation usability tests. These objectives were met. For example, the calculated task completion accuracy was 99.66% for all tasks for first-time nurse users with minimal training. A few minor usability problems were uncovered that were subsequently fixed without major changes to the GUI or that affected critical safety-related tasks.

The risk analysis was iterated and revised as the product development matured. FMEAs were updated for safety-critical risks associated with three product areas: the user interface, the mechanical and electrical subsystems, and the product manufacturing process. Some detailed-implementation problems were found and fixed, but overall the risk of continuing into full-scale production, operations, and support was minimal. Systems engineering continued into the Operations phase, primarily to address customer change requests and problem reports, and to participate in planning for a broader product line of IV pumps.

Overall, customer satisfaction, sales, and profits from the Symbiq IV pump have been strong, and satisfaction levels among the management, financial, customer, end-user, developer, maintainer, regulatory, and medical-community stakeholders have been quite high. This largely reflects the extensive stakeholder involvement in the system's formulation, analysis, and process commitment decision milestones.

1.3 The Fundamental System Success Theorem and Its Implications

In the Introduction, we presented overviews of the Fundamental System Success Theorem and the System Success Realization Theorem [6,7]. The Fundamental System Success Theorem states:

> *A system will be successful if and only if it makes winners of its success-critical stakeholders.*

The proof of "if" was summarized as follows:

1. Everyone significant is a winner.
2. Nobody significant is left to complain.

Some external critics may complain that the system did not use their favorite technology, but if they are not success-critical, they cannot affect the success of the project for the success-critical stakeholders.

The proof of "only if" was summarized as follows:

1. Nobody wants to lose.
2. Prospective losers will refuse to participate, or will counterattack.
3. The usual result is lose-lose.

The proof is elaborated by example in three frequently occurring instances of the primary stakeholders in an enterprise involving a customer contracting with a developer for a software system that will benefit a community of users, as shown in Table 1-2 [8].

In Case 1, the customer and developer attempt to win at the expense of the user by skimping on effort and quality. When presented with the product, the user refuses to use it, leaving everyone a loser with respect to expectations.

In Case 2, the developer and the user attempt to win at the expense of the customer (usually on a cost-plus contract) by adding numerous low-value "bells and whistles" to the product. When the customer's budget is exhausted without a resulting value-added product, again everyone is a loser with respect to expectations.

In Case 3, the user and the customer compile an ambitious set of features to be developed and pressure competing developers to bid low or lose the competition. Once a contract is signed, the surviving bidder will usually counterattack by colluding with the user or the customer to convert the project into Case 2 (adding user bells and whistles with funded engineering change proposals) or Case 1 (by minimally interpreting vague contract terms for user help, maintenance diagnostics, and so on). Again, everyone is a loser.

The Failure Story and Success Story presented earlier in this chapter also illustrate the Fundamental System Success Theorem. The Too-Good Road Surface Assessment Robot shows that it takes only one losing success-critical stakeholder looking bad to turn a technically outstanding product into an unsuccessful operational one. The Next-Generation Intravenous Medical Pump success story shows how much effort Hospira went to in identifying and satisfying its financial, doctor, nurse, administrator, and safety assurance stakeholders via business case analyses, interviews, surveys, prototypes, and safety analyses in the process of defining and developing their product.

TABLE 1-2 Win-Lose Generally Becomes Lose-Lose

Proposed Solution	"Winner"	Loser
Quick, cheap, sloppy product	Developer and customer	User
Lots of "bells and whistles"	Developer and user	Customer
Driving too hard a bargain	Customer and user	Developer

One implication of the Fundamental System Success Theorem is that it is risky to use terms such as "optimize," "minimize," and "maximize" in project guidance. As Nobel Prize winner Herbert Simon showed in his book *Models of Man* [9], success in multiple-stakeholder situations is achieved not by optimizing, minimizing, or maximizing of individual criteria, but rather by *satisficing* with respect to the stakeholders' multiple criteria. In the latter case, the stakeholders do not get everything they want, but obtain an outcome that is better than their previous situation. Another implication is that several practices are necessary to achieve a stakeholder win-win situation, as discussed next.

1.4 The System Success Realization Theorem and Its Implications

As discussed in the previous section, the Fundamental System Success Theorem does not tell us how to realize and maintain a win-win state. This requires the System Success Realization Theorem:

Making winners of your success-critical stakeholders requires:

1. Identifying all of the success-critical stakeholders (SCSs).
2. Understanding how the SCSs want to win.
3. Having the SCSs negotiate a win-win set of product and process plans.
4. Controlling progress toward SCS win-win realization and adaptation to change.

The next four sections elaborate these four success-realization elements.

1.4.1 Identifying All of the SCSs

A good way to identify your system's SCSs is via the ICSM's Concurrency View, shown in Figure 0-6 in the Introduction. The first three rows in Figure 0-6 cover the concurrent activities most prominent at the beginning of the Exploration phase: Envisioning Opportunities, System Scoping, and Understanding Needs. They involve exploring what is unsatisfactory with the current system of interest (which may be an individual system, a product line of similar systems, or an enterprise that includes a number of product lines and individual systems) and identifying alternative candidates for improving it. The Understanding Needs activity generally involves using existing feedback from the system's current SCSs (end-users, operators, administrators, maintenance and support personnel, suppliers, distributors, customers, system-level managers, higher-level managers, and perhaps others) to determine what needs fixing to make the system better serve their needs. This activity will produce a baseline set of SCSs.

The Envisioning Opportunities activity may involve ways to improve or extend the current system by modernizing its aging infrastructure, extending its capabilities, capitalizing on emerging technology, or forming strategic partnerships with organizations having complementary capabilities that would enable the current system to better serve the existing customers and users, or to serve a broader base of customers and users. Alternatively, it may involve setting up a new organization to pursue a new technology or business opportunity. In either case, such activities are likely to extend the baseline set of SCSs, or perhaps to reduce the baseline by phasing out or divesting existing product lines or services.

The System Scoping activity during the Exploration phase will perform an initial winnowing of the candidate initiatives, based on top-level feasibility evidence and business-case analysis. It will also identify further SCSs, such as finance specialists, venture capitalists, or other research and development sponsors.

The later parts of the Exploration phase and the Valuation phase will involve the concurrent engineering of system goals/objectives/requirements; the concurrent top-level architecting and designing of the human, hardware, and software aspects of alternative system solutions and their top-level life-cycle plans; and a top-level analysis of the relative feasibility of the candidate solutions. These activities will also involve iteration of the earlier needs, opportunities, and system scoping analyses. In addition, they will identify further candidate SCSs, such as systems engineers, systems developers, system assurance personnel, and, as needed, contract management personnel, business process engineering personnel, business management personnel, and specialists in needed technical and human factors disciplines.

The Foundations phase may identify further SCSs as the project works out its success-critical preparations for development, transition, and operations. These may include representatives of organizations concerned with safety, security, or other general-public concerns; representatives of critical supply-chain management functions; and representatives of diverse customers receiving specially developed versions of the developed system.

All of these stakeholders add up to a rather formidable set of SCSs. The good news is that most projects will involve a relatively minimal subset of the potential SCSs—frequently just representatives of the four major life-cycle roles of end-user, acquirer, developer, and maintainer, with others brought in on an as-needed basis. For smaller, less-critical projects, the roles of end-user, acquirer, and maintainer can often be merged into a single SCS, as with agile methods. And for many system issues, only a small number of stakeholders are SCSs.

1.4.2 Understanding How the SCSs Want to Win

The activities discussed in the preceding subsection will not only identify SCSs, but also bring to light many of their win conditions or value propositions with respect to the system being defined. A good example is the information about what is unsatisfactory with the current system of interest. Other examples include information on opportunities to improve or extend the current system, and desired capabilities identified in exploring improved concepts of operation. Beyond these, references such as the National Research Council report, *Human–System Integration in the System Development Process* [10], identify further methods for eliciting stakeholders' desired capabilities, such as field observation, task and workflow analysis, participatory analysis, scenario development, prototyping, executable models and simulations, stories and use cases, and concept mapping.

The dependency ratings refer only to direct dependencies. For example, system developers, acquirers, and administrators are concerned with safety or security only to the extent that a system's information suppliers, users, and dependents are concerned with them. In turn, information suppliers and system dependents are concerned with reliability and availability only to the extent that these help provide their direct concerns with security and safety. Further information on how the priorities of system functional capabilities and quality attributes vary by stakeholder role is provided in Chapter 2.

1.4.3 Having the SCSs Negotiate a Win-Win Set of Product and Process Plans

As seen in Table 1-3, the relative priorities for different quality attributes vary by stakeholder role. This is also the case for functional capabilities, which means that the SCSs will often have to negotiate mutually satisfactory or win-win combinations of system capabilities and quality attributes. In general, this means that each stakeholder will not get everything he or she wants, but will get an outcome that is better than the current situation.

These methods are good for identifying capabilities, but not as effective for identifying the system's desired quality attributes. Fortunately, some research results (such as those in Table 1-2) provide a top-level baseline for how the major quality attributes vary by system stakeholder. Most of the terms in Table 1-3 are reasonably self-explanatory, but two may require further explanations. System dependents are people who are not involved in the system's development or operation, but also dependent on some of its attributes (e.g., safety for airline passengers and medical patients). System controllers perform real-time control of a system (e.g., airline pilots or electric power distribution controllers). Stakeholders may belong to multiple classes: an airline pilot is both a system controller and a system-dependent passenger, for example.

For more than 15 years, we have been developing, applying, and evolving methods, processes, and tools for diverse stakeholders to express their win conditions, to identify conflicts among the win conditions, and to negotiate win-win agreements [11,12,13]. The six generations of WinWin toolsets have been used on more than 200 projects, with increasing success rates in speed and stakeholder satisfaction in using the approach and tools. The latest version has used a Facebook style that has made it much easier for nontechnical stakeholders to use the toolset, and to remain involved in renegotiating changes as a project progresses.

TABLE 1-3 Top-Level Stakeholder/Value Dependencies: Quality Attributes

Dependability Attributes	Information Suppliers	System Dependents	Information Brokers	Information Consumers Mission – critical	Information Consumers Mission – uncrit.	System Controllers	Developers	Maintainers	Administrators	Acquirers
Protection										
Safety		**		**		**				
Security	*	**	**	**		**				
Privacy	**		**	*	*					
Robustness										
Reliability		*	*	**		**		*	*	
Availability		*	*	**		**		*	*	
Survivability		*	*	**		**		*	*	
Quality of Service										
Performance			**	**	*	**		*	*	
Accuracy, Consistency	**		**	**	*	**			*	
Usability	*		*	**	**	**			*	
Evolvability			*	**	*	*		**	*	**
Interoperability			**							**
Correctness							*			**
Cost							*			**
Schedule			*	**	*	*	**			**
Reusability							**	*		*

** Critical
* Significant
() Insignificant or indirect

Figure 1-3 depicts the relationship between the various elements of a WinWin equilibrium. It is defined as having all of the stakeholders' Win Conditions covered by Agreements to include the Win Condition among all of the stakeholders, with no outstanding Issues. This is true by default at the beginning of the process. When a stakeholder enters a Win Condition, the other stakeholders can discuss it and decide whether to agree with (a modification of) it as part of the system definition. If all of the stakeholders agree, the Win Condition is covered by an Agreement, and the WinWin equilibrium is preserved.

If stakeholders disagree, they should submit Issues saying why they disagree, and ideally indicating what needs to be done to enable them to agree. The resulting loss of the WinWin equilibrium due to an outstanding Issue needs to be addressed by stakeholders submitting Options to resolve the Issue. Almost always, the resulting discussions and evolution of the Options result in a resolution of the Issue and restoration of the WinWin equilibrium. If not, it is best to recognize this fact early and either rescope the project or terminate it, as we have seen that a win-lose situation almost always leads to a lose-lose result.

An excellent source for creating options for mutual gain is *Getting to Yes* [14]. At the enterprise level, an excellent set of patterns of success and examples for developing a success-oriented culture is a Mitre report, *Patterns of Success in Systems Engineering* [15]. Based on extensive project analyses, this report includes several social patterns of success, such as establishing a Circle of Trust among stakeholders, and organizing around networks versus nodes. Moreover, it identifies several technical patterns of success, such as "Seeing Is Believing" via prototyping and multiple-stakeholder views, and planning to replan versus planning the work and blindly working the plan. From a stakeholder value standpoint, some good techniques for expediting win-win convergence are expectations management [16] and matching people's tasks to their win conditions.

The key principles in matching people's tasks to their win conditions involve *searching out win-win situations* and *expanding the option space to create*

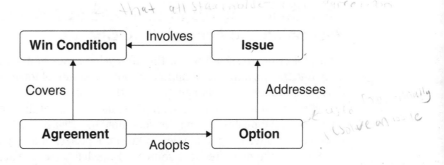

FIGURE 1-3 The WinWin Equilibrium Model

win-win situations. Some effective techniques available to the project manager for searching out win-win situations include the following [17]:

- Breaking options into parts (functions, activities, increments, phases), and configuring combinations of suboptions into win packages for each participant. For example, under some conditions, establishing a separate leader for successive system increments has worked well, particularly if the increments are large, with different technical and/or organizational centers of gravity.
- Realigning options along win-win axes. For example, some projects have successfully shifted the authority and responsibility for quality assurance from the developer, who may consider it a bore, to the maintainer, who will consider it a major win-leverage opportunity.

Among the effective techniques available to the project manager for expanding the option space to create win-win situations are the following:

- Linking tasks to future options and career paths ("Quality assurance may be a bore, but it's a ticket to a fast-track career path").
- Expanding the scope of a task ("Quality assurance should not be a bore. I think you could lead the way in helping us make quality assurance a more proactive function in getting us quality products. That would be a real achievement").
- Linking tasks to extra rewards ("Rescuing this integration and test mess will be a killer, but I'll make sure you get a good bonus and lots of kudos if you succeed").
- Providing extra support ("This schedule is very ambitious, but I'll provide your team with the first-class tools and facilities you'll need to meet it").
- Surfacing new options ("We can't develop all the functions in 12 months, but if we do an incremental development, we can satisfy your top-priority needs in 12 months").

1.4.4 Controlling Progress toward SCS Win-Win Realization and Adaptation to Change

As a project progresses through the life-cycle phases and stages, it will increasingly find that its initial assumptions about the nature of its product plans and process plans will undergo change. Some of these changes will preserve or strengthen the win-win equilibrium, but others will cause aspects of the project to change into a win-lose relationship among the stakeholders. Clearly, such changes need to be monitored, analyzed, and handled to keep the project in a win-win equilibrium.

Some of the most frequent sources of needed corrective action are destabilizing changes in the following areas:

- The value propositions of the SCSs
- The organizational relationships among the SCSs
- The need to accommodate new SCSs
- The competitive marketplace and emerging technology
- The project's feasibility evidence and business case
- The infrastructure upon which the system is built
- The interfaces between the system and its co-dependent external systems
- The key personnel involved in the project
- The financial or other resources required for the project
- The regulations that the project needs to satisfy

When such changes are destabilizing, the relevant SCSs need to revisit their previous negotiated win-win solution and determine the most cost-effective way to recover a win-win equilibrium. In outsourcing situations, it is best to identify the relevant destabilizers as project stability assumptions that will need to be addressed if they become invalid.

References

[1] Latimer, D.T. IV. *Effectiveness of Engineering Practices for the Acquisition and Employment of Robotic Systems.* PhD dissertation, Department of Computer Science, University of Southern California, May 2008.

[2] Weinberg, G., and Schulman, E. "Goals and Performance in Computer Programming." *Human Factors.* 1974;16(1):70–77.

[3] Pew, R., and Mavor, A. *Human–System Integration in the System Development Process.* NAS Press, 2007.

[4] Pew and Mavor, 2007.

[5] Pyster, A., et al. *The Systems Engineering Body of Knowledge (SEBoK).* 2012. www.sebokwiki.org.

[6] Boehm, Barry, and Ross, Rony. "Theory-W Software Project Management Principles and Examples." *IEEE Transactions on Software Engineering.* 1989;15(7):902–916.

[7] Boehm, Barry, and Jain, Apurva. "A Value-Based Theory of Systems Engineering." *Proceedings, INCOSE,* 2006.

[8] Boehm, Barry, Huang, LiGuo, Jain, Apurva, and Madachy, Ray. "The Nature of Information System Dependability: A Stakeholder/Value Approach," Technical Report USC-CSE-2004-520, http://csse.usc.edu/csse/TECHRPTS/2004/2004_main.html.

[9] Simon, H. *Models of Man*. Wiley, 1957.

[10] Pew and Mavor, 2007.

[11] Boehm, B., Lee, M. J., Bose, P., and Horowitz, E. *Software Requirements Negotiation and Renegotiation Aids: A Theory-W Based Spiral Approach*. 17th International Conference on Software Engineering (ICSE'95), ACM-IEEE, May 1995, p. 243.

[12] Boehm, B., Grunbacher, P., and Briggs, R. "Developing Groupware for Requirements Negotiation: Lessons Learned/" *IEEE Software*. May/June 2001;46–55.

[13] Kukreja, N., and Boehm, B. "Process Implications of Social Networking-Based Requirements Negotiation Tools." *Proceedings, ICSSP 2012,* June 2012.

[14] Fisher, R., and Ury, W. *Getting to Yes*. Houghton Mifflin, 1981.

[15] Rebovich, G., and DeRosa, J. *Patterns of Success in Systems Engineering*. MITRE Product MP 110369. Bedford, MA: Mitre Corporation, November 2011.

[16] Karten, N. *Managing Expectations*. Dorset House, 1994.

[17] Boehm and Ross, 1989.

2

The Second Principle: Incremental Commitment and Accountability

"Thus grief still treads upon the heels of pleasure
Married in haste, we may repent at leisure"

—William Congreve, *The Old Batchelour*, 1693

"Trust is built through effective commitments. Trust is lost through inconsistent behavior on matters of importance. If trust has been cultivated and grown over time ... the project will be highly resilient to problems."

—Scott Berkun, *The Art of Project Management*, Chapter 12, O'Reilly, 2005

Successful system development projects are built on a bedrock of trust. If people don't trust each other, they will cut down on sharing information and helping each other out. They will gird themselves in contractual overhead and bureaucracy, and build Pearl Harbor files to be able to blame others if the project gets into trouble—and such behavior is often precisely what gets the project into trouble. And as stated earlier, trust is built through effective commitments.

Watts Humphrey, in *Managing the Software Process* [1], has identified six critical elements of effective commitments:

1. The person making the commitment does so willingly.
2. The commitment is not made lightly; that is, the work involved, the resources, and the schedule are carefully considered.
3. There is agreement between the parties as to what is to be done, by whom, and when.
4. The commitment is openly and publicly stated.
5. The person responsible tries to meet the commitment, even if help is needed.
6. Prior to the committed date, if something changes that impacts either party relative to the commitment, advance notice is given and a new commitment is negotiated.

While this looks like a heavyweight set of conditions, once a basis for trust is built up among people—even those initially unfamiliar with each other—the conditions become understood within the common framework of the task under consideration. For example, the documented content of the commitments might be based on stories or capability descriptions rather than complete, consistent, traceable, testable requirements. And if meeting a fixed schedule is critical, the agreement may include the option of dropping lower-priority features to meet the schedule. Another definition of trust is that each party has confidence that the other parties feel accountable for the commitments they have made.

→ To be accountable for a commitment, it is important to neither promise nor expect more than can be delivered. In a world of rapidly changing mission priorities, new technologies, competitive challenges, and organizational relationships, total commitment to the full details of a product to be delivered five years later is a very risky bet. It is easy to see how incremental commitments are more satisfactory than total up-front commitments.

Understanding the Cone of Uncertainty [2,3,4], shown in Figure 2-1, helps to appreciate commitments in this context of change. Early in a system's life cycle,

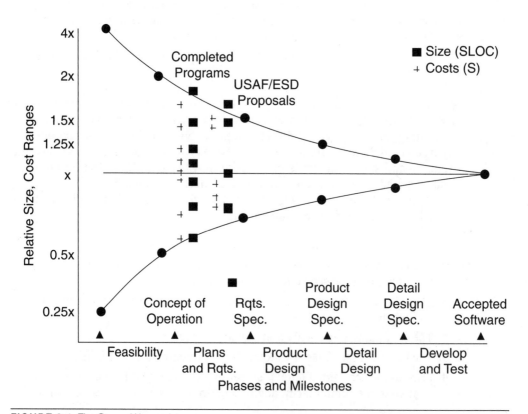

FIGURE 2-1 The Cone of Uncertainty

there are many possible system capabilities and solutions to consider, leading to a wide range of system costs. Particularly in competitive procurements, it is tempting to make bids and proposals at the lower edge of the Cone of Uncertainty. This is often rationalized through optimistic assumptions such as "The A team will perform on the project," "The COTS products will do everything right," or "It shouldn't take *that* much effort to turn the prototypes into products." Often, such temptations are mirrored with similar behavior by acquirers who are trying to sell their programs, resulting in a "conspiracy of optimism." This usually results in a project's actual costs far outrunning the optimistic estimates and creating a large overrun.

Even with less optimistic assumptions, committing to a fixed-price contract at an early date would run a large risk of promising more than you can deliver and overrunning your agreed-upon budget. Instead, it is preferable to do some prototyping, architecting, or COTS evaluations before committing to a fixed price (or, as discussed in the Introduction, to use a poker or blackjack approach rather than a roulette approach).

2.1 A Failed Total-Commitment Project: Bank of America's MasterNet

In the 1950s and 1960s, Bank of America (BofA) was the leading pioneer in banking automation with its electronic check processing capability. Subsequent BofA leaders had other interests, allowing BofA's banking automation capabilities to degrade over time. In 1981, BofA's new president, Sam Armacost, had an agenda to regain its automation leadership by "leapfrogging into the 1990s." After an in-house effort that spent $6 million and failed to develop a workable trust management system, Armacost appointed a new executive vice president of the trust management department, Clyde Claus, with the charge of either modernizing the department or discontinuing it.

2.1.1 Case Study History

In a partial implementation of ICSM Principle 1, Claus set up a Voice of the Customer approach to interview representatives of the various banks and trust management organizations that would be employing MasterNet's services, to determine which services the system should provide to them. This resulted in a very large set of customer-desired requirements, covering more than 100 types of assets and the need to comply with numerous federal and state requirements. The resulting software comprised 3.5 million lines of code.

Given the 1981 BofA in-house development failure, Claus began looking for an external company with a successful trust management system development record, and reusable software assets that could enable a large amount of trust management software to be built quickly. This search ended with Claus entering negotiations with Steven Katz, the CEO of Premier Systems, which had developed several successful trust management systems for smaller banks. Katz indicated that if he could reuse his current trust management software, he could develop the full set of desired capabilities in the 9 months and $22 million budgeted for MasterNet.

Unfortunately, Claus's systems engineering personnel had been transferred to a corporate systems engineering group, so they were unable to perform a detailed analysis of Katz's proposal. Because BofA didn't see any superior options, Claus and his management went ahead and signed a contract for Katz to proceed in March 1984, with the full system delivery due in December 1984. By then, Katz had 100 programmers working on the project, but it was far from complete, as the software was not as reusable as expected, it did not scale up well to BofA's large-bank needs, and numerous "devils in the details" slowed the development down.

BofA's management did not wish to announce another failure. Instead, they agreed to increase the budget and extend the schedule to build a critical-mass trust management capability. After a large number of features had been developed in 1985–1986, Claus decided to showcase the new MasterNet system in a major public relations event to demonstrate "the industry's most sophisticated technology for handling trust accounts." The event went moderately well, but it did not demonstrate scalability because the Prime computer hardware and software supporting Premier Systems' trust management capabilities could not scale up to BofA's trust management workload.

During 1986, Claus began preparing for the conversion and cutover to MasterNet, beginning with the transfer of the $38 billion worth of institutional trust customers. The initial platform was a 1 million instructions per second (MIPS), 8 megabytes of main memory Prime computer, which was seriously underpowered. Even with an upgrade to a three 16-megabyte, 8-MIPS processor configuration (along with a lot of operating system and data management system rework), the system could not process the workload. Subsequently, 21 of the 24 Prime disk drives failed and needed to be replaced.

System problems continued during 1987. Two more processors were added, but crashes continued, and monthly reports were up to two months late. Clients began dropping off, with BofA's base dwindling from 800 to 700 accounts and from $38 billion to $34 billion in institutional assets. The Prime-based trust system did not interoperate well with the rest of BofA's IBM mainframe systems. Eventually, in May 1988, BofA transferred its whole trust business to other banks, after an overall expenditure of $80 million and more than four years of project effort. The previous president, Tom Clausen, replaced Armacost in late 1986, and Claus resigned in October 1987. Further descriptions of MasterNet are available from other sources [5,6].

2.1.2 Relation to ICSM Principles

Numerous factors contributed to the failed MasterNet project, but the main one was the total-commitment violation of Principle 2 to entrust Katz and Premier Systems with the implementation of the full 3.5 million lines of software, without incrementally determining whether this solution was feasible and compatible with the rest of BofA's IBM mainframe systems. By over-focusing on the Voice of the Customer in committing to the full wish list of capabilities, and neglecting both the voices of the maintainers in choosing an incompatible Prime-based system and the voices of BofA top management and investors in neglecting to perform a full risk analysis of the project's feasibility, the project was also in violation of Principle 1 (i.e., considering the interests of all the success-critical stakeholders). Principle 1 also played a role in this case, because the value propositions of stakeholders can change over time, so there needs to be a continuing means of adapting the system, where reasonable, to those changing values. Moreover, as we will see, the MasterNet project was in violation of Principle 4 regarding evidence-based and risk-based decision making.

Figure 2-2 summarizes the results of several studies performed at USC on the root causes of failed projects [7,8,9]. The studies concluded that the main causes of project failure tended to be projects adopting a total-commitment development approach without considering issues of development feasibility with respect to the full range of success-critical stakeholders. The studies found that the key stakeholder classes common to virtually all projects (users, acquirers, developers, maintainers)

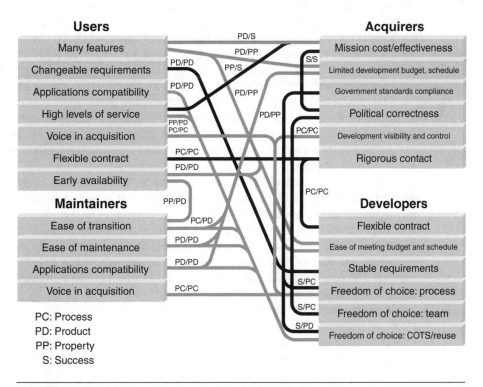

FIGURE 2-2 The Value Proposition Model-Clash Spider Web. The gray lines show MasterNet model clashes.

consistently had serious incompatibilities among their top value propositions or success models.

The upper-left part of Figure 2-2 shows the most frequent value propositions or win conditions of people in the user role (for MasterNet, the trust departments of banks for which the project team was creating MasterNet—i.e., the "voice of the customer"). The "many features" product model (PD) added up to 3.5 million lines of code. The "applications compatibility" product model (PD) meant interoperability with BofA's other IBM mainframe/OS-360/COBOL applications. The "high levels of service" property model (PP) meant near-instant response time, 24/7 availability, and ease of use, among other characteristics. The "voice in acquisition" process model (PC) often meant, "I'm not sure I'll need this, but since you're asking, I'll put it on the list." The "early availability" property model (PP) meant, "We need it all as soon as possible."

The BofA acquirers in the upper-right part of Figure 2-2, bereft of much systems engineering support, interpreted the "mission cost-effectiveness" success model (S) as committing to satisfy the full set of user wishes on a highly ambitious budget ($22 million) and schedule (9 months). The project team tried to achieve this by choosing Premier Systems and its reusable models and software, but Premier Systems' product model (PD) value proposition of developer "freedom of choice: COTS/reuse"—using Prime computer equipment—clashed with the IBM mainframe/OS-360/COBOL applications compatibility product model (PD) of the users and maintainers; the high levels of service (performance, reliability) property (PP) model of the users, and the ease of transition and maintenance product models (PD) of the maintainers. Further explanations can be found in the references cited earlier.

The gray lines in Figure 2-2 show that the MasterNet project was caught in a "spider web" of the most frequent product–process–property–success "model clashes" among the most common stakeholder roles of user, acquirer, developer, and maintainer that can cause projects to fail. The black lines come from analyses of other failed projects.

There was a great deal of uncertainty about the ability of Premier Systems to develop at least a partial face-saving trust management system, yet the MasterNet management decided to go ahead with a total commitment to their approach. This decision violated ICSM Principle 2. In addition, Principle 1 was violated by neglecting the maintainer and user value propositions of application compatibility, ease of transition, and ease of maintenance. Most serious, though, was the decision to go forward with no evidence that the Premier solution was feasible with respect to the other value propositions, in violation of Principle 4.

A much better ICSM approach would have been to create a representative sample of the MasterNet workload and to engage Premier Systems in a 60-day exercise to demonstrate how well its system could handle the workload. Based on subsequent experience, it seems clear that this pilot would have failed, and the ICSM decision arrow corresponding to too high and unaddressable risk could have been chosen as an evidence-based off-ramp, saving Bank of America $80 million that the company could have used on more feasible projects.

2.2 A Successful Incremental-Commitment Project: The TRW Software Productivity System

The spiral model was originally developed at TRW in 1978 as a way to help the company evolve away from its over-commitment to the waterfall model in its corporate software development policies and standards. Its initial formulation showed how a project could use risk considerations to determine whether a project should be done as a pure waterfall process, a pure evolutionary prototyping process, or a mixture of the two. This model was first used for the full definition and development of a software-intensive system when TRW embarked on the development of a corporate software productivity system, as part of a corporate initiative to improve productivity in all of its divisions.

Since TRW was using its own money rather than the government's money to fund the project, it found the spiral model to be a good way to converge incrementally on the definition of the SPS, and to develop the system incrementally while being linked to an initial user project rather than being fully developed before being offered to user projects. This enabled the initial spiral model project to also be the initial Incremental Commitment Spiral Model project [10,11].

2.2.1 Getting Started: The Exploration Phase

Scene: Bob Williams's office, late 1979. Bob is the vice president/general manager of the 2000-person Software and Information Systems Division, one of six divisions in the TRW Defense and Space Systems Group (DSSG). Barry is his chief engineer and advanced technology business area manager.

Bob: I've just come back from a DSSG general managers' offsite about improving productivity. Corporate in Cleveland is making a big push to get the auto parts divisions to be more competitive with the Japanese, and wants everybody in TRW to focus on improving their productivity. It looks like the company will put up money for productivity initiatives if there's a good business case for them. I think it's worth a try. Do you think you can put something together for us?

Barry: Sure. This fits with a lot of improvements we've talked about but haven't found funding for. Our TRW version of the COCOMO model provides us with a good framework for a business case. It shows how much our productivity goes up or down as we change some of the cost drivers like tool support, turnaround time, reusing components, and people factors. This last would fit with your ideas about multiple career paths for our people. We could probably use some of our local area network technology to get everybody interactively working and communicating. And we could probably get added support from some of the Defense Department's Ada initiatives. Is corporate looking for a full-up proposal?

Bob: Well, if we were proposing to spend the government's money, that's what we would do. But here they're spending the company's money, and want a clearer idea of their options and what everybody's ideas are before they commit to spend a lot of money. So we have a couple of months to put a white paper together. Why don't you do a part-time study with Ray Wolverton and a couple of the Ada guys and put a draft together. And let's get everybody involved by doing a survey of what people think would best help them improve their productivity.

Barry: Great. We'll get right on it and give you a progress report in a couple of weeks.

From this starting point, Tables 2-1, 2-2, and 2-3 summarize the progression of the TRW Software Productivity System (SPS) project through what are now called the ICSM Stage I Exploration, Valuation, and Foundations phases. Subsequently, its ICSM Stage II Development and Operations activities were incremental, in that Increment 1 focused on the SPS infrastructure and the early life-cycle tools needed first by the pilot project, with subsequent increments focusing on the pilot project's later-phases tool needs.

TABLE 2-1 TRW Software Productivity System: Exploration Phase

Objectives	Significantly increase software productivity
Constraints	At reasonable cost Within context of TRW culture ▪ Government contracts; high-tech, people-oriented, security-critical developments
Alternatives	Management: project organization, policies, planning, control Personnel: staffing, incentives, training Technology: tools, workstations, methods, reuse Facilities: offices, communications
Risks	May be no high-leverage improvements Improvements may violate constraints
Risk resolution	Internal surveys Analyze cost model Analyze exceptional projects Literature search
Risk-resolution results	Some alternatives infeasible ▪ Single corporate time-sharing system: security Mix of alternatives can produce significant gains
Plan for next phase	Six-person task force for six months More extensive surveys and analysis ▪ Internal, external, economic Develop analysis of alternatives, top-level concept of operation and business case
Commitment	Fund next phase

2.2.2 SPS Exploration Phase

The SPS Exploration phase involved five part-time participants over a two-month period. As indicated in Table 2-1, the objectives and constraints were expressed at a very high level and in qualitative terms like "significantly increase" and "at reasonable cost." Some of the alternatives considered, primarily those in the "technology" area, could lead to development of a software product, but the possible attractiveness of a number of non-software alternatives in the management, personnel, and facilities areas could have led to a conclusion not to embark on a software development activity. The primary risk areas involved possible situations in which the company would invest a good deal, only to find that:

- The resulting productivity gains were not significant and/or
- Potentially high-leverage improvements were not compatible with some aspects of the "TRW culture."

The risk-resolution activities undertaken in the Exploration phase were primarily surveys and analyses, including structured interviews of software developers and managers; an initial analysis of productivity leverage factors identified by the constructive cost model (COCOMO); and an analysis of previous projects at TRW exhibiting high levels of productivity.

The risk-analysis results indicated that significant productivity gains could be achieved at a reasonable cost by pursuing an integrated set of initiatives in the four major areas. However, some candidate solutions, such as a software support environment based on a single, corporate, mainframe-based time-sharing system, were found to be in conflict with TRW constraints requiring support of different levels of security-classified projects. Thus, even at a very high level of generality of objectives and constraints, the Exploration phase was able to answer basic feasibility questions and eliminate significant classes of candidate solutions.

The plan for the Valuation phase involved commitment of 12 person-months compared to the 2 person-months invested in Exploration (during these phases, all participants were part-time). As with the current Valuation phase, its intent was to produce an analysis of alternatives and a recommended top-level concept of operation and business case.

2.2.3 SPS Valuation Phase.

Table 2-2 summarizes the Valuation phase along the lines given in Table 2-1 for the Exploration phase. The features of Table 2-2 compare to those of Table 2-1 as follows:

- The level of investment was greater (12 versus 2 person-months).
- The objectives and constraints were more specific ("double software productivity in five years at a cost of $10,000 per person" versus "significantly increase productivity at a reasonable cost").

- Additional constraints surfaced, such as the preference for TRW products—in particular, a TRW-developed local area network (LAN) system.
- The alternatives analyzed were more detailed ("SREM, PSL/PSA or SADT, as requirements tools, etc." versus "tools"; "private/shared" terminals" and "smart/dumb" terminals versus "workstations").
- The risk areas identified were more specific ("TRW LAN price-performance within a $10,000-per-person investment constraint" versus "improvements may violate reasonable cost constraint").
- The risk-resolution activities were more extensive (including the benchmarking and analysis of a prototype TRW LAN being developed for another project).

TABLE 2-2 TRW Software Productivity System: Valuation Phase

Objectives	Double software productivity in five years
Constraints	$10,000 per person investment Within context of TRW culture Government contracts, high tech, people oriented, security Preference for TRW products
Alternatives	Office: private/modular/... Communication: LAN/star/concentrators/... Terminals: private/shared; smart/dumb Tools: SREM/PSL-PSA/...; PDL/SADT/... CPU: IBM/DEC/CDC/...
Risks	May miss high-leverage options TRW LAN price/performance Workstation cost
Risk resolution	Extensive external surveys, visits TRW LAN benchmarking Workstation price projections
Risk-resolution results	Operations concept: private offices, TRW LAN, personal terminals, VAX server Begin with primarily dumb terminals; experiment with smart workstations Defer operating system, tools selection
Plan for next phase	Partition effort into software development environment (SDE), facilities, and management initiatives Address high-risk SDE elements: LAN, infrastructure scalability, UNIX user interface Develop first-increment and life-cycle plans Six full-time experts for six months
Commitment	Commit an upcoming pilot project to use SDE Commit the SDE to support the project Focus Increment 1 plans on pilot-project priorities Form representative steering group

- The result was a fairly specific operational concept document, involving private offices tailored to software work patterns and personal terminals connected to VAX super minicomputers via the TRW LAN. Some choices were specifically deferred to the next round, such as the choice of operating system and specific tools.
- The life-cycle plan and the plan for the next phase involved a partitioning into separate activities to address management improvements, facilities development, and development of the first increment of a software development environment.
- The commitment step involved more than just an agreement with the plan. It committed to apply the environment to an upcoming 100-person pilot software project and to develop an environment focusing on the pilot project's needs. It also specified forming a representative steering group to ensure that the separate activities were well coordinated and that the environment would not be overly optimized around the pilot project.

TABLE 2-3 TRW Software Productivity System: Foundations Phase

Objectives	User-friendly system Integrated software, office-automation tools Support all project personnel Support all life-cycle phases
Constraints	Customer-deliverable SDE ⇨ portability Stable, reliable service
Alternatives	OS: VMS/AT&T UNIX/Berkeley UNIX/ISC Host-target/fully portable tool set Workstations: Zenith/LSI-11/...
Risks	Mismatch to pilot-project needs and priorities User-unfriendly system ■ 12-language syndrome; experts-only UNIX performance, support Workstation/mainframe compatibility
Risk resolution	Pilot-project surveys, requirements participation Survey of UNIX-using organizations Workstation study
Risk-resolution results	Top-level requirements specification Host-target with UNIX host UNIX-based workstations Build user-friendly front end for UNIX Initial focus on tools to support early phases
Plan for next phase	Overall development plan ■ For tools: SREM, RTT, PDL, office automation ■ For front end: compatible language for tools ■ For LAN: equipment, facilities 15 full-time personnel for 8 months to IOC
Commitment	Proceed with plans

2.2.4 SPS Foundations Phase

Table 2-3 shows the corresponding steps involved during the Foundations phase of defining the SPS. A key decision was to clarify that the objective was project productivity and not just programmer productivity. TRW's government projects were highly document-intensive, and integration of software development support and office support was a main objective.

The initial risk-identification activities during the Foundations phase showed that several system requirements hinged on the decision between a host-target system or a fully portable toolset and the decision between VMS and UNIX as the host operating system. These requirements included the functions needed to provide a user-friendly front end, the operating system to be used by the workstations, and the functions necessary to support a host-target operation. To keep these requirements in synchronization with the others, a special minispiral was initiated to address and resolve these issues. The resulting review led to a commitment to a host-target operation using UNIX on the host system, at a point early enough to work the operating system–dependent requirements in a timely fashion.

Addressing the risks of mismatches to the user-project's needs and priorities resulted in substantial participation of the user-project personnel in the requirements definition activity. This led to several significant redirections of the requirements, particularly toward supporting the early phases of the software life cycle into which the user project was embarking, such as an adaptation of the software requirements engineering methodology (SREM) tools for requirements specification and analysis.

Besides UNIX and its companion tools, the overall set of tools included a number of user-interface incompatibilities (the 12-language syndrome referred to the variety of languages needed for programming, compiling, build making, version control, job control, requirements, design, test management, and other tasks). A high-priority effort was directed toward developing a front end for these tools that minimized their incompatibilities.

The incremental commitment level was increased from 12 to 36 person-months, followed by a planned increase to 120 person-months for developing the initial operational capability for the pilot project.

2.2.5 Overall Project Results

The Software Productivity System developed and supported using the spiral model avoided the identified risks and achieved most of the system's objectives. The SPS grew to include more than 300 tools and 1.3 million instructions; 93% of the instructions were reused from previous project-developed, TRW-developed, or external-software packages. By 1986, more than 25 projects had used all or portions of the system. All of the projects fully using the system had increased their productivity by at least 50%; indeed, most had doubled their productivity (when compared with cost-estimation model predictions of their productivity using traditional methods).

However, one risk area—that projects with non-UNIX target systems would not accept a UNIX-based host system—was underestimated. Some projects accepted the host-target approach, but for various reasons (such as customer constraints and zero-cost target machines), a good many did not. As a result, the system was less widely used on TRW projects than expected. This and other lessons learned were incorporated into a spiral approach to developing a next-generation software development environment reflecting new generations of networking, hardware, and software technologies. More details and further discussion may be found in a number of papers [12,13,14].

2.3 The Two Cones of Uncertainty and the ICSM Stages I and II

The primary drivers for the incremental-commitment approaches in ICSM Stages I and II are the two Cones of Uncertainty shown in Figure 2-3.

The first Cone of Uncertainty reflects uncertainties in the nature of the system to be developed and in the applicability of various candidate solution approaches.

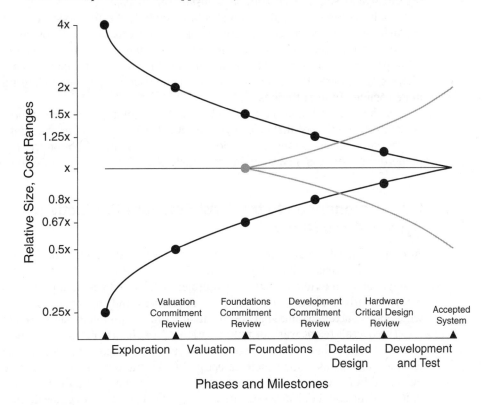

FIGURE 2-3 The Two Cones of Uncertainty

Total commitment to a particular set of requirements and solution approaches during the early phases of system definition can be highly risky (a wide range of uncertainty corresponds with a high probability of lost value, and probability of loss multiplied size of loss is the accepted definition of risk exposure). Examples from Chapter 1 are the total commitment to the best-possible technical solution in the Too-Good Robot failure story, leading to total loss of the investment in the robot's development; and the extensive incremental investments in the Abbott Laboratories–Hospira success story, in buying information to reduce risk via market surveys, business case analyses, field studies, prototypes, and safety analyses, as it proceeded through its Exploration, Valuation, and Foundations phases.

The second Cone of Uncertainty reflects uncertainties in whether the best solution determined at the end of Stage I will still be the best solution after a lengthy single-pass, total-commitment development period. In olden times of slow changes in technology, competition, market demands, organizations, and leadership, the single-pass approach was not too risky. But now and increasingly in the future, the pace of changes in these factors is rapidly increasing, and total commitment to the requirements for a three-year single-pass development of a new system is likely to find that the three-year-old delivered solution is obsolete or noncompetitive.

Again with respect to the examples in Chapter 1, the Too Good Robot project could have delivered a scalable but simpler initial capability, but opted for the single-pass full capability. The Hospira infusion pump project could have tried for a full product line of up to six-channel pumps, but instead started with an initial offering of combinable one- and two-channel pumps and a scalable architecture for more complex future offerings.

Further discussion of the risks to be avoided in total-commitment approaches in complex multiple-stakeholder systems are discussed next, in the context of addressing clashes among the various stakeholders' desired product, process, property, and success models, using the MasterNet failure story as an example.

2.3.1 Comparison to the TRW Software Productivity System Case Study

Although it used the cost drivers in a software cost estimation model to explore options and estimate likely impacts, the TRW-SPS project did not define productivity solely in terms of increasing a project's delivered source lines of code per person-month. Rather, it also surveyed developers and managers to determine which other factors would improve the quality of their products and work life.

The overall result was not only creation of a software development environment and tools, but also an improved work environment and development of technical as well as management career paths. Several options were explored and evaluated in increasing detail during each definition phase, and the results, feasibility evidence, and risk assessments were reviewed and used to guide decisions at the equivalent of the ICSM Validation, Foundations, and Development Commitment

Reviews. Also, the project was bonded to an initial TRW production project to ensure that the system would meet real users' needs. The end results were not perfect (the home-built forms management package was expensive to maintain and fell behind COTS capabilities, and the lack of platform independence limited its usage), but software productivity and personnel satisfaction were significantly improved.

2.4 Alternative Incremental and Evolutionary Development Models

The primary models of incremental and evolutionary development focus on different competitive and technical challenges. The time phasing of each model is shown in Figure 2-4 in terms of the increment (1, 2, 3, ...) content with respect to the definition (Df), development (Dv), and production, support, and utilization (PSU) stages used in the Life-Cycle Models knowledge area in the Systems Engineering Body of Knowledge [15,16]. The Definition stage corresponds to the ICSM Stage I; the Development stage corresponds to the ICSM Development phase for each increment; and the PSU stage corresponds to the ICSM Production and Operations phase for the increment.

The Figure 2-4 notation $Df_{1..N}$ indicates that the initial stage produces specifications not just for the first increment, but rather for the full set of increments. These are assumed to remain stable for the prespecified sequential model but are expected to change for the evolutionary concurrent model. The latter's notation (Dv_1 and Df_{2R} in the same time frame; PSU_1, Dv_2, and Df_{3R} in the same time frame; and so on) indicates that the plans and specifications for the next increment are being rebaselined by a systems engineering team concurrently with the development of the current increment and the PSU of the previous increment. This offloads the work of handling the change traffic from the development team and significantly improves the team's chances of finishing the current increment on budget and schedule.

To select an appropriate life-cycle model, it is important to first gain an understanding of the main archetypes and where they are best used. Table 2-4 summarizes each of the primary models of single-step, incremental, and evolutionary development in terms of examples, strengths, and weaknesses, followed by explanatory notes.

The *Prespecified Single-Step* and *Prespecified Multistep* models from Table 2-4 are not evolutionary. Prespecified multistep models split the development so as to field an early initial operational capability, followed by several preplanned product improvements (P3Is). An alternative version splits up the work but does not field the intermediate increments. When requirements are well understood and stable, the prespecified models enable a strong, predictable process. When requirements are emergent and/or rapidly changing, they often require expensive rework if they lead to undoing architectural commitments.

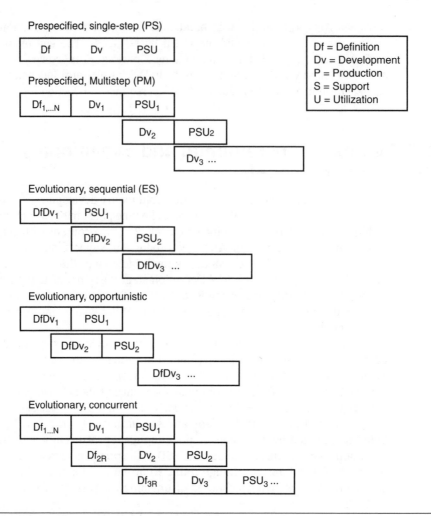

FIGURE 2-4 Primary Models of Incremental and Evolutionary Development

The *Evolutionary Sequential* model involves an approach in which the initial operational capability for the system is rapidly developed and is upgraded based on operational experience. Pure agile software development fits this model. If something does not turn out as expected and needs to be changed, it will be fixed in 30 days at the time of its next release. Rapid fielding also fits this model for larger or hardware–software systems. Its major strength is to enable quick-response capabilities in the field. With pure agile development, the model can fall prey to an easiest-first set of architectural commitments that break when, for example, system developers try to scale up the workload by a factor of 10 or to add security as a new feature in a later increment. For rapid fielding, using this model may prove expensive when the quick mash-ups require extensive rework

TABLE 2-4 Primary Models of Incremental and Evolutionary Development

Model	Examples	Pros	Cons
Prespecified single-step	Simple manufactured products: nuts, bolts, simple sensors	Efficient, easy to verify	Difficulties with rapid change, emerging requirements (complex sensors, human-intensive systems)
Prespecified multistep	Vehicle platform plus value-adding preplanned product improvements (PPPIs)	Early initial capability, scalability when stable	Emergent requirements or rapid change, architecture breakers
Evolutionary sequential	Small: agile Larger: rapid fielding	Adaptability to change, smaller human-intensive systems	Easiest first; late, costly fixes; systems engineering time gaps; slow for large systems
Evolutionary opportunistic	Stable development, maturing technology	Mature technology upgrades	Emergent requirements or rapid change, system engineering time gaps
Evolutionary concurrent	Rapid, emergent development, systems of systems	Emergent requirements or rapid change, stable development increments, SysE continuity	Overkill on small or highly stable systems

to fix incompatibilities or to accommodate off-nominal usage scenarios, but the rapid results may be worth it.

The *Evolutionary Opportunistic* model can be adopted in cases that involve deferring the next increment until a sufficiently attractive opportunity presents itself, the desired new technology is mature enough to be added, or other enablers such as scarce components or key personnel become available. It is also appropriate for synchronizing upgrades of multiple COTS products. It may be expensive to keep the systems engineering and development teams together while waiting for the enablers, but again, it may be worth it.

The *Evolutionary Concurrent* model involves a team of systems engineers concurrently handling the change traffic and rebaselining the plans and specifications for the next increment, so as to keep the current increment development stabilized. An example and discussion are provided in Table 2-5 in the next subsection.

2.4.1 Incremental and Evolutionary Development Decision Table

Table 2-5 provides some criteria for deciding which of the processes associated with the primary classes of incremental and evolutionary development models to use.

The *Prespecified Single-Step* process exemplified by the traditional waterfall or sequential Vee model is appropriate if the product's requirements can be specified in advance and have a low probability of significant change, and if there is no

TABLE 2-5 Incremental and Evolutionary Development Decision Table

Model	Stable, Prespecifiable Requirements?	OK to Wait for Full System to Be Developed?	Need to Wait for Next-Increment Priorities?	Need to Wait for Next-Increment Enablers?*
Prespecified single-step	Yes	Yes		
Prespecified multistep	Yes	No		
Evolutionary sequential	No	No	Yes	
Evolutionary Opportunistic	No	No	No	Yes
Evolutionary concurrent	No	No	No	No

*Example enablers: technology maturity; external-system capabilities; needed resources; new opportunities.

value or chance to deliver a partial product capability. A good example of this case would be the hardware for an Earth resources monitoring satellite that would be infeasible to modify after it goes into orbit.

The *Prespecified Multistep* process splits up the development with the objective of fielding an early initial operational capability and several P3Is. It is best if the product's full capabilities can be specified in advance and have a low probability of experiencing significant change. This process is useful in cases when waiting for the full system to be developed may incur a loss of important and deliverable incremental mission capabilities. A good example would be a well-understood and well-prioritized sequence of software upgrades for the on-board Earth resources monitoring satellite.

The *Evolutionary Sequential* process develops an initial operational capability and upgrades it based on operational experience, as exemplified by agile methods. It is most appropriate in cases when there is a need to get operational feedback on an initial capability before defining and developing the next increment's content. A good example would be the software upgrades suggested by experiences with the satellite's payload, such as the identification of which kind of multi-spectral data collection and analysis capabilities are best for which kind of agriculture under which weather conditions.

The *Evolutionary Opportunistic* process defers the next increment until its new capabilities are available and mature enough to be added. It is best used when the increment does not need to wait for operational feedback, but it may need to wait for next-increment enablers such as technology maturity, external system capabilities, needed resources, or new value-adding opportunities. A good example of such a case would be the need to wait for agent-based satellite anomaly trend analysis and mission-adaptation software to become predictably stable before incorporating it into a scheduled increment.

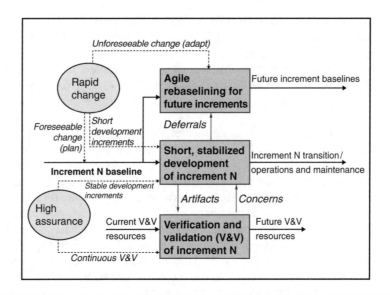

FIGURE 2-5 Evolutionary Concurrent Rapid Change Handling and High Assurance

The *Evolutionary Concurrent* process, as realized in the ICSM [17] and shown in Figure 2-5, has a continuing team of systems engineers handling the change traffic and rebaselining the plans and specifications for the next increment, while also keeping a development team stabilized for on-time, high-assurance delivery of the current increment and employing a concurrent verification and validation (V&V) team to perform continuous defect detection to enable even higher assurance levels.

A good example of this case would be the satellite's ground-based mission control and data handling software's next-increment rebaselining to adapt to new COTS releases and continuing user requests for data processing upgrades. The satellite example illustrates the various ways in which the complex systems of the future, different parts of the system, and its software may evolve in a number of ways, once again affirming that there is no one-size-fits-all process for software evolution. However, Table 2-5 can be quite helpful in determining which processes are the best fits for evolving each part of the system, and the three-team model in Figure 2-5 provides a way for projects to develop the challenging software-intensive systems of the future that will need both adaptability to rapid change and high levels of assurance.

2.5 Development as C²ISR

The rapid-change-driven need to deliver high-assurance incremental capabilities on short fixed schedules means that each increment needs to be kept as stable as possible. This is particularly the case for large, complex systems, in which having the developers try to address a high level of rebaselining traffic during development can easily lead to chaos. In keeping with the use of the spiral model as a risk-driven process model generator, the risks of destabilizing the development process turn this center portion of the project into a stabilized, waterfall-like build-to-specification process. It involves making foreseeable changes easier via tailorable design patterns, with unforeseeable change traffic being routed elsewhere.

The need for high assurance of each increment also makes it cost-effective to invest in a team of appropriately skilled personnel who will continuously verify and validate the increment as it is being developed. This team, which would comprise verification and validation (V&V) experts, would identify problems and defects as close to their point of occurrence as possible, thereby reducing rework time and effort. Team members would also prepare for and execute continuous testing of the increment under development, as discussed later. If they detected a potential show-stopper problem, they would work with the developers to determine whether a temporary workaround would enable the increment to be safely delivered on time, or whether the project should be halted immediately and remain stationary until the show-stopper is fixed.

"Routing the change traffic elsewhere" does not imply deferring the change impact analysis, change negotiation, and rebaselining until the beginning of the next increment. With a single development team and rapid rates of change, this would require a team optimized to develop products based on stable plans and specifications to spend much of the next increment's scarce calendar time performing tasks that are much better suited to the skills of agile teams. Stabilizing the development team enables at least part of the Stage II activity to be managed via the traditional fixed-price, build-to-requirements specification, and purchasing-agent acquisition metaphor.

The appropriate metaphor for "addressing rapid change" is not a build-to-specification metaphor or a purchasing-agent metaphor, but rather an adaptive "command–control–intelligence–surveillance–reconnaissance" (C^2ISR) metaphor. It involves an agile team performing the first three activities of the C^2ISR "observe, orient, decide, act" (OODA) loop for the next increments, while the plan-driven development team is performing the "act" activity for the current increment. "Observing" involves monitoring changes in relevant technology and COTS products, whether in the competitive marketplace, in external interoperating systems, or in the environment; it also entails monitoring progress on the current increment to identify slowdowns and likely scope deferrals. "Orienting" involves performing change impact analyses, risk analyses, and tradeoff analyses to assess candidate rebaselining options for the upcoming increments. "Deciding" involves stakeholder renegotiation of the content of upcoming increments, architecture rebaselining, and the degree of COTS upgrading to be done to prepare for the next increment. It also comprises updating the future increments' feasibility evidence to ensure that their renegotiated scopes and solutions can be achieved within their budgets and schedules.

A successful rebaseline effort means that the plan-driven development team can hit the ground running at the beginning of the "Act" phase of developing the next increment, and the agile team can hit the ground running on rebaselining definitions of the increments beyond. Nevertheless, a challenge remains in defining the observe–orient–decide process by which the agile team works. To handle unpredictable, asynchronous change traffic, it is not possible to do a sequential "observe, then orient, then decide" process. Instead, the ICSM defines a triage process by which each change request is handled, as shown in Figure 2-6. For example, it handles unforeseen change requests involving new technology or COTS opportunities; changing requirements and priorities; changing external interfaces; low-priority current increment features being deferred to a later increment; and user requests based on experience with currently fielded increments (including defect fixes).

In the context of the agile rebaselining team in Figure 2-4, the chart in Figure 2-6 shows how the agile team interacts with the change proposers, current-increment development team, and managers of future increments to evaluate the proposed changes and their interactions with one another, and to negotiate rebaselined packages for the next increment. Again, there is no precise way to forecast the budget and schedule of this team's workload. Within an available budget and schedule, the agile team will perform a continuing "handle now; incorporate in next increment rebaseline; defer-or-drop" triage in the top "Assess Changes, Propose Handling" phase. Surges in demand must be matched by surges in needed expertise and funding support.

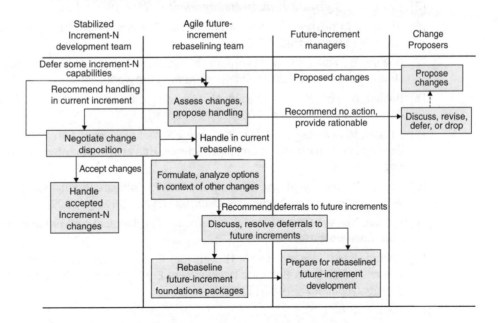

FIGURE 2-6 The Agile Rebaselining Team C²ISR Triage Model

The current-increment development team may be performing the increment in several iterations. In that case, the team members may respond to the rebaselining team's proposed changes to the current increment by reprioritizing their current-increment backlog, with the possibility of some lower-priority features being time-boxed out of the current increment. Alternatively, they may work directly with the rebaselining team and the operational stakeholders to accommodate a high-priority need by identifying some low-priority current-increment features that can be deferred to future increments. Such negotiations—occurring between the right people at the right time—are a common feature of the ICSM. They are supportive of the first ICSM principle and key to the value of incremental and iterative approaches.

References

[1] Humphrey, W. *Managing the Software Process*. Reading, MA: Addison-Wesley Professional, 1989.

[2] Bauman, H. C. "Accuracy Considerations for Capital Cost Estimation." *Industrial & Engineering Chemistry*. April 1958.

[3] Boehm, B. *Software Engineering Economics*. Upper Saddle River, NJ: Prentice Hall, 1981.

[4] McConnell, S. *Software Project Survival Guide*. Microsoft Press, 1997.

[5] Flowers, S. *Software Failure: Management Failure*. Wiley, 1996.

[6] Glass, R. *Software Runaways: Monumental Software Disasters*. Upper Saddle River, NJ: Prentice Hall, 1997.

[7] Boehm, B., and Port, D. "Escaping the Software Tar Pit: Model Clashes and How to Avoid Them." *ACM Software Engineering Notes*. January 1999;36–48.

[8] Boehm, B., Port, D., and Al-Said, M. "Avoiding the Software Model-Clash Spiderweb." *IEEE Computer*. 2000;33(11):120–122.

[9] Al-Said, M. *Detecting Model Clashes during Software Systems Development*. PhD dissertation, Department of Computer Science, University of Southern California, December 2003.

[10] Boehm, B., and Penedo, M. "Memories of TRW's Software Productivity Project." In A. Stellman and J. Greene, eds. *Beautiful Teams*. O'Reilly, 2009.

[11] Boehm, Barry. "A Spiral Model of Software Development and Enhancement." *IEEE Computer*. 1988;21(5):61–72.

[12] Boehm, Barry, Penedo, Maria H., Stuckle, E. Don, Williams, Robert D., and Pyster, Arthur B. "A Software Development Environment for Improving Productivity." *Computer*. 1984;17(6):30–44.

[13] Boehm, 1988.

[14] Boehm and Penedo, 2009.

[15] Pyster, A., et al. *The Systems Engineering Body of Knowledge (SEBoK)*. 2012. www.sebokwiki.org.

[16] Boehm, B., and Lane, J. "Using the Incremental Commitment Model to Integrate System Acquisition, Systems Engineering, and Software Engineering." *CrossTalk.* October 2007;4–9.

[17] Boehm, B., and Lane, J. *DoD Systems Engineering and Management Implications for Evolutionary Acquisition of Major Defense Systems.* SERC RT-5 report. March 2010. USC-CSSE-2010-500.

3

The Third Principle: Concurrent Multidiscipline Engineering

"Do everything in parallel, with frequent synchronizations."

—Michael Cusumano and Richard Selby, *Microsoft Secrets,* 1995

"As the correct solution of any problem depends primarily on a true understanding of what the problem really is, and wherein lies its difficulty, we may profitably pause upon the threshold of our subject to consider first, in a more general way, its real nature: the causes which impede sound practice; the conditions on which success or failure depends; the directions in which error is most to be feared. Thus we shall attain that great perspective for success in any work—a clear mental perspective, saving us from confusing the obvious with the important, and the obscure and remote with the unimportant."

—Arthur M. Wellington, *The Economic Theory of the Location of Railroads*, 1887

The first flowering of systems engineering as a formal discipline focused on the engineering of complex physical systems such as ships, aircraft, transportation systems, and logistics systems. The physical behavior of the systems could be well analyzed by mathematical techniques, with passengers treated along with baggage and merchandise as a class of logistical objects with average sizes, weights, and quantities. Such mathematical models were very good in analyzing the physical performance tradeoffs of complex system alternatives. They also served as the basis for the development of elegant mathematical theories of systems engineering.

The physical systems were generally stable, and were expected to have long useful lifetimes. Major fixes or recalls of fielded systems were very expensive, so it was worth investing significant up-front effort in getting their requirements to be complete, consistent, traceable, and testable, particularly if the development was to be contracted out to a choice of competing suppliers. It was important not to overly constrain the solution space, so the requirements were not to include design choices, and the design could not begin until the requirements were fully specified.

Various sequential process models were developed to support this approach, such as the diagonal waterfall model, the V-model (a waterfall with a bend upward in the middle), and the two-leg model (an inverted V-model). These were effective in developing numerous complex physical systems, and were codified into government and standards-body process standards. The manufacturing process of assembling physical components into subassemblies, assemblies, subsystems, and system products was reflected in functional-hierarchy design standards, integration and test standards, and work breakdown structure standards as the way to organize and manage the system definition and development.

The fundamental assumptions underlying this set of sequential processes, prespecified requirements, and functional-hierarchy product models began to be seriously undermined in the 1970s and 1980s. The increasing pace of change in technology, competition, organizations, and life in general made assumptions about stable, prespecifiable requirements unrealistic. The existence of cost-effective, competitive, incompatible commercial products or other reusable non-developmental items (NDIs) made it necessary to evaluate and often commit to solution components before finalizing the requirements (the consequences of not doing this will be seen in the failure case study in Chapter 4). The emergence of freely available graphic user interface (GUI) generators made rapid user interface prototyping feasible, but also made the prespecification of user interface requirement details unrealistic. The difficulty of adapting to rapid change with brittle, optimized, point-solution architectures generally made optimized first-article design to fixed requirements unrealistic.

As shown in the "hump diagram" of Figure 0-5 in the Introduction, the ICSM emphasizes the principle of concurrent rather than sequential work for understanding needs; envisioning opportunities; system scoping; system objectives and requirements determination; architecting and designing of the system and its hardware, software, and human elements; life-cycle planning; and development of feasibility evidence. Of course, the humps in Figure 0-5 are not a one-size-fits-all representation of every project's effort distribution. In practice, the evidence- and risk-based decision criteria discussed in Figures 0-7 and 0-8 in the Introduction can determine which specific process model will fit best for which specific situation. This includes situations in which the sequential process is still best, as its assumptions still hold in some situations. Also, since requirements increasingly emerge from use, working on all of the requirements and solutions in advance is not feasible—which is where the ICSM Principle 2 of incremental commitment applies.

This establishes the context for the "Do everything in parallel" quote at the beginning of this chapter. Even though preferred sequential-engineering situations still exist in which "Do everything in parallel" does not universally apply, it is generally best to apply it during the first ICSM Exploratory phase. By holistically and concurrently addressing during this beginning phase all of the system's hardware, software, human factors, and economic considerations (as described in the Wellington quote at the beginning of the chapter), projects will generally be able to determine their process drivers and best process approach for the rest of the system's life cycle. Moreover, as discussed previously, the increasing prevalence of process drivers such as emergence, dynamism, and NDI support will make concurrent approaches increasingly dominant.

Thus suitably qualified, we can proceed to the main content of Chapter 3. Our failure and success case studies are two different sequential and concurrent approaches to a representative complex cyber–physical–human government system acquisition involving remotely piloted vehicles (RPVs). The remaining sections will discuss best practices for concurrent cyber–physical–human factors engineering, concurrent requirements and solutions engineering, concurrent development and evolution engineering, and support of more rapid concurrent engineering.

An example to illustrate ICSM concurrent-engineering benefits is the unmanned aerial system (UAS; i.e., RPV) system enhancement discussed in Chapter 5 of the NRC's *Human–System Integration* report [1]. These RPVs are airplanes or helicopters operated remotely by humans. The systems are designed to keep humans out of harm's way. However, the current RPV systems are human-intensive, often requiring two people, and often considerably more, to operate a single vehicle. The increase in need to operate numerous RPVs is causing a strong desire to modify the 1:2 (one vehicle controlled by two people) ratio to allow for a single operator to operate more than one RPV, as shown in Figure 3-1.

A recent advanced technology demonstration of an autonomous-agent-based system enabled a single operator to control four RPVs flying in formation to a crisis area while compensating for changes in direction to avoid adverse weather conditions or no-fly zones. Often, such demonstrations to high-level decision makers, who are typically focused on rapidly getting innovations into the competition

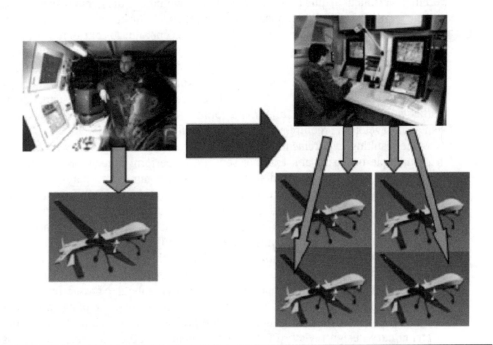

FIGURE 3-1 Vision of 4:1 Remotely Piloted Vehicle System (from Pew and Mavor, 2007)

space, will lead to commitments to major acquisitions before the technical and economic implications have been worked out (good examples have been the Iridium satellite-based personal telephone system and the London Ambulance System).

Based on our analyses of such failures and complementary successes (e.g., the rapid-delivery systems of Federal Express, Amazon, and Walmart), the failure and success stories in this chapter illustrate failure and success patterns in the RPV domain. In the future, the technical, economic, and safety challenges for similarly autonomous air vehicles will become even more complex, as with Amazon's recent concept and prototype of filling the air with tiny, fully autonomous, battery-powered helicopters rapidly delivering packages from its warehouse to your front door.

In this chapter, the demonstration of a 4:1 vehicle:controller ratio capability highly impressed senior leadership officials viewing the demo, and they established a high-priority rapid-development program to acquire and field a common agent-based 4:1 RPV control capability for use in battlefield-based, sea-based, and home-country–based RPV operations.

3.1 Failure Story: Sequential RPV Systems Engineering and Development

This section presents a hypothetical sequential approach representative of several recent government acquisition programs, which would use the demo results to create the requirements for a proposed program that used the agent-based technology to develop a 4:1 ratio system that enabled a single operator to control four RPVs in battlefield-based, sea-based, and home-country–based RPV operations. A number of assumptions were made to sell the program at an optimistic cost of $1 billion and schedule of 40 months. Enthusiasm was such that the program, budget, and schedule were established, and a multi-service working group of experienced battlefield-based, sea-based, and home-country–based RPV controllers was established to develop the requirements for the system.

The resulting requirements included the need to synthesize status information from multiple on-board and external sensors; to perform dynamic reallocation of RPVs to targets; to perform self-defense functions; to communicate status and observational information to central commanders and other RPV controllers; to control RPVs in the same family but with different releases having somewhat different controls; to avoid harming friendly forces or noncombatants; and to be network-ready with respect to self-identification when entering battle zones, establishing security credentials and protocols, operating in a publish–subscribe environment, and participating in replanning activities based on changing conditions. These requirements were included in a request for proposal (RFP) that was sent out to prospective bidders.

The winning bidder provided an even more impressive demo of agent technology and a proposal indicating that all of the problems were well understood, that a preliminary design review (PDR) could be held in 120 days, and that the cost would be only $800 million. The program managers and their upper management were delighted at the prospect of saving $200 million of the taxpayers' money, and they established a fixed-price contract to develop the 4:1 system to the requirements in the RFP in 40 months, with a System Functional Requirements Review (SFRR) in 60 days and a PDR in 120 days.

At the SFRR, the items reviewed were transcriptions and small elaborations of the requirements in the RFP. They did not include any functions for coordinating the capabilities, and included only sunny-day operational scenarios. There were no capabilities for recovering from outages in the network, from the loss of RPVs, or from incompatible sensor data, or for tailoring the controls to battlefield-based, sea-based, or home-country–based control equipment. The contractor indicated that it had hired some ex-RPV controllers who were busy putting such capabilities together.

However, at the PDR, the contractor could not show feasible solutions for several critical and commonly occurring scenarios, such as coping with network outages, missing RPVs, and inconsistent data; having the individual controllers coordinate with each other; performing self-defense functions; tailoring the controls to multiple equipment types; and satisfying various network-ready interoperability protocols. As has been experienced in practice [2], such capabilities are much needed and difficult to achieve.

Because the schedule was tight and the contractor had almost run out of systems engineering funds, management proposed to address the problems by using a "concurrent engineering" approach of having the programmers develop the software capabilities while the systems engineers were completing the detailed design of the hardware displays and controls. Having no other face-saving alternative to declaring the PDR to be a failure, the customers declared the PDR to be passed.

Actually, proceeding into development while completing the design is a pernicious misuse of the term "concurrent engineering," as there is not enough time to produce feasibility evidence and to synchronize and stabilize the numerous off-nominal approaches taken by the software developers and the hardware-detail designers. The situation becomes even worse when portions of the system are subcontracted to different organizations, which will often reuse existing assets in incompatible ways. The almost-certain result for large systems is one or more off-nominal architecture-breakers that require large amounts of rework and throwaway software to reconcile the inconsistent architectural decisions made by the self-fulfilling "hurry up and code, because we will have a lot of debugging to do" programmers. Figure 3-2 shows the results of such approaches for two large TRW projects, in which 80% of the rework resulted from the 20% of problem fixes resulting from critical off-nominal architecture-breakers [3].

As a result, after 40 months and $800 million in expenditures, some RPV control components were developed but were experiencing integration problems, and even after descoping the performance to a 1:1 operator:RPV ratio, several problems were still unresolved. For example, the hardware engineers used their traditional approach to defining interfaces in terms of message content (e.g., "The sensor data crossing an interface is defined in terms of the following units, dimensions,

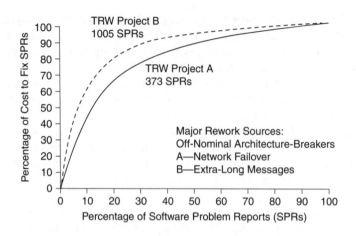

FIGURE 3-2 Results of Creating or Neglecting Off-Nominal Architecture-Breakers

coordinate systems, precision, frequency, or other characteristics"). They then took full earned value credit for defining the system's interfaces. However, the RPVs were operating in a Net-centric system of systems, where interface definition includes protocols for joining the network, performing security handshakes, publishing and subscribing to services, leaving the network, and so on. As there was no earned value left for defining these protocols, they remained undefined while the earned value system continued to indicate full credit for interface definition. The resulting rework and overruns could be said to result from off-nominal architecture breakers or from shortfalls in the concurrent engineering of the sensor data processing and networking aspects of the system, and from shortfalls in accountability for results.

Eventually, the 1:1 capability was achieved and the system delivered, but with reduced functionality, a cost of $3 billion, and a schedule of 80 months. Even worse, the hasty patching to get the first article delivered left the customer with a brittle, poorly documented, poorly tested system that would be the source of many expensive years of system ownership and sub-par performance.

3.2 Success Story: Concurrent Competitive-Prototyping RPV Systems Development

A concurrent incremental-commitment approach to the agent-based RPV control opportunity, using the ICSM process and competitive prototyping, would recognize that there were a number of risks and uncertainties involved in going from a single-scenario proof-of-principle demo to a fieldable system needing to operate in more complex scenarios. It would decide that it would be good to use prototyping as a way of buying information to reduce the risks, and would determine that a reasonable first step would be to invest $25 million in an Exploration phase. This would initially involve the customer and a set of independent experts developing operational scenarios and evaluation criteria from the requirements in Section 3.1 (to synthesize status information from multiple on-board and external sensors; to perform dynamic reallocation of RPVs to targets; to perform self-defense functions; and so on). These would involve not only the sunny-day use cases but also selected rainy-day use cases involving communications outages, disabled RPVs, and garbled data.

(Customer reviews reqs and IOS eval. criteria)

The customer would identify an RPV simulator that would be used in the competition, and would send out a request for information to prospective competitors to identify their qualifications to compete. Based on the responses, the customer would then select four bidders to develop virtual prototypes addressing the requirements, operational scenarios, and evaluation criteria, and providing evidence of their proposed agent-based RPV controllers' level of performance. The customer would then have the set of independent experts evaluate the bidders' results. Based on the results, it would perform an evidence- and risk-based Valuation Commitment Review to determine whether the technology was too immature to merit further current investment as an acquisition program, or whether the system performance, cost, and risk were acceptable for investing the next level of resources in addressing the problems identified and developing initial prototype physical capabilities.

As was discovered much more expensively in the failure case described earlier, the prospects for developing a 4:1 capability were clearly unrealistic. The competitors' desire to succeed led to several innovative approaches, but also to indications that having a single controller handle multiple-version RPV controls would lead to too many critical errors. Overall, however, the prospects for a 1:1 capability were sufficiently attractive to merit another level of investment, corresponding to a Valuation phase. This phase was funded at $75 million, some of the more ambitious key performance parameters were scaled back, the competitors were down-selected to three, and some basic-capability but multiple-version physical RPVs were provided for the competitors to control in several physical environments.

The evaluation of the resulting prototypes confirmed that the need to control multiple versions of the RPVs made anything higher than a 1:1 capability infeasible. However, the top two competitors provided sufficient evidence of a 1:1 system feasibility that a Foundations Commitment Review was passed, and $225 million was provided for a Foundations phase: $100 million for each of the top competitors, and $25 million for customer preparation activities and the independent experts' evaluations.

In this phase, the two competitors not only developed operational RPV versions, but also provided evidence of their ability to satisfy the key performance parameters and scenarios. In addition, they developed an ICSM Development Commitment Review package, including the proposed system's concept of operation, requirements, architecture, and plans, along with a Feasibility Evidence Description providing evidence that a system built to the architecture would satisfy the requirements and concept of operation, and be buildable within the budget and schedule in the plan.

The feasibility evidence included a few shortfalls, such as remaining uncertainties in the interface protocols with some interoperating systems, but each of these was covered by a risk mitigation plan in the winning competitor's submission. The resulting Development Commitment Review was passed, and the winner's proposed $675 million, 18-month, three-increment Stage II plan to develop an initial operational capability (IOC) was adopted. The resulting 1:1 IOC was delivered on budget and 2 months later than the original 40-month target, with a few lower-priority features deferred to later system increments. Figure 3-3 shows the comparative timelines for the Sequential and Concurrent approaches.

Of the $1 billion spent, $15 million was spent on the three discontinued Exploration-phase competitors, $40 million was spent on the two discontinued Valuation-phase competitors, and $100 million was spent on the discontinued Foundations-phase competitor. Overall, the competitive energy stimulated and the early risks avoided made this a good investment. However, the $125 million spent on the experience built up by the losing finalist could also be put to good use by awarding the finalist with a contract to build and operate a testbed for evaluating the RPV system's performance.

Actually, it would be best to announce such an outcome in advance, and to do extensive team building and award fee structuring to make the testbed activity constructive rather than adversarial.

While the sequential and concurrent cases were constructed in an RPV context from representative projects elsewhere, they show how a premature total commitment without adequate resources for and commitment to early concurrent engineering of the modeling, analysis, and feasibility assessment of the overall system will often lead to large overruns in cost and schedule, and performance that is

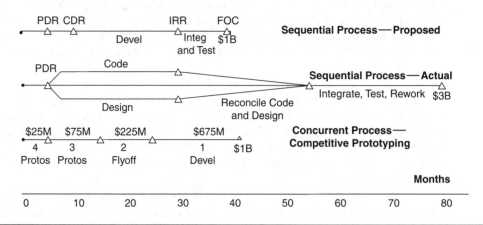

FIGURE 3-3 Comparative Timelines

considerably less than initially desired. However, by "buying information" early, the concurrent incremental commitment and competitive prototyping approach was able to develop a system with much less late rework than the sequential total commitment approach, and with much more visibility and control over the process.

The competitive prototyping approach spent about $155 million on unused prototypes, but the overall expenditure was only $1 billion as compared to $3 billion for the total-commitment approach, and the capability was delivered in 42 versus 80 months, which indicates a strong return on investment. Further, the funding organizations had realistic expectations of the outcome, so that a 1:1 capability was a successful realization of an expected outcome, rather than a disappointing shortfall from a promised 4:1 capability. In addition, the investment in the losing finalist could be put to good use by capitalizing on its experience to perform an IV&V role.

Competitive prototyping can lead to strong successes, but it is also important to indicate its potential failure modes. These include under-investments in prototype evaluation, leading to insufficient data for good decision making; extra expenses in keeping the prototype teams together and productive during often-overlong evaluation and decision periods; and choosing system developers too much on prototyping brilliance and too little on ability to systems-engineer and production-engineer the needed products [4]. These problem areas are easier to control in competitions among in-house design groups, where they are successfully used by a number of large corporations.

3.3 Concurrent Development and Evolution Engineering

As good as the success story in Section 3.2 appears to be, it could have a fatal flaw that is shared by many outsourced system acquisitions—namely, its primary focus on satisfying today's requirements as quickly and inexpensively as possible. This may build architectural decisions into the system that make it difficult to adapt to new opportunities or competitive threats. From an economic standpoint, this approach neglects the Iron Law of System Evolution:

> *For every dollar invested in developing a sustained-use system, be prepared to pay at least two dollars on the system's evolution.*

Data from hardware-intensive systems indicates that the average percentage of life-cycle cost spent on operations and support (O&S%) is a relatively small 12% for single-use consumables, but is 60% for ships, 78% for aircraft, and 84% for ground vehicles [5]. For software-intensive systems, O&S% figures from seven studies range from 60–70% to more than 90% [6].

Even so, many projects (and some system acquisition guidance documents) continue to emphasize such practices as "maximizing system performance while minimizing system acquisition costs." Such practices generally lead to brittle, point-solution architectures that overly constrain evolution options and inflate evolution costs, and to a lack of key system deliverables for reducing operations and support costs, such as maintenance and diagnostic tools and documentation, test case inputs and outputs, and latest-release COTS components. (COTS vendors generally support only their latest three releases. In one maintenance study, we encountered a system that was delivered with 120 COTS products, 66 of which were on releases that were no longer supported by the vendors.)

[handwritten margin note: Ops can be costly and neglected]

Several good practices for avoiding such situations can be applied in the initial ICSM Exploration phase. These include early addressing of post-deployment and aftermarket considerations such as development of a full operations concept description, including the following considerations:

- Identification and involvement of key operations and maintenance stakeholders
- Agreement on their roles and responsibilities
- Inclusion of total ownership costs in business case analyses
- Addressing of post-deployment supply chain management alternatives
- Identification of development practices and deliverables needed for successful operations and maintenance

Since operations and maintenance costs can consume 60% to 90% of an enterprise's resources, it is also important to build up a knowledge base on their nature, and to apply the knowledge to reduce their costs and difficulties. For example, this was done for the two TRW projects summarized in Figure 3-2. As indicated in Figure 3-2, their major sources of rework effort were found to be off-nominal architecture-breakers. This source of risk was added to the TRW risk management review guidelines for future projects. Also, their additional major sources of life-cycle change were determined to be hardware–software interfaces, new algorithms, subcontractor interfaces, user interfaces, external application interfaces, COTS upgrades, database restructuring, and diagnostic aids, as shown in Table 3-1.

[handwritten margin note: Investing in sys engineering and understanding off-nominal architecture breakers can lead to savings later on]

Following Dave Parnas's information-hiding principles [7], these sources of change were encapsulated in the architectures of similar projects, and additional systems engineering effort was devoted to addressing off-nominal architecture breakers. As detailed in the next chapter, by investing more effort in systems engineering and architecting, the highly successful Command Center Processing and Display System-Replacement (CCPDS-R) system [8] flattened the usual exponential growth in cost to make changes even later in the life cycle. The resulting savings in total cost of ownership are shown in Figure 3-4 [9]. This figure indicates that the added investment in CCPDS-R was recouped via rework reduction by the end of the initial development cycle, and generated increasing savings in later cycles.

TABLE 3-1 Projects A and B Cost-to-Fix Data (Hours)

Category	Project A	Project B
Extra-long messages		3404 + 626 + 443 + 328 + 244 = 5045
Network failover	2050 + 470 + 360 + 160 = 3040	
Hardware-software interface	620 + 200 = 820	1629 + 513 + 289 + 232 + 166 = 2832
Encryption algorithms		1247 + 368 = 1615
Subcontractor interface	1100 + 760 + 200 = 2060	
GUI revision	980 + 730 + 420 + 240 + 180 = 2550	
Data compression algorithm		910
External applications interface	770 + 330 + 200 + 160 = 1460	
COTS upgrades	540 + 380 + 190 = 1110	741 + 302 + 221 + 197 = 1461
Database restructure	690 + 480 + 310 + 210 + 170 = 1860	
Routing algorithms	494 + 198 = 692	
Diagnostic aids	360	477 + 318 + 184 = 979
Total	**13,620**	**13,531**

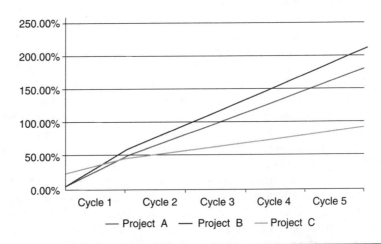

FIGURE 3-4 TOC's for Projects A, B, and C (CCPDS-R) Relative to Baseline Costs

3.4 Concurrent Engineering of Hardware, Software, and Human Factors Aspects

Not every system has all three hardware, software, and human factors aspects. When a system does have more than one of these aspects, however, it is important to address them concurrently rather than sequentially. A hardware-first approach will often choose best-of-breed hardware components with incompatible software or user interfaces; provide inadequate computational support for software growth; create a late software start and a high risk of a schedule overrun; or commit to a functional-hierarchy architecture that is incompatible with layered, service-oriented software and human-factors architectures [10].

Software-first approaches can similarly lead to architectural commitments or selection of best-of-breed components that are incompatible with preferred hardware architectures or make it hard to migrate to new hardware platforms (e.g., multiprocessor hardware components). They may also prompt developers to choose software-knows-best COTS products that create undesirable human–system interfaces. Human-factors-first approaches can often lead to the use of hardware–software packages that initially work well but are difficult to interoperate or scale to extensive use.

Other problems may arise from assumptions by performers in each of the three disciplines that their characteristics are alike, when in fact they are often very different. For systems having limited need or inability to modify the product once fielded (e.g., sealed batteries, satellites), the major sources of life-cycle cost in a hardware-intensive system are realized during development and manufacturing. However, as we noted earlier, hardware maintenance costs dominate (60–84% of life-cycle costs cited for ships, aircraft, and ground vehicles). For software-intensive systems, manufacturing costs are essentially zero. For information services, the range of 60% to 90% of the software life-cycle cost going into post-development maintenance and upgrades is generally applicable. For software embedded in hardware systems, the percentages would be more similar to those for ships and such. For human-intensive systems, the major costs are staffing and training, particularly for safety-critical systems requiring continuous 24/7 operations. A primary reason for this difference is indicated in rows 2 and 3 of Table 3-2. Particularly for widely dispersed hardware such as ships, submarines, satellites, and ground vehicles, making hardware changes across a fleet can be extremely difficult and expensive. As a result, many hardware deficiencies are handled via software or human workarounds that save money overall but shift the life-cycle costs toward the software and human parts of the system.

As can be seen when buying hardware such as cars or TVs, there is some choice of options, but they are generally limited. It is much easier to tailor software or human procedures to different classes of people or purposes. It is also much easier to deliver useful subsets of most software and human systems, while delivering a car without braking or steering capabilities is infeasible.

TABLE 3-2 Differences in Hardware, Software, and Human System Components

Difference Area	Hardware/ Physical	Software/Cyber/ Informational	Human Factors
Major life-cycle cost sources	Development; manufacturing; multilocation upgrades	Life-cycle evolution; low-cost multilocation upgrades	Training and operations labor
Nature of changes	Generally manual, labor-intensive, expensive	Generally straightforward except for software code rot, architecture-breakers	Very good, but dependent on performer knowledge and skills
Incremental development constraints	More inflexible lower limits	More flexible lower limits	Smaller increments easier, if infrequent
Underlying science	Physics, chemistry, continuous mathematics	Discrete mathematics, logic, linguistics	Physiology, behavioral sciences, economics
Testing	By test engineers; much analytic continuity	By test engineers; little analytic continuity	By representative users
Strengths	Creation of physical effects; durability; repeatability; speed of execution; 24/7 operation in wide range of environments; performance monitoring	Low-cost electronic distributed upgrades; flexibility and some adaptability; big-data handling, pattern recognition; multitasking and relocatability	Perceiving new patterns; generalization; guiding hypothesis formulation and test; ambiguity resolution; prioritizing during overloads; skills diversity
Weaknesses	Limited flexibility and adaptability; corrosion, wear, stress, fatigue; expensive distributed upgrades; product mismatches; human-developer shortfalls	Complexity, conformity, changeability, invisibility; common-sense reasoning; stress and fatigue effects; product mismatches; human-developer shortfalls	Relatively slow decision making; limited attention, concentration, multitasking, memory recall, and environmental conditions; teaming mismatches

The science underlying most of hardware engineering involves physics, chemistry, and continuous mathematics. This often leads to implicit assumptions about continuity, repeatability, and conservation of properties (mass, energy, momentum) that may be true for hardware but not true for software or human counterparts. An example is in testing. A hardware test engineer can generally count on covering a parameter space by sampling, under the assumption that the responses will be a continuous function of the input parameters. A software test engineer will have many discrete inputs, for which a successful test run provides no assurance that the neighboring test run will succeed. And for humans, the testing needs to be done by the operators and not test engineers.

A good example of integrated cyber–physical–human systems design is the detailed description of the Hospira medical infusion pump success story in Chapter 1. It included increasing risk-driven levels of detail in field studies and hardware–software–user interface prototyping; task analysis; hardware and software component analysis, including usability testing; and hardware–software–human safety analyses. Example prototypes and simulations included the following:

- Hardware industrial design mockups
- Early usability tests of hardware mockups
- Paper prototypes for GUIs with wireframes consisting of basic shapes for boxes, buttons, and other components
- GUI simulations using Flash animations
- Early usability tests with hardware mockups and embedded software that delivered the Flash animations to a touchscreen interface that was integrated into the hardware case

3.5 Concurrent Requirements and Solutions Engineering

With respect to the content of the Feasibility Evidence Description view of the ICSM in Figure 0-6 in the Introduction, the term "requirements" includes the definition of the system's operational concept and its requirements (the "what" and "how well" the system will perform). The term "solutions" includes the definition of the system–hardware–software–human factors architecture elements, and the project's plans, budgets, and schedules (the "how" and "how much").

For decades, and even today, standard definitions of corporate and government system development and acquisition processes have stipulated that the Requirements activity should produce complete, consistent, traceable, and testable requirements before any work was allowed on the solutions. Initially, there were some good reasons for this sequential approach. Often, requirements were inserted that were really solution choices, thus cutting off other solution choices that could have been much better. Or in many situations, developers would generate solutions before the requirements were fully defined or understood, leading to numerous useless features or misguided architectural commitments that led to large overruns. At the time, most systems were relatively simple and requirements were relatively stable, so that the risk of spending more time specifying them was less than the risk of expensive overruns.

However, the sequential requirements-first approach is a poor fit to most human approaches to practical problem solving. Figure 3-5 shows a representative result from a study of how people work when developing solutions, concurrently obtaining insights all the way from operational concepts to low-level solution components [11].

For more complex systems, teams of people will be similarly exploring and understanding multiple levels of problems and solutions and coordinating their

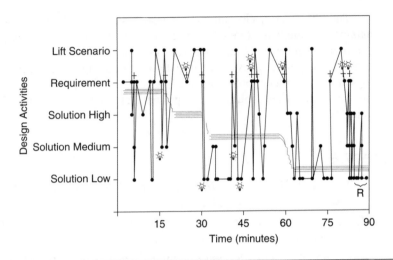

FIGURE 3-5 Human Problem Understanding and Solving: An Elevator (Lift) System Example

progress, capitalizing on many insights that are not available if they are locked into a sequential, reductionist, requirements-first approach. Also, they will have difficulties in developing key evidence such as business cases for the system, which require both estimates of system benefits (needing information about the requirements), and estimates of costs (needing information about the solutions).

Further, as systems become more complex and human-interactive, users become less able to specify their requirements in advance ("Which decision aids do I want to see on the computer screen or in the cockpit? I don't know, but I'll know it when I see it"—the IKIWISI syndrome). Also, as users gain experience in interactively using a system, new requirements emerge that may not be supportable by the architecture developed for the initial requirements (e.g., capabilities to cancel or undo commands, produce trend analyses, or decision outcome predictions).

Such hard-to-specify or emergent requirements are addressable via prototyping or solutions exploration, but these are not allowed in literal interpretations of sequential, requirements-first approaches, which tend to get ossified by layers of regulations, specifications, standards, contracting practices, and maturity models. One of the authors (Boehm) found himself in the difficult position of having led much of the effort to define the sequential, waterfall-oriented TRW Software Development Policies and Standards in the 1970s, along with training courses, review criteria, and corporate public relations materials—and then trying to convince projects in the 1980s to use counterculture techniques such as human-interface prototyping ("Prototyping is not allowed. It's developing solutions before we fully define the requirements").

The ICSM's principles and practices such as evidence- and risk-driven decision making provide ways to evolve to concurrent versus sequential requirements and solutions engineering. These considerations will be covered in the next chapter. Also, further details such as evidence-based process guidance are covered in Chapter 13. In addition, methods, processes, and tools for concurrent-engineering risk assessment and award-fee contracting are provided on the ICSM website at http://csse.usc. edu/ICSM.

References

[1] Pew, R., and Mavor, A. *Human–System Integration in the System Development Process.* NAS Press, 2007.

[2] Beidel, E. "Efforts Under Way to Harden Unpiloted Aircraft for Contested Airspace." *National Defense.* July 2011.

[3] Boehm, B., Valerdi, R., and Honour, E. "The ROI of Systems Engineering: Some Quantitative Results for Software-Intensive Systems." *Systems Engineering.* 2008;11(3):221–234.

[4] Ingold, D. "Results of a Survey on Competitive Prototyping for Software-Intensive Systems." USC-CSSE Technical Report USC-CSSE-2008-841. October 2008. http://csse.usc.edu/csse/TECHRPTS/2008/2008_main.html.

[5] Redman, Q. *Weapon System Design Using Life Cycle Costs.* Raytheon Presentation, NDIA, 2008.

[6] Koskinen, J. "Software Maintenance Fundamentals." In P. Laplante (Ed.), *Encyclopedia of Software Engineering.* Taylor & Francis Group, 2009.

[7] Parnas, D. "Designing Software for Ease of Extension and Contraction." *IEEE Transactions in Software Engineering.* March 1979;128–137.

[8] Royce, W. *Software Project Management: A Unified Framework.* Reading, MA: Addison-Wesley Professional, 1998.

[9] Boehm, B., Lane, J., and Madachy, R. "Total Ownership Cost Models for Valuing System Flexibility." *Proceedings of CSER 2011.* March 2011.

[10] Maier, M. "System and Software Architecture Reconciliation." *Systems Engineering.* 2006;9(2):146–159.

[11] Guindon, R. "Designing the Design Process: Exploring Opportunistic Thoughts." *Human–Computer Interaction.* 1990;5.

4

The Fourth Principle: Evidence- and Risk-Based Decisions

"Look before you leap."

—Anonymous proverb

"He who hesitates is lost."

—Anonymous proverb

Principle 3 emphasizes having a variety of systems engineers and stakeholders concurrently understanding the system's needs, envisioning opportunities, exercising prototypes, and developing, verifying, and validating operations concepts, requirements, architectures, and life-cycle plans. Without some mechanism to synchronize and stabilize all of this concurrency, this could be a recipe for chaos.

One of the several contributions of Principle 4 is to serve as a means to synchronize and stabilize the concurrent activities and system artifacts. As discussed in explaining Figure 0-6 (the ICSM Concurrency View), what is reviewed at ICSM decision milestones is the evidence that the various concurrently developed artifacts satisfy a combined set of feasibility criteria for the system. This implies that the system's operational concept, requirements, architecture, work breakdown structure, plans, budgets, and schedules need to be sufficiently complete and consistent (i.e., synchronized and stabilized) to be able to support the production of convincing evidence.

Having evidence serve as the principal decision criterion at milestone decision reviews is a considerable step forward from traditional schedule-based or event-based reviews. An initial step forward in systems engineering and acquisition guidance was to progress from schedule-based major project reviews (the contract says that the Preliminary Design Review is scheduled for September 30, so we'll have it then, whether we have a preliminary design or not) to event-based reviews (the Preliminary Design Review will be held when there is a preliminary design to review).

This is better, but frequently leads to "Death by PowerPoint and SysML" reviews. These present much design detail, but there is little time to determine

97

whether the design will meet the system's key performance parameters. Such evidence of feasibility is generally desired, but is generally considered as an optional appendix and not a project deliverable. Thus, it is often neglected when budgets are tight and when contractual earned-value increments, progress payments, and award fees are based on producing a design and not evidence of its feasibility. As with schedule-based reviews, there will be a temptation at this point to consider the project innocent of risk until proven guilty, and to proceed into the later phases with a great deal of undiscovered risk, which will be much more expensive to address as technical debt later.

feasibility evidence guides ICSM reviews

In an ICSM evidence-based review, the feasibility evidence is a first-class deliverable. As such, its planning and preparation becomes subject to earned value management and is factored into progress payments and award fees. Investments in feasibility evidence have been found to pay off significantly in development rework avoidance. In a regression analysis of 161 software projects, rework due to shortfalls in architecture and risk resolution evidence grew from 18% added effort for small (10,000 source lines of code) projects to 91% added effort for very large (10 million source lines of code) projects [1].

The link between evidence-based and risk-based decision making is that shortfalls in evidence are uncertainties or probabilities of loss, and that the fundamental decision quantity for risk exposure is measured by the following expression:

converse of each other

$$\text{Risk Exposure} = \text{Probability(Loss)} * \text{Size(Loss)}$$

Up to now, we have been using "risk" as the key concept in reducing downstream losses in uncertain situations, but we should now point out that this rather negative viewpoint has a positive counterpart called opportunity management, for which

$$\text{Opportunity Exposure} = \text{Probability (Gain)} * \text{Size (Gain)}$$

Actually, these two concepts are the converses of each other, as a decision not to pursue an opportunity results in a loss of opportunity exposure, whose probability and size of loss can be considered to be a risk exposure. This idea will be elaborated upon in Chapter 11 on risk-opportunity assessment and control.

As seen in the earlier discussion of growth of rework versus system size, it is less risky to proceed with evidence shortfalls on a small project with a small cost of rework, than to forge ahead with a very large project with a very large cost of rework. Even on a large project, though, shortfalls in evidence are not necessarily reasons to terminate the project or to invest in more evidence. If the opportunity exposure is high and the window of opportunity is closing rapidly, the risk of delay is high and proceeding at least incrementally with a small amount of evidence can be the best decision.

Thus, we can see that Principle 4 brings all of the other principles together. It involves concerns with the stakeholders' value propositions in making decisions as in Principle 1; with proceeding incrementally as in Principle 2; and with synchronizing and stabilizing the concurrent activity as prescribed in Principle 3. We will elaborate on this integration at the end of this chapter, in addition to referencing later chapters in Part IV that elaborate on feasibility evidence planning, preparation, and review; risk assessment and risk control techniques; and production of key evidence elements such as cost and schedule estimates.

4.1 Failure Story: The Unaffordable Requirement

In the early 1980s, a large government organization contracted with TRW to develop an ambitious information query and analysis system. The system would provide more than 1000 users, spread across a large building complex, with powerful query and analysis capabilities for a large and dynamic database.

The customer specified the system using a classic sequential-engineering waterfall development model. Based largely on user need surveys, an oversimplified high-level performance analysis, and a short deadline for getting the To-Be-Determineds out of the requirements specification, they fixed into the contract a requirement for a system response time of less than 1 second. It satisfied the System Requirements Review criteria of being unambiguous, testable, and free of design commitments.

Subsequently, the software architects found that subsecond performance could be provided only via a highly customized design that attempted to anticipate query patterns and cache copies of data so that each user's likely data would be within 1 second's reach (a 1980s precursor of Google). The resulting hardware architecture had more than 25 super-midicomputers (an earlier term for a computer with performance and capacity between that of a minicomputer and a mainframe) busy caching data according to algorithms whose actual performance defied easy analysis. The scope and complexity of the hardware-software architecture brought the estimated cost of the system to nearly $100 million, driven primarily by the requirement for a 1-second response time.

Faced with this unattractive prospect (far more than the customer's budget for the system), the customer and developer decided to develop a prototype of the system's user interface and representative capabilities to test. The results showed that a 4-second response time would satisfy users 90% of the time. A 4-second response time, with special handling for high-priority transactions, dropped development costs closer to $30 million. Thus, the premature specification of a 1-second response time neglected the risk of creating an overly expensive and time-consuming system development. Fortunately, in this case, the only loss was the wasted effort on the expensive-system architecture and a 15-month delay in delivery (see Figure 4-1). More frequently, such rework is done only after the expensive full system is delivered and found still too slow and too expensive to operate.

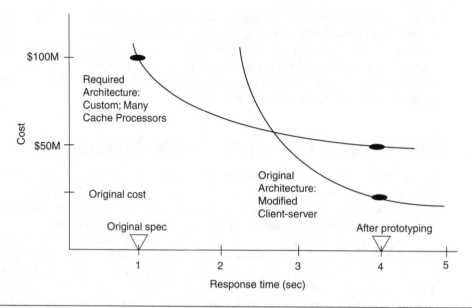

FIGURE 4-1 Problems Encountered without Feasibility Evidence

4.1.1 Problem Avoidance with Principle 4

Had the developers been required to deliver a Feasibility Evidence Description (FED) showing evidence of feasibility of the 1-second response time, they would have run benchmarks on the best available commercial query systems, using representative user workloads, and would have found that the best that they could do was about a 2.5-second response time, even with some preprocessing to reduce query latency. They would have performed a top-level architecture analysis of custom solutions, and concluded that such 1-second solutions were in the $100 million cost range. They would have shared these results with the customer in advance of any key reviews, and found that the customer would prefer to explore the feasibility of a system with a commercially supportable response time. They would have done user interface prototyping and found much earlier that the 4-second response time was acceptable 90% of the time.

As some uncertainties still existed about the ability to address the remaining 10% of the queries, the customer and developer would have agreed to avoid repeating the risky specification of a fixed response time requirement. The customer and developer would instead have defined a range of desirable-to-acceptable response times, with an award fee provided for faster performance. They would also have agreed to reschedule the next milestone review to give the developer time and budget to present evidence of the most feasible solution available, using the savings over the prospect of a $100 million system development as the rationale. This would have put the project on a more solid success track over a year before the actual project discovered and rebaselined itself, and without the significant expense that went into the unaffordable architecture definition.

For example, the customer and developer would negotiate response time ranges. They would agree on a range between a 2-second response time as desirable and a 4-second response time as acceptable, with some 2-second special cases being identified. Next they would benchmark commercial system add-ons to validate their feasibility. Finally, they would present the solution and feasibility evidence at a suitably scheduled Preliminary Design Review (with evidence, roughly equivalent to an ICSM Foundations Commitment Review). The result would be an acceptable solution with minimal delay.

4.1.2 Other Lessons Learned

As seen in Figure 4-1, the best architectural solution is a discontinuous function of the response time requirement level. Thus, a "Build it quick and tune it later" strategy can lead to big trouble, as the tuning to an increasing workload is likely to run into an unachievable architecture-breaker barrier with extremely expensive rework involved in switching to a more scalable architecture. Similarly, attempts to automate the derivation of a system's architecture from its functional requirements are likely to commit to an architecture with similar architecture-breaker discontinuities.

Further, one can see that the cost of a system is not necessarily a function of its number of requirements. Changing the required response time by one character from 1 to 4 seconds in a 2000-page requirements specification reduced the cost by a factor of more than 3. Unlike functional requirements that have local impacts that additively influence system costs, quality attributes have system-wide impacts that often multiplicatively influence system costs.

4.2 Success Story: CCPDS-R

A Principle 4 success story is the Command Center Processing and Display System Replacement (CCPDS-R), a project to reengineer the command center aspects of the U.S. early missile warning system. It covered not only the software but also the associated system engineering and computing hardware procurement. The software effort involved more than 1 million lines of Ada code, across a family of three related user capabilities. The developer was TRW; the customer was the U.S. Air Force Electronic Systems Center (USAF/ESC); the users were the U.S. Space Command, the U.S. Strategic Command, the U.S. National Command Authority, and all nuclear-capable Commanders in Chief. The core capability was developed on a 48-month fixed-price contract between 1987 and 1991. While this was admittedly a long while ago in software time, the project closely mirrors current systems being developed in government and the private sector, so it remains relevant as an example [2].

The project had numerous high-risk elements. One was the extremely high dependability requirements for a system of this nature. Others were the ability to reengineer the sensor interfaces, the commander situation assessment and decision-aid displays, and the critical algorithms in the application. Software infrastructure challenges included distributed processing using Ada tasking and the ability to satisfy critical-decision-window performance requirements. Many of these aspects underwent considerable change during the development process. The project involved 75 software personnel, most of whom had training in Ada programming but had not applied it to real projects.

CCPDS-R used standard Department of Defense (DoD) acquisition procedures, including a fixed-price contract and the documentation-intensive DoD-STD-2167A software development standards. However, by creatively reinterpreting the DoD standards, processes, and contracting mechanisms, USAF/ESC and TRW were able to perform with agility, deliver on budget and on schedule, fully satisfy their users, and receive Air Force awards for outstanding performance.

4.2.1 CCPDS-R Evidence-Based Decision Milestones

The DoD acquisition standards were acknowledged, but their milestone content was redefined to reflect the stakeholders' success conditions. The usual DoD-STD-2167A Preliminary Design Review (PDR) to review paper documents and briefing charts around month 6 was replaced by a PDR at month 14 that demonstrated working software for all the high-risk areas, particularly the network operating system, the message-passing middleware, and the graphic user interface software. The PDR also reviewed the completeness, consistency, and traceability of all of the Ada package interface specifications, as verified by the Rational Ada compiler and R-1000 toolset. Thus, a great deal of system integration was done before the software was developed.

TRW invested significant resources into a package of message-passing middleware that handled much of the Ada tasking and concurrency management, and provided message ports to accommodate the insertion of sequential Ada packages for the various CCPDS-R application capabilities. For pre-PDR performance validation, simulators of these functions could be inserted and executed to determine system performance and real-time characteristics. Thus, not only software interfaces but also system performance could be validated prior to code development, and stubs could be written to provide representative module inputs and outputs for unit and integration testing. Simulators of external sensors and communications inputs and outputs were developed in advance to support continuous testing. Also, automated document generators were developed to satisfy the contractual needs for documentation.

Evidence of achievable software productivity was provided via a well-calibrated cost and schedule estimation model—in this case, an Ada version of the Constructive Cost Model (Ada COCOMO), which was available for CCPDS-R. It was used to help developers, customers, and users better understand how much functional capability could be developed within an available budget and schedule, given the personnel, tools, processes, and infrastructure available to the project.

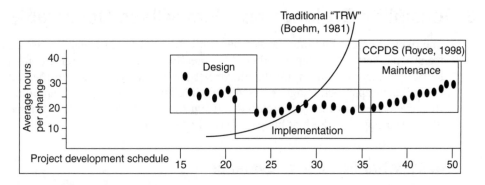

FIGURE 4-2 Cost of Changes versus Time: CCPDS-R

Another major advantage of the Ada COCOMO cost/performance tradeoff analyses was the ability to determine and enable the savings achieved via reuse across the three different installations and user communities.

Since the CCPDS-R plans and specifications were machine processable, the project was able to track progress and change at a very detailed level. This enabled the developers to anticipate potential downstream problems and largely handle them via customer collaboration and early fixes, rather than experiencing delayed problem discovery and expensive technical contract-negotiation fixes. Figure 4-2 shows one such metrics-tracking result: the cost of making CCPDS-R changes as a function of time.

For CCPDS-R, the message-passing middleware and modular applications design enabled the project to be highly agile in responding to change, as reflected in the low growth in cost of change shown in Figure 4-1. Further, the project's advance work in determining and planning to accommodate the commonalities and variabilities across the three user communities and installations enabled significant savings in software reuse across the three related CCPDS-R system versions.

4.2.2 Other Innovative CCPDS-R Practices

USAF/ESC and TRW agreed that the contract award fee for good performance would not just go into the TRW corporate profit coffers. Instead, a significant part was set aside for individual project performer bonuses. This not only enhanced motivation and teamwork, but also made the CCPDS-R project personnel turnover the lowest in TRW large-project history.

The architecture of the system was organized around the performers' skill levels. In particular, previous project experience at TRW and elsewhere had shown high risks of having inexperienced personnel deal with concurrency and Ada tasking constructs. For CCPDS-R, experienced Ada developers wrote the concurrency architecture and the Ada tasking software. The junior programmers were given sequential modules to develop, while being trained by TRW in Ada tasking and concurrency skills for the future.

4.3 Feasibility Evidence as a First-Class Deliverable

The risks of proceeding into development without evidence of feasibility are clear from a plethora of examples other than the Unaffordable Requirement failure story. Two more examples are the MasterNet project in Chapter 2 and the Total-Commitment approach to agent-based RPVs in Chapter 3. Thus, it is important to treat evidence as a first-class project deliverable, rather than as an optional appendix to be dropped at the first budget or schedule crunch.

4.3.1 What Feasibility Evidence Is

Figure 4-3 shows the content of a Feasibility Evidence Description. Chapter 13 includes description of FED content and risk-based guidance and checklists for tailoring the content up from a simple starting point. This is most effective when accomplished as a collaborative activity between the customer and the developer.

Once the FED is applied on a contract, its evidence content becomes a first-class deliverable. There should be a plan and a budget for generating its content, and mechanisms such as periodic reviews and an earned value management capability or an agile burn-down equivalent for tracking its progress with respect to its plan. As additional understanding of the project risks accumulates, the items in the FED can be rebaselined up or down. A portion of the contract's award fee should be allocated to the successful development and independent review of the resulting feasibility evidence.

Feasibility Evidence Description Content

Evidence *__provided by developer__* and *__validated by independent experts__* that if the system is built to the specified architecture, it will:

- Satisfy the requirements: capability, interfaces, level of service, and evolution
- Support the operational concept
- Be buildable within the budgets and schedules in the plan
- Generate a viable return on investment
- Generate satisfactory outcomes for all of the success-critical stakeholders
- Resolve all major risks by treating shortfalls in evidence as risks and covering them by risk management plans
- Serve as basis for stakeholders' commitment to proceed

FIGURE 4-3 Feasibility Evidence Description (FED) Content

4.3.2 What Feasibility Evidence Development Isn't

Feasibility evidence development is not evidence appreciation. Frequently, systems engineers involved in developing models and simulations to evaluate feasibility become so engrossed in the elegance and detail of their models that they do not complete them until after the key decision milestone for which they are needed is past. As with many other systems engineering and development "how much is enough" questions, the best way to address this is to balance the risks of doing too little evidence development against the risks of doing too much.

Some key drivers in this regard are the project's size and criticality, which point toward having more evidence, and the project's rate of requirements and technology change, which point away from generating a lot of evidence that will quickly become obsolete. These decision drivers are quantified in Figure 4-4 in the next subsection.

Also, obtaining evidence isn't equivalent to generating evidence. Often, a well-prepared phone call to a representative previous-project user of a prospective COTS product being evaluated for project use will produce evidence of feasibility or infeasibility that is far superior to weeks of COTS product exercise. As a first-class

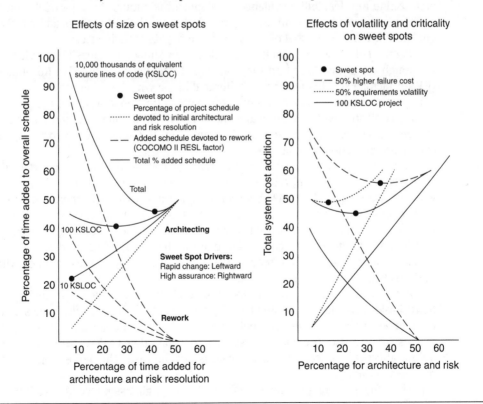

FIGURE 4-4 Size, Volatility, and Criticality Effects on Feasibility Evidence Sweet Spots

deliverable, the FED's development should be preceded by careful planning and evaluation of alternative ways of obtaining evidence.

Feasibility evidence development is also not analysis paralysis. Often, COTS or cloud services evaluations become caught in a delay loop in which a new vendor announcement becomes an excuse to delay making a decision until the actual glories of the vendor announcement are available and can be evaluated. If users need new capabilities soon or the product being developed has a short market window, the project cannot afford to wait. At best, it should do a quick assessment of how much of the announcement is likely to be vaporware, and how the system could be architected to accommodate the new COTS product or service if and when its glories become reality.

4.3.3 How Much Feasibility Evidence Development Is Enough?

Size, criticality, and volatility are key decision drivers for focusing on agile or architected approaches. Nevertheless, critical questions remain about how much architecting and feasibility evidence development is enough for a particular project. Here we provide a quantitative approach that has helped projects address this question. It extends the ROI of investments in feasibility evidence.

Figure 4-4 shows the results of a risk-driven "how much feasibility evidence is enough" analysis, based on the COCOMO II Architecture and Risk Resolution (RESL) factor [3]. This factor was calibrated along with 22 others to 161 project data points. It relates the amount of extra rework effort on a project to the percent of project effort devoted to software-intensive system architecting and feasibility evidence development. The analysis indicated that the amount of rework was an exponential function of project size.

A small (10,000 equivalent source lines of code—10 KSLOC) project could fairly easily adapt its architecture to rapid change via refactoring or its equivalent, with a rework penalty of 14% between minimal and extremely thorough architecture and risk resolution. However, a very large (10,000 KSLOC) project would incur a corresponding rework penalty of 91%, covering such effort sources as integration rework due to large-component interface incompatibilities and critical performance shortfalls. You can imagine the impact of more software combined with the complexity of very large projects.

Actually, the RESL factor includes several other architecture-related attributes besides the amount of architecting investment, such as available personnel capabilities, architecting support tools, and the degree of architectural risks requiring resolution. Also, the analysis assumes that the other COCOMO II cost drivers do not affect the project outcomes, which is not the case. This tends to move the numbers to the right.

The effects of rapid change (volatility) and high assurance (criticality) on the sweet spots are shown in the right-hand graph in Figure 4-4. Here, the solid lines represent the average-case cost of rework, architecting, and total cost for a 100-KSLOC project as shown at the left. The dotted lines show the effect on the cost of architecting and total cost if rapid change adds 50% to the cost of architecture and risk resolution. Quantitatively, this moves the sweet spot from roughly 20% to 10% of effective architecture investment (but actually 15% due to the 50% cost penalty). Thus, large investments in architecture and other documentation do not have a positive return on investment due to the high costs of documentation rework for rapid-change adaptation.

The dashed lines at the right in Figure 4-4 represent a conservative analysis of the effects of failure cost of architecting shortfalls on the project's effective business cost and architecting sweet spot. It assumes that the costs of architecture shortfalls include not only added rework, but also losses to the organization's operational effectiveness and productivity. These are conservatively assumed to add 50% to the project-rework cost of architecture shortfalls to the organization. In most cases for high-assurance systems, the added cost would be considerably higher.

Quantitatively, this moves the sweet spot from roughly 20% to more than 30% as the most cost-effective investment in architecting for a 100-KSLOC project. Note that the sweet spots are actually relatively flat "sweet regions" extending from 5% to 10% to the left and right of the sweet spots. However, moving to the edges of a sweet region increases the risk of significant losses if some project assumptions turn out to be optimistic.

Again, the effects of other factors may affect the location of a given project's "how much evidence is enough" sweet spot. A good cross-check is to use the Constructive Systems Engineering Cost Model (COSYSMO)[4] to estimate the project's amount of needed systems engineering effort. A third approach is to use the risk-based decision heuristic of balancing the risks of doing too little evidence generation against the risks of doing too much (the balance between "Look before you leap" and "He who hesitates is lost.").

4.4 How Much of Anything Is Enough?

The risk-based decision heuristic of balancing the risks of doing too little evidence generation against the risks of doing too much can be applied to most decisions involved in system definition, development, and evolution. How much system scoping, planning, prototyping, COTS evaluation, requirements detail, spare capacity, fault tolerance, safety, security, environmental protection, documenting, configuration management, quality assurance, peer reviewing, testing, use of formal methods, and feasibility evidence are enough? The best answer can generally be found by considering and balancing the risks of doing too little against the risks of doing too much. This answer, however, will generally not be the same for all parts of the system. The higher-risk parts of the system will need more attention to detail than the lower-risk parts, so as to reduce both the probability and the size of loss involved in getting it wrong.

If there is any meta-principle underlying the four principles and other practices in the ICSM, it is this *Meta-Principle of Balance:*

Balancing the risk of doing too little and the risk of doing too much will generally find a middle-course sweet spot that is about the best you can do.

Of course, there is nothing new about this idea. It's what Herb Simon was talking about in preferring satisficing to optimizing; what Aristotle was talking about with the Golden Mean; what the Confucians talk about with the Doctrine of the Mean; and what the Buddhists talk about with the Middle Way. With all of these advocates, it seems like a pretty good underlying meta-principle.

4.5 Summing Up the Principles

The definition of the spiral principles has gone through several iterations, including, for example, a joint effort by USC and the CMU Software Engineering Institute that resulted in the definitions of six Spiral Invariants and six Hazardous Spiral Look-Alikes [5]. Subsequent continuing experience in applying the Spiral Invariants led to their consolidation into the four principles just explained in Chapters 1–4.

Table 4-1 summarizes how the four principles reinforce each other to more rapidly and cost-effectively deliver value to a system's stakeholders. The rows in Table 4-1 show how the application of each principle improves the cost-effectiveness of applying the other three principles, in terms of value delivered to the stakeholders across the system's evolving life cycle. The columns show how each principle's cost-effectiveness is improved by the other three principles.

For example, row 1 begins by showing how applying Principle 1 on Stakeholder Value-Based Guidance improves the cost-effectiveness of applying Principle 2 on Incremental Commitment and Accountability by better identifying the system's success-critical stakeholders and enabling them to more rapidly and fully understand each other's value propositions, and to work out better decisions on which stakeholders are best suited to have primary and secondary responsibilities and authority to perform the system's life-cycle definition, development, and evolution functions. Similarly, column 1 begins by showing how applying Principle 2 improves the cost-effectiveness of applying Principle 1, in that the incremental commitment of the stakeholders to their responsibilities and authority as the life cycle proceeds leads to more rapid and incremental mutual understanding and buildup of mutual trust in each other, which in turn leads to more agility in responding to the continuing flow of changes impacting the system's definition and evolution. This strengthening of Principle 1 is what enables it to improve the cost-effectiveness of Principle 3 shown in row 1, in enabling more rapid convergence on mutually satisfactory system solutions. Thus, Principle 3 is strengthening Principle 1 in column 1 by speeding up the growth of stakeholders' mutual

TABLE 4-1 How the Principles Reinforce Each Other and Deliver Value More Rapidly

Improves→ ↓Applying	1. Stakeholder Value-Based System D&E	2. Incremental Commitment, Accountability	3. Concurrent Multidiscipline System D&E	4. Evidence- and Risk-Based Decisions
1. Stakeholder Value-Based Guidance		Understands other stakeholders' value propositions Works out stakeholder responsibilities and authority Better decisions	Rapidly converges on mutually satisfactory solutions Faster decisions	Focuses evidence generation on highest-value issues Cost-effective decisions
2. Incremental Commitment and Accountability	Builds trust in other stakeholders Increases agility in responding to change		Triage of changes enables consistent, feasible near-term and longer-term decisions	Ensures adequate resources for evidence development
3. Concurrent Multidiscipline Engineering	Speeds up understanding of other stakeholders' value propositions	Enables more rapid and continuing focus on highest-level issues		Enables more cost-effective, timely generation of evidence and the resulting decisions
4. Evidence- and Risk-Based Decisions	Provides stakeholders with evidence of value	Avoids commitments to infeasible solutions	Synchronizes and stabilizes concurrency	

understanding of each other's value propositions ... and so on with Principle 4 and the other parts of Table 4-1. Underlying it all is the *Meta-Principle of Balance: Balancing the risk of doing too little and the risk of doing too much will generally find a middle-course sweet spot that is about the best you can do.*

Next, Part II describes how the ICSM applies and nurtures the four principles through a flexible framework of phases, stages, and anchor points. To do so, we provide an example systems development project in the medical systems domain as it proceeds through the phases and stages of the ICSM life cycle.

References

[1] Boehm, B., Valerdi, R., and Honour, E. "The ROI of Systems Engineering: Some Quantitative Results for Software-Intensive Systems." *Systems Engineering.* 2008;11(3):221–234.

[2] Royce, W. *Software Project Management: A Unified Framework.* Reading, MA: Addison-Wesley Professional, 1998.

[3] Boehm, B., Abts, Chris, Brown, A. Winsor, Chulani, Sunita, Clark, Bradford K., Horowitz, Ellis, Madachy, Ray, Reifer, Donald J., and Steece, Bert. *Software Cost Estimation with COCOMO II* (with CD-ROM). Englewood Cliffs, NJ: Prentice Hall, 2000.

[4] Valerdi, R. *The Constructive Systems Engineering Cost Model (COSYSMO): Quantifying the Costs of Systems Engineering Effort in Complex Systems.* VDM Verlag, 2008.

[5] Boehm, B., and Hansen, W. "Understanding the Spiral Model as a Tool for Evolutionary Acquisition." *CrossTalk.* May 2001.

The Seven Ages of Man, from Petit's Almanack, 1525.

Shakespeare's Beautiful Idea on the Seven Ages of Man (1792), Joseph C. Gear. Folger Shakespeare Library Digital Image Collection [ART File S528a4 no.48a-b]

Part II

ICSM Life Cycle and Stage I: Incremental Definition

"...When we mean to build,
We first survey the plot, then draw the model;
And when we see the figure of the house,
Then must we rate the cost of the erection;
Which if we find outweighs ability,
What do we then but draw anew the model
In fewer offices, or at last desist
To build at all? Much more, in this great work,
Which is almost to pluck a kingdom down
And set another up, should we survey
The plot of situation and the model,
Consent upon a sure foundation,
Question surveyors, know our own estate,
How able such a work to undergo,
To weigh against his opposite; or else
We fortify in paper and in figures,
Using the names of men instead of men:
Like one that draws the model of a house
Beyond his power to build it; who, half through,
Gives o'er and leaves his part-created cost
A naked subject to the weeping clouds
And waste for churlish winter's tyranny."

—Bardolph, *Henry IV*, Part II, Act 1, Scene 3

Shakespeare provided beautifully crafted descriptions of mundane occurrences. Whether "the Ages of Man" from *As You Like It* or Bardolph's ruminations on a half-built home while considering the size of an army, Shakespeare defines steps and phases with grace, humor, and accuracy. It is now our duty to consider the ICSM life cycle, albeit in words woefully short of William's art.

In this part, we begin by describing the overall ICSM life cycle, its stages and phases, and the ways in which it relates to other life-cycle models. We then delve into Stage I and its phases in greater detail. Throughout this description and continuing in Part III and Part IV, we make use of a case study based on the development of an emergency health response unit to illustrate the activities in each lifecycle phase.

- Chapter 5 addresses the entire ICSM life cycle.
- Chapter 6 begins the discussion of Stage I with the Exploration phase.
- Chapter 7 continues the walk through the life cycle with the Valuation phase.
- Chapter 8 completes the discussion of Stage I with the Foundations phase.

5

The ICSM Life Cycle

"When you first start off trying to solve a problem, the first solutions you come up with are very complex and most people stop there. But if you keep going, and live with the problem and peel more layers of the onion off, you can often times arrive at some very elegant and simple solutions. Most people just don't put in the time or energy to get there."

—Steve Jobs

B efore we begin a detailed discussion of the ICSM phases, it is useful to first discuss the complete ICSM lifecycle to better put the phase activities in perspective. This chapter discusses the ICSM lifecycle, how it compares with other lifecycle models, and then concludes with an overview of Stage I. Finally, at the end of this chapter, we introduce a case study that we will use throughout the ICSM phases to illustrate ICSM concepts and how they might be applied to an actual project.

5.1 ICSM Life Cycle

The best view of the ICSM for this discussion is the Phased View, illustrated in Figure 5-1. This view shows how the overall lifecycle process divides naturally into two major stages. Stage I, Incremental Definition, covers the up-front growth in system understanding, definition, feasibility assurance, and stakeholder commitment. Stage I leads to a larger Stage II commitment to implement a feasible set of specifications and plans for incremental development and operations of the desired system. This view also illustrates the risk-driven focus of the ICSM as well as its iterative and incremental approach to development, and the role of feasibility evidence in supporting the decision at each commitment review.

5.2 Comparison of ICSM to Other Life-Cycle Models

Those familiar with other system development life-cycle models may wonder how the ICSM aligns to these models. Figure 5-2 compares these life-cycle models and shows that in concept, these models have much in common. Most break the life

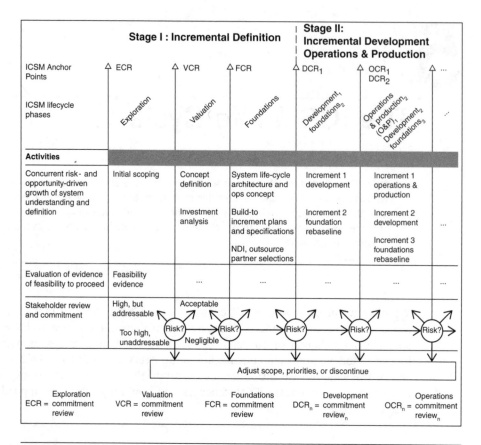

	Stage I : Incremental Definition			Stage II: Incremental Development Operations & Production		
ICSM Anchor Points	△ ECR	△ VCR	△ FCR	△ DCR_1	△ OCR_1 DCR_2	△ ...
ICSM lifecycle phases	*Exploration*	*Valuation*	*Foundations*	*Development₁ foundations₂*	*Operations & production₂ (O&P)₁ Development₃ foundations₃*	..
Activities						
Concurrent risk- and opportunity-driven growth of system understanding and definition	Initial scoping	Concept definition / Investment analysis	System life-cycle architecture and ops concept / Build-to increment plans and specifications / NDI, outsource partner selections	Increment 1 development / Increment 2 foundation rebaseline	Increment 1 operations & production / Increment 2 development / Increment 3 foundations rebaseline	...
Evaluation of evidence of feasibility to proceed	Feasibility evidence	...	...	...	...	...
Stakeholder review and commitment	High, but addressable / Too high, unaddressable	Acceptable / Negligible				
	Risk?	Risk?	Risk?	Risk?	Risk?	
			Adjust scope, priorities, or discontinue			

Exploration	Valuation	Foundations	Development	Operations
ECR = commitment review	VCR = commitment review	FCR = commitment review	DCR_n = commitment $review_n$	OCR_n = commitment $review_n$

FIGURE 5-1 Overview of ICSM Stages and Phases.

cycle into a number of phases separated by some form of review. Even though the key phases are not exactly aligned across the various models, they have common goals and engineering activities. For example, the ICSM Development phase combines the IEEE 1220 detailed design and FAIT (fabrication, assembly, integration, and test) phases. While addressing some of the Exploration and Valuation phase activities, the Scaled Agile Framework* is primarily intended for development and operations, so it maps more closely to the Foundations, Development, and Production and Operations phases of the ICSM.

The fact that these model diagrams look somewhat alike does not mean they operate in a similar fashion. The ICSM is not a one-size-fits-all process— it is intended to be adapted to fit the characteristics of a given project within a

---

*Information on SAFe and the SAFe graphics in Figure 5-2 are adapted from Scaled Agile Framework (scaledagileframework.org) and are based on the work of the Scaled Agile Framework organization led by Dean Leffingwell.

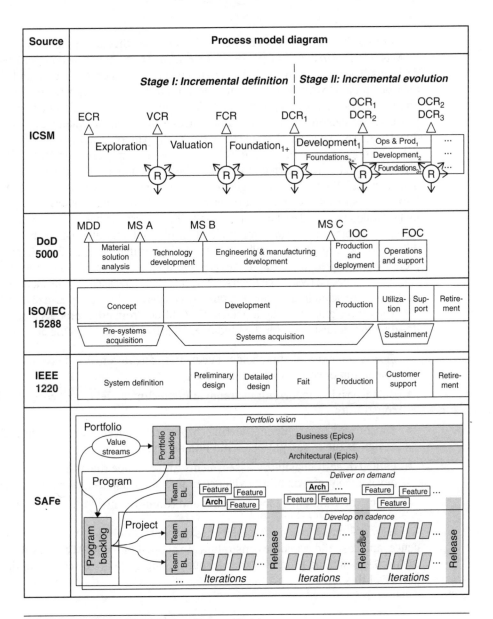

Source	Process model diagram
ICSM	*Stage I: Incremental definition* | *Stage II: Incremental evolution* ECR, VCR, FCR, DCR₁, OCR₁/DCR₂, OCR₂/DCR₃ Exploration, Valuation, Foundation₁₊, Development₁ / Foundations₂₊, Ops & Prod₁ / Development₂ / Foundations₃₊
DoD 5000	MDD, MS A, MS B, MS C, IOC, FOC Material solution analysis, Technology development, Engineering & manufacturing development, Production and deployment, Operations and support
ISO/IEC 15288	Concept, Development, Production, Utilization, Support, Retirement Pre-systems acquisition, Systems acquisition, Sustainment
IEEE 1220	System definition, Preliminary design, Detailed design, Fait, Production, Customer support, Retirement
SAFe	Portfolio — Value streams — Portfolio backlog — Portfolio vision — Business (Epics) — Architectural (Epics) Program — Program backlog — Project — Team BL — Feature/Arch — Deliver on demand — Develop on cadence — Iterations — Release

FIGURE 5-2 Comparison of Various Process Models

development ecosystem, and its phases may be combined, repeated, or over-
lapped. Project characteristics that may impact life-cycle definitions include the
level of maturity of the requirements, expected system size and complexity, level
of expected innovation, maturity of candidate technologies, environmental constraints and standards, affordability, and schedule constraints, as well as the experience base of both the acquiring and developing organizations.

Two significant differences between ICSM and the other process models is that the ICSM is *risk-driven* and requires *feasibility evidence* to make critical program life-cycle decisions. The risk-driven (circle-R) decision points make it explicitly clear and acceptable for a project to evolve in different directions based on risks. Experienced managers and engineers often overlap sequential phases to cope with risks and opportunities. However, as demonstrated in the Unaffordable Requirement failure case study in Chapter 4, less-experienced people tend to take the path of least resistance and follow the sequential plans, either blissfully unaware of or simply ignoring identified risks. This has often been somewhat facetiously called "risk admiration" as opposed to "risk management." When risks are negligible, the ICSM encourages phases to be combined into a more streamlined process. Likewise, when risks are unacceptably high (e.g., too many "unknowns"), decisions must be made to invest further in feasibility assessments, technology maturation, or exploration of additional alternatives before committing to the next phase. Finally, if risks are higher than stakeholder tolerance, the project is most likely too weak to survive, and it should be terminated or some other exit activity selected to salvage the useful work taken. This aspect of the model is illustrated in more detail in the examples provided as part of the ICSM phase discussions.

The third significant way in which ICSM differs from other process models is in its adherence and support for the fundamental principles that lead the developers to:

- Clearly understand stakeholder needs and resolve conflicts between competing or conflicting requirements
- Balance risks, opportunities, innovation, technical debt,[†] and cost-schedule constraints
- Encourage concurrent engineering throughout concept development and design at the cyber, physical, and human levels
- Establish early feasibility assessments and manage the associated development of feasibility evidence to inform decision-making processes
- Ensure accountability for decisions and commitments

How risk management, feasibility assessments, development of feasibility evidence, and cost and schedule constraints are applied in the ICSM and used to guide the decision-making processes throughout the life cycle are discussed in detail in Part IV of this book.

[†] *Technical debt* is a term coined by Ward Cunningham and refers to delayed technical work or rework that is incurred when shortcuts are taken or short-term needs are given precedence over the longer-term objectives. It is the result of intentional decisions that impact the viability of a system and usually incur interest (i.e., additional cost) to eliminate. The intentional decisions may be focused on processes/methods, documentation, capabilities, schedule, funding, or other things in the life cycle. These decisions commit the project to a certain direction. Although the impact may not be evident, it must be understood to manage the tradespace and potential technical debt.

5.3 Stage I: Deciding Why, What, When, Who, Where, How, and How Much

As we saw in Part I, we are in an era where many of our system development and major enhancement projects fail after considerable investments in time and dollars. Analyses of these failed projects show that often development starts without clear direction, resulting in wasted effort, rework, and technical debt, somewhat similar to the recent U.S. Affordable Care Act system (healthcare.gov) experience. By changing our early system development patterns of thought and applying systems thinking to the problem or need at hand, we can establish better foundations for system development success.

ICSM Stage I consists of the incremental phases that converge on defining the system to be developed based on clear stakeholder needs, business value, technology maturity, and feasibility with respect to cost and schedule. Each of the Stage I incremental definition phases is intended to help stakeholders, system engineers, and architects better understand system needs and explore options for meeting those needs. An analysis of alternative solutions focuses on both technical feasibility and business value, and considers how well each alternative meets the cost and schedule parameters. As strong alternatives are identified, a top-level design or architecture is developed for each and further analyzed with respect to desired performance and ability to meet the desired needs.

The duration of the generic Stage I can be anywhere from one week to several years and can depend on a multitude of factors, such as the size and complexity of the desired capability and capability requirements; how much innovation the stakeholders are willing to invest in; the size, complexity, and technical feasibility of candidate solutions; and the cost and schedule of the initial development and expected total costs of ownership. For example:

- A small, cohesive, agile-methods, developer–customer team tasked with developing a new capability using a mature infrastructure can form and begin incremental development using Kanban, Scrum, eXtreme Programming (XP), Crystal, or other agile methods in a week.
- A large, complex new software system or set of systems such as an airport baggage handler system may take two to four years to develop the system concept, mature new technologies to automate multisource data collection and baggage tracking, develop protocols and conventions for system operation, simulate and analyze candidate routing algorithms, and develop specifications and plans for Stage II development. These specifications and plans are at the "build-to" level for the initial increment and at a much higher conceptual level for future increments unless the future increments contain high-risk/high-impact elements that must be addressed earlier in the development process. Future increment specifications and plans are elaborated in detail for the later increments "just in time" to better anticipate and accommodate downstream changes in system objectives, technology, and interoperating systems.

As shown in the "Stakeholder review and commitment" row in Figure 5-1, each project's ICSM roadmap is determined by the arrows chosen in response to risk assessments and stakeholder commitment decisions at its anchor-point milestone reviews. A small agile project tends to follow the negligible-risk arrows and combines the Valuation and Foundations phases to develop the foundations necessary to support an agile development process in Stage II. In contrast, an ultra-large, immature-technology project may apply a form of competitive prototyping as discussed in Chapter 3—for example, funding four small competitive concept-definition and validation activities in the Exploratory phase, three larger follow-on Valuation activities, and two considerably larger Foundations activities, and choosing at each anchor-point milestone the best-qualified approaches to proceed with based on the feasibility and risk evaluations presented at each anchor-point milestone review. In still other cases, the reviews might indicate that certain essential technologies or infrastructure incompatibilities need more work before proceeding into the next phase.

The rest of the Part II chapters explain the Stage I phases in detail. For each phase we describe the phase in terms of the entry criteria and inputs at the start of the phase, the activities performed during the phase, and the exit criteria and outputs and the end of the phase. As part of this discussion, we provide:

- A set of questions that should be addressed during the phase
- Types of feasibility assessments and evidence that might be used
- Potential pitfalls that will lead to inadequate or non-optimal solutions, technical debt, excessive costs, or lower market share
- Major risks to watch for at the end of each phase that will lead to later problems if not adequately mitigated
- Guidance on how the phase activities scale from small to large projects
- How the four key ICSM principles guide the phase activities.

5.4 ICSM Case Study

To help illustrate many of the ICSM concepts throughout the rest of this book, we provide an easy-to-understand, but relatively rich case study in the field of health care, the Medical First Responder System (MedFRS). This section summarizes the MedFRS statement of need.

Ensayo is a small urban, semirural region in the western United States that covers about 400 square miles and has a population of about 300,000 people. The region currently has 10 ambulances that are augmented by 4 regional fire trucks with a paramedic on board. There are four hospitals in the region, two of which are designated as Level 1 trauma centers.

Current first responder systems that provide emergency health care in the field consist of multiple systems installed on first responder platforms. Currently, this platform is an ambulance, but it may eventually include a helicopter or a boat as well. Current platforms have added many systems over time to help the first responders treat people. However, with the variety of systems now on the platform, the suite of systems is complex, not easy to use, and taking up valuable space needed to actually treat the person. As a result, the proliferation of these disparate systems has reached the point where it is impacting patient safety.

To remedy this situation, the Ensayo regional area government has put together an initiative to consolidate current first responder systems into a well-integrated system of systems as well as provide new capabilities to support treatment of critical patients. This system of systems is called the Medical First Responder System. The MedFRS is a system that will integrate a variety of first responder systems onto a single computer that can link to a regional trauma center. The computer will preferably be a ruggedized commercial laptop computer or handheld device, and will simplify the operation and interoperation of these first responder systems while providing for patient privacy and safety. The MedFRS integration includes the patient monitoring and treatment systems and the standardization of system protocols, interfaces, and key data (e.g., electronic patient records).

Key desired features for MedFRS include the ability to:

1. Integrate the constituent systems
2. Provide telemedicine capabilities to key trauma care facilities in the region
3. Connect to a variety of medical devices and telemetry systems using standard interfaces and providing a common user "look and feel" across the devices and systems, including consistent yet distinguishable alarms and messages
4. Incorporate an electronic health record compatible with regional health care facilities and trauma centers
5. Provide a high level of patient privacy and safety
6. Integrate information from patient "smart" stents that monitor blood chemistry and pressure into the telemedicine system once the stents have received U.S. Food and Drug Administration (FDA) approval
7. Provide a learning capability for future improved patient care.

Note that MedFRS as described in this book is not a complete example. Rather, aspects of such a system development effort are used to illustrate key ICSM concepts and application.

6

Exploration Phase

"Making the familiar strange and the strange familiar."

—First attributed to the German poet Novalis (1772–1801)

The genesis of a new need or system typically starts with an identified problem or a desire to perform an activity "better." "Better" can be defined in many ways—automation of manual tasks, faster, cheaper, safer, more securely, and more accurately, to name but a few possibilities. Solutions for this need (or capability) can range from relatively simple to extremely complex, with each solution providing a potentially different level of acceptability, cost, and time to realization. The goal of this phase is to spend time exploring alternative solutions to identify candidate(s) that will potentially provide a sufficient return on the investment made to acquire and use the solution over time. To conduct this exploration, it is important to take time to

- Understand the capability (or set of capabilities) and its importance to the target stakeholders and users
- Identify various ways for providing the capability
- Evaluate the feasibility of providing the capability within acceptable cost and schedule limits, enterprise-fit constraints, and current technology maturity

It is also at this point that innovation and creativity can be of most value in identifying candidate solutions to an identified need. The tradespace is open to consider a realm of possibilities, whether it be a new process, repurposing an existing system or process, or a new system or set of systems.

6.1 What Is the Exploration Phase?

The Exploration phase starts with an identified need or capability that might have a technology-based solution. The goal of this phase is to conduct preliminary investigations to better understand the need and identify some potential options for providing the needed capability (or set of capabilities) that appear doable within

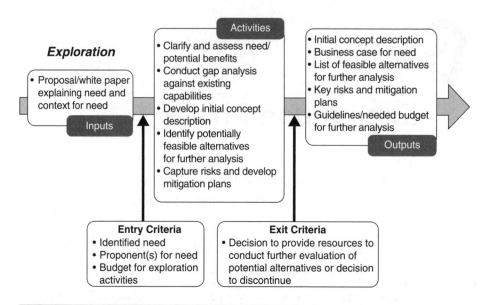

FIGURE 6-1 Exploration Process Overview

cost and schedule targets and enterprise-fit constraints. Figure 6-1 provides an overview of the Exploration phase, showing the inputs and entry criteria that trigger the phase, the high-level activities performed in this phase, and the outputs and exit criteria that determine the conclusion of this phase.

An Exploration phase begins not only with an identified need (or capability), but also with a proponent for that need who can make a case that there exists an enterprise or organizational gap, inadequate capability, or market niche to be addressed and worthy of further exploration and investment. The first "commitment" to enter an Exploration phase, the Exploration Commitment Review (ECR), is typically based on a proposal or white paper that has been developed by one or more proponents.

The proponent provides the motivating force to get a new project, initiative, or enterprise started. As shown in Table 6-1, proponents can be organization leaders with goals, authority, and resources; entrepreneurs with goals and resources; inventors with goals and ideas; or consortia with shared goals and distributed leadership and resources.

The proposal or white paper provided by the proponent succinctly explains the need, including why there is a need and why that need should be addressed. The proposal or white paper may also provide additional details related to the conditions or environment in which the need is critical as well as the consequences if the need is not addressed or, in the case of a newly identified market niche, a preliminary market analysis including potential competitors and a rough estimate of the return on investment for the new product.

TABLE 6-1 Common Types of Proponents

Type	Goals	Authority	Ideas	Resources
Leader with baseline agenda	X	X	X	X
Leader with open agenda	X	X		X
Entrepreneur with baseline agenda	X		X	X
Entrepreneur with open agenda	X			X
Inventor with goals and ideas	X		X	
Consortium with shared goals	X	(X)		(X)

The Exploration phase activities shown in Figure 6-1 are guided by a set of questions. Typical questions for this phase are:

- What is the real need?
- Who wants it and why?
- Who is/are the key proponent(s)?
- How strong is the business case? What is the expected market share?
- Who are the other stakeholders/competitors that can impact success?
- What will its impact be on current enterprise/market capabilities or systems (good or bad)?
- Are there nontechnology options for addressing the need?
- Can existing systems be modified to address the new need?
- What are the supporting technologies and opportunities?
- Can we find the right personnel, partners, suppliers, and subcontractors?
- What are the key technologies we will depend on?
- What are the obstacles to success and how can they be avoided?
- What are other nontechnology aspects that will impact cost, schedule, and overall success (e.g., regulatory, legal, political, cultural)?

By focusing on these aspects and questions, the potential solutions spaces are explored. For those needs that cannot be met by nontechnology solutions or changes to existing systems, a business case is developed and a risk assessment conducted for the proposed new system or set of systems. If the proposed new system will require a new innovation or maturing a relatively new technology, more detailed feasibility evidence may be required to support the commitment review to proceed further. If the proposed system will require a major financial investment, the stakeholders and decision makers may want to pursue multiple solutions and fund a competitive prototyping activity. The level of investment in this phase is related to the level of investment anticipated for the solution system and the associated risks with developing the system.

How the Exploration activities are approached depends on the type of organization—that is, whether the organization is an acquirer or a potential supplier. Two types of organizations might be involved in this process:

▪ Government entity or business needing to fill a "mission" or "business" gap/opportunity
▪ Organizations that make/sell products or product lines or provide services (e.g., cloud services).

The first one is an "acquirer" organization typically looking for a solution for its organization. The goal of an acquiring organization is to achieve the most cost-effective solution while meeting the organization's current needs and enhancing future value.

Making or selling products or services in a commercial environment has some different drivers: the need to produce something that people want. Therefore, a market analysis is often part of the exploration process, along with an analysis of how much it will take to develop the product/service versus how much the organization can charge for the product/product license/service.

As we have noted, the level of formality and rigor in this phase depends on the size, complexity, and anticipated costs and risks of the system under consideration. For smaller, less risky software systems and applications that will provide a new capability within an enterprise, the Exploration and Valuations phases are often combined. For larger, more complex systems, especially those that will be exploring innovative solutions or developing and maturing a new technology, the Exploration phase is much more rigorous and may require considerable investigations, prototype developments, or technology demonstrations before a commitment is made to proceed further.

6.2 What Are the Potential Pitfalls during Exploration?

Understanding *what* to do is not sufficient to ensure success in the Exploration phase. In addition, one needs to consider "how much," who to include in decisions, how the potential solution spaces will fit within the enterprise, as well as what is sufficient evidence to proceed. These considerations lead to a set of common pitfalls that can result in significant technical debt or a discontinued project late in the development life cycle after a considerable investment:

▪ Inadequate plans, budget, or schedule for the Exploration activities
▪ Omitting or neglecting key stakeholders
▪ Poor project fit to enterprise strategy
▪ Weak marketplace or competition analysis
▪ Excessive, overly constrained, or incompatible key performance parameters
▪ Insufficient exploration of nontechnical solutions

- Insufficient time to pursue innovative solutions
- Inadequate next-phase plans
- Over-focusing on requirements for system/product users and overlooking other key stakeholders (such as maintainers and stakeholders of interoperating systems) and their needs
- Prematurely imposing requirements constraints that disqualify other sufficient solution opportunities (such as commercial-off-the-shelf [COTS] products or modifications to existing systems)
- Quickly converging on requirements that lead to obsolete solutions
- Overgeneralization of the initial product or service
- Neglecting growth trends in user needs or basing requirements on technologies with limited growth potential (such as inability to accommodate workload growth or SoS interoperability, or easiest-first solutions that cannot be extended later)

Consideration of these potential pitfalls during the Exploration phase and its commitment review will lead to a stronger commitment decision to either explore more, proceed, or discontinue.

6.3 Potential Major Risks to Watch for at the End of Exploration

After a certain amount of exploration, an organization needs to make a "go/no go" decision with respect to the next phase. This may be driven by proposal due dates, funding deadlines, potential marketing/product-announcement events, or other external events and opportunities. Not all of the questions will have solid answers. However, if indicators point toward funding the next phase, it is critical to clearly identify key risks at this point and establish risk mitigation plans for them. Some key risks to watch for at this point include the following:

- Overly optimistic plans, schedules, and estimates for the next phase commitments
- Key technologies that are not yet mature enough
- Success-critical stakeholders that have either not been consulted or are not in agreement with the need or candidate approaches
- Overly risk-adverse decision makers leading to "analysis paralysis"
- Overly risk-embracing decision makers eager to commit to the next phase with insufficient understanding of the needs and information about candidate approaches and a philosophy that "we can always fix it later if it is not quite right"
- Inadequate consideration of barriers to entry and strategies for "crossing the chasm"

- Critical engineering staff shortfalls
- Weak critical links in the candidate supply chains

Ways to identify, analyze, mitigate, track, and manage risks are discussed in Chapter 15.

6.4 How Exploration Scales from Small to Large, Complex Systems

The level of exploration performed typically depends on how well the problem and solution spaces are understood; the expected level of key performance requirements such as timing, precision, accuracy, security, and safety; and the size, complexity, precedence, and cost of the anticipated solution. The goal is to explore the problem and solutions spaces no more and no less than is required to have necessary evidence to support the business decision process. For example:

- For a new capability that can be developed through modifications and enhancements to existing systems, the Exploration phase may be combined with the Stage I Valuation phase and maybe even the Foundations phase. The existing systems provide a well-understood solution space and mature foundations.

- For a new set of capabilities that may require an innovative solution, the development of one or more new systems, or the maturation of new technologies, more rigorous research, prototyping, and feasibility assessments are required. In these situations, each phase should be worked in succession until there is sufficient evidence of a solution that satisfies the cost and schedule constraints or the evidence indicates that there is no reasonable solution within acceptable cost and schedule constraints. The level of detail of the evidence should not be uniform, but rather risk driven.

The key guide for Exploration tailoring should be this question: What does it take to provide sufficient answers to the Exploration questions listed earlier to make a reasonable business decision to proceed or to discontinue the project?

6.5 Role of Principles in Exploration Activities

To summarize the Exploration phase, we turn to the four ICSM principles. It is in this initial phase that the success-critical stakeholders for a need or capability are identified, these stakeholders are called upon to help define the need and refine the associated system concepts, alternatives are identified and evaluated to the extent that there is evidence to support the feasibility of each approach going forward, and risks and limitations of each alternative are identified along with adequate mitigation plans. At the culmination of these activities, the organizational decision makers are called upon to commit to the next phase with the current concept and alternatives, adjust the scope

TABLE 6-2 ICSM Principles as Applied to the Exploration Phase

Principle	Application in Exploration Phase
Stakeholder value-based guidance	Identification of success-critical stakeholders
	Identification of each stakeholder's priorities or value for each key system capability or feature
	Stakeholders' negotiation of a mutually satisfactory solution space
Concurrent multidiscipline engineering	Identification of candidate solutions
	Evaluation of cyber, physical, and human factor aspects of each alternative for meeting the stakeholders' identified capability needs or opportunities, indicating where each alternative strongly supports a given capability, adequately supports a given capability, or does not support a given capability at all
Evidence- and risk-based decisions	Evidence of the viability of the top alternatives
	Risks and associated mitigation plans for the top alternatives
Incremental commitment and accountability	One of the following decisions:
	Commitment to evaluate top alternatives in the Valuation phase with an appropriate budget and schedule
	Conduct additional exploration activities to consider additional alternatives, further investigate key technologies, or develop better risk mitigation plans
	Adjust scope and priorities before proceeding to the next phase with an appropriate budget and schedule
	Conclude that there is sufficient information and little risk in combining one or more Stage 1 phases
	Discontinue the project

and priorities before proceeding, or discontinue the project. Table 6-2 summarizes the role of the ICSM principles in the Exploration phase in this decision.

6.6 Exploration for the MedFRS Initiative

With the Ensayo chief information officer (CIO) commitment to explore MedFRS further, an engineering team was established to review and refine the needs statement through consultations with medical personnel and other stakeholders and to then identify and explore a spectrum of alternatives for providing the desired improvements and new capabilities.

The goal of MedFRS is to provide emergency health care in the field in a cost-effective manner that improves patient outcomes. MedFRS will integrate a variety of first responder systems within a single platform, preferably a ruggedized commercial laptop computer or handheld device, and will simplify the operation and interoperation of these systems while providing for patient privacy and safety. The MedFRS integration will include patient monitoring and treatment systems and the standardization of system protocols, interfaces, and key data (e.g., electronic health records).

One of the first investigations was to determine if any other regional areas had implemented a similar initiative and if so, how they had done it and the results that they had achieved. Two areas were found that had implemented telemedicine systems on first responder vehicles: Tucson, Arizona, and East Baton Rouge Parish, Louisiana.

The Tucson effort began in 2006 and was deployed in late 2007 with the help of $3.8 million in federal grants. It used a WiFi network specifically for mobile tele-trauma care and was available only within the city. Due to somewhat unreliable WiFi connections and a lack of additional funding after the grant funds were used, the telemedicine capability was discontinued. However, the Tucson first responders continue to transmit electronic patient care reports over the network and communicate with the trauma centers using their other communications systems.

East Baton Rouge Parish began its effort to include telemedicine capabilities on first responder vehicles in 2009. Its approach was to implement the capabilities in three phases, starting with a prototype on a single first responder platform using 3G cellular technology. Phase 2 provided the capability to share information between all area emergency rooms and prehospital providers, leaving the implementation of the telemedicine capability using 4G cellular technology to Phase 3. Phase 3 is currently in the early stages.

After reviewing the Tucson and East Baton Rouge Parish experiences and conducting preliminary interviews with Ensayo key stakeholders, the MedFRS engineering team decided that the key required features for the initial version of MedFRS would include the following abilities:

- Integrate first responder medical systems
- Connect to a variety of medical devices and telemetry systems, to initially include cardiac monitors, blood pressure monitors, defibrillators, pulse oximeters, and intravenous (IV) infusion pump monitors
  - Using "standard" interfaces
  - Providing a common "look and feel" across the devices and systems, including consistent alarms and messages
- Initially transmit patient information to the trauma center using current communications systems
- Incorporate an electronic health record compatible with regional health care facilities and trauma centers
- Provide for a high level of patient privacy and safety

Based on the Tucson experience and the East Baton Rouge approach, it was decided to defer the telemedicine capabilities. However, initial explorations identified some additional features that were added to the future options list:

- Integrate information from patient "smart" stents that monitor blood chemistry and pressure into the telemedicine system as soon as the stents have received U.S. Food and Drug Administration (FDA) approval
- Require retina authentication for access to any controlled substances that first responders may carry (newly discovered capability currently under development)
- Provide a learning capability for future improved patient care

As a result of preliminary analysis of the initial features, the MedFRS engineering team decided to conduct additional exploration activities. These activities and the resulting findings are summarized in Table 6-3. Table 6-4 summarizes the MedFRS findings and risks identified as part of the exploration activities.

TABLE 6-3 Exploration Needs Refinement and Feasibility Analysis Summary

Exploration Activity	Summary of Findings
Prototyping to determine feasibility of candidate MedFRS computers and ability of existing computers to support the number and variety of expected interfacing devices and systems	Several laptop computer models were identified that can interface to a considerable number of devices and systems through either Ethernet or wireless connections. These devices can use the platform communications system or wireless connections to communicate and share information with the regional trauma centers. Additional handheld devices (e.g., tablets, iPads, smartphones) are available to extend the MedFRS capabilities outside of the platform and to the site of the injured person.
Research to determine the power requirements for MedFRS and identify how the requisite amount of power might be supplied on the first responder vehicle without adversely impacting vehicle performance	The power requirements associated with the initial set of systems and devices to be part of MedFRS are well within the current power limits available on the current emergency responder systems. However, the current power supplies take up a considerable amount of space that could be better used for the patient area and future devices. Smaller, more compact power supplies have been identified, but they have not yet been certified for emergency equipment.
Research to determine the types of protocols and interfaces that must be supported by the MedFRS computers based on priorities of desired capabilities	Current first responder vehicles are outfitted with a variety of devices from different vendors. Some of the devices have interfaces that allow them to be connected to laptop devices, but some of the older devices on a few of the platforms are stand-alone models, requiring manual entry of information into the laptop for incorporation into an electronic health record. Some (but not all) of the devices can connect to the small handheld wireless interfaces.
Research to determine the maximum number of MedFRS systems that can operate simultaneously in the Ensayo region	There were initial concerns that in a major catastrophe where a considerable number of victims are being treated in a given area, the wireless capability might become degraded. However, discussions with area wireless service providers indicate that additional cell towers can be mobilized and moved quickly to an emergency area to support peak needs. In addition, there are concerns that information could be entered into the wrong patient record when a first responder is working with multiple victims. There are methods available to attach a bar-code tag to each patient so that the bar code can be read and used to determine the actual patient record for the data.
Research to determine the current emergency room and telemedicine systems supported at the various regional trauma centers, any current upgrade plans, and stakeholders' key quality attributes	This research was conducted using role-based simulation and observations in the emergency rooms at the regional trauma centers. The current telemedicine capabilities at each local trauma center limit the number of concurrent telemedicine sessions to five. This limitation is in part due to the number of personnel available to interact with the telemedicine systems as well as take care of trauma patients already at the trauma center. There are currently no plans to upgrade any of these systems.

TABLE 6-4 Example Summary of MedFRS Exploration Phase

Objectives and business case	Improve major-trauma health care provided by first responders from site of incident to trauma center
	Improve emergency patient outcomes overall
	Reduce emergency patient recovery times and costs
Constraints	Estimated cost for system upgrades: $2 million
	Estimated cost for additional personnel: $1 million/year
	No down time for existing capabilities during transition to new capabilities provided by MedFRS
	Interoperability with Ensayo trauma centers and hospitals
Alternatives	Devices and systems:
	Expand current capabilities using current devices and systems and over time migrate to a standard set of devices and systems.
	Use a single vendor to provide the medical devices and systems as well as the computers to which the devices interface—would require early up-front replacement of noncompliant devices and systems, but would simplify and reduce the amount of software required to integrate devices and systems. However, current potential vendors are slow to adopt newer technologies and provide full-feature devices.
	Networks and communications:
	Start with existing networks and communications systems knowing that their limits will be reached as more networked devices are associated with a given platform, then upgrade with 4G cellular as needed.
	Migrate as soon as possible to 4G communications with a capacity to handle number of devices/systems expected in the first three years.
Risks	Obtaining consensus from hospitals and trauma centers for compatible electronic health record and telemedicine capabilities
	Providing the power needed to support all of the devices and systems on the various platforms
	Providing necessary communications from the field to the trauma center for multiple first responders
	Target cost of $2 million for upgrades and $1 million for additional medical/first responder personnel
Risk mitigation	Further research and benchmarking in the Valuation phase
	Electronic patient record evaluation and consensus building in the Valuation phase
Risk-resolution results	Obtained preliminary information from a large cellphone company showing that communications from the field to the trauma center should not be a significant problem for even large catastrophes, as the cellphone company has the ability to add mobile towers to an area of interest fairly quickly. However, if the catastrophe is extensive in area, available resources might become saturated.
Plan for next phase	Refine and elaborate alternatives
	Evaluate top alternatives for devices and systems further
	Identify acceptable electronic health record alternatives and begin consensus building at key trauma facilities
	Conduct benchmark tests on candidate networks and communications systems to confirm published specs
	Update cost and schedule estimates for MedFRS based on more detailed information generated in the Valuation phase
Commitment	Fund next phase

7

Valuation Phase

"80% of a company's profits come from 20% of its customers...."

"80% of a company's profits come from 20% of the time its staff spends."

—Richard Koch

If the Exploration commitment review leads to a decision to proceed, the project enters into the Valuation phase, in which team members further analyze alternative solutions and provide evidence that there is at least one viable solution before proceeding into the Foundations phase. The definition of "viable" is based on both a technology/performance assessment and a cost/schedule assessment.

7.1 What Is the Valuation Phase?

The Valuation phase is the second phase of the ICSM life cycle, in which a more rigorous analysis of alternative solutions is conducted. It often includes analyses of return on investment (ROI) and total cost of ownership for key alternatives. The goals and objectives of the Valuation phase are twofold:

- Elaborate the analyses of alternative solutions, to include sufficient feasibility evidence and a detailed business case for each.
- Identify key risks associated with each alternative and ensure that each risk is resolved or covered by a risk mitigation plan.

During this phase, the solution tradespace is rigorously investigated, looking for "sweet spots" to balance user needs with cost-effective solutions. For "extreme" requirements or requirements that push the limits of current technology or cost/schedule constraints, a range of options is evaluated to determine a candidate set of solutions that are "good enough" and provide flexibility to incorporate the "extreme requirements" at some point in the future.

For relatively immature technologies that are part of one or more alternatives, a technology development strategy is defined and initiated. By the end of this phase, the engineering team should be close to identifying key infrastructure components

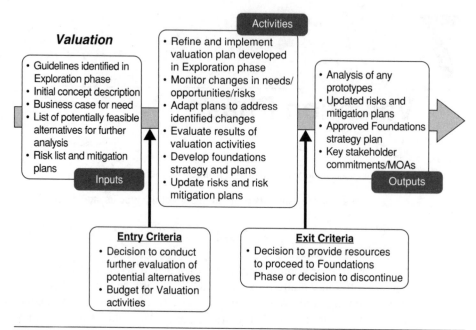

FIGURE 7-1 Valuation Process Overview

for each alternative. After a thorough analysis of feasibility evidence, identified risks, technology development strategies, estimated costs, and the expected ROI, success-critical stakeholders decide the next steps for addressing the user needs. Figure 7-1 provides an overview of the Valuation phase, showing the inputs and entry criteria that trigger the phase, the high-level activities performed in this phase, and the outputs and exit criteria that determine the conclusion of this phase.

Like the Exploration phase, the Valuation-phase activities are guided by a set of questions. Typical questions for this phase are:

- What are the "extreme" requirements with respect to existing capabilities and generally available solutions?
- Will less extreme performance/capability suffice? If so, what are the various levels of acceptability?
- If COTS products are in the candidate solution spaces:
  - How much tailoring (e.g., adaptation, customization, initialization) will be required?
  - What will this tailoring effort entail?
  - Will this tailoring need to be reimplemented each time the product is upgraded?
  - How flexible is the product?

- How scalable is the product?
- How interoperable is it with other planned COTS products/systems?
- How stable is the vendor?
- How many customers are using the current version of the COTS product?
- How satisfied are these customers?
- If new technologies are being considered in the solution space,
  - How mature are they?
  - Have they been used in similar applications?
  - Do they scale to the desired level?
  - If not sufficiently mature, what is the status of efforts to get the technology to the desired maturity level?
- Do any of the alternatives under consideration require some level of innovation? If so:
  - Have innovation efforts been funded?
  - What is the progress to date?
- Are there any new stakeholders? If so, what are their win conditions?
- Is anyone else trying to develop a similar capability? If so, might a joint effort work?
- Are any public–private partnerships available to support technology/product development?
- What are the expected costs (development and total cost of ownership, including any recurring costs associated with COTS products such as annual license fees) for the top alternatives?
- What is the expected return on investment?

The answers to the applicable questions will drive feasibility assessments, prototype development, product evaluations, and benchmarking activities.

7.2 What Are the Potential Pitfalls during Valuation?

Many of the potential Valuation pitfalls that can lead to significant technical debt or a discontinued project late in the development life cycle after a considerable investment are similar to those in the Exploration phase. It is important to do sufficient engineering and evaluation in this phase to ensure decisions are backed by concrete evidence while not straying into "analysis paralysis." The potential pitfalls in this phase include:

- Inadequate Valuation budget and schedule
- Neglecting success-critical stakeholders, particularly those associated with external interoperating systems

- Neglecting viable alternatives
- Inadequate COTS product or purchased-services evaluations
- Easiest-first approaches to feasibility assessments, which leads to potentially not having the needed budget to complete the most critical assessments
- Prototyping shortfalls, especially in scalability and off-nominal cases
- Delays in feasibility evidence description and business-case preparation
- Shortfalls in feasibility evidence descriptions or success-critical stakeholder agreements without risk mitigation plans
- Shortfalls in competitive prototyping strategy
- Inadequate Foundations plans, budget, or schedule

Consideration of these potential pitfalls during the Valuation phase and its commitment review will lead to a stronger commitment decision to either explore more, proceed to Foundations, or discontinue the project.

7.3 Major Risks to Watch for at End of Valuation

Again, after a certain amount of valuation effort, an organization needs to make a "go/no go" decision with respect to the next phase. Not all of the Valuation questions will have solid answers. However, if indicators point toward funding the next phase, it is critical to clearly identify key risks at this point and establish risk mitigation plans for them. Some key risks to watch for at this point include the following:

- Key technologies that are not yet mature enough
- New technology that will not provide a significantly better capability than current capability
- Maturation of new technology that will cost too much or take too long to meet the need
- Alternatives that depend on other systems or COTS products that are not well aligned with current needs and requirements and may not evolve in the desired direction over time
- Candidate COTS products or purchased services that are provided by an unstable vendor or a vendor that has a record of support problems
- Reliance on older legacy systems that are close to the end of their life
- Success-critical stakeholders that have either not been consulted or are not in agreement with the need or candidate approaches
- Overly risk-adverse decision makers, leading to "analysis paralysis"

- Overly risk-embracing decision makers, eager to commit to the next phase with insufficient understanding of the needs and information about candidate approaches and a philosophy that "we can always fix it later if it is not quite right"
- Overly optimistic plans, schedules, and estimates for the next phase commitments

Ways to identify, analyze, mitigate, track, and manage risks are discussed in Chapter 15.

7.4 How Valuation Scales from Small to Large, Complex Systems

The level of valuation performed typically depends on how well the problem and solution spaces are understood; the expected level of system performance such as scalability, timing/response time, precision, accuracy, security, and safety and the ability of the alternatives to meet these requirements; and the size, complexity, precedence, and cost of the anticipated solution. The goal is to explore the problem and solution spaces no more and no less than is required to have necessary evidence to support the business decision to proceed to the Foundations phase. For example:

- As mentioned in the Exploration phase, for a new capability that can be developed through modifications and enhancements to existing systems, the Valuation phase may be combined with the Stage I Exploration phase and maybe even the Foundations phase. The existing systems provide a well-understood solution space and mature foundations.
- For a new set of capabilities that may require an innovative solution, the development of one or more new systems, or the maturation of new technologies, more rigorous research, prototyping, and feasibility assessments are required during the Valuation phase. In this case, the Valuation assessments build upon and expand the high-level assessments conducted in the Exploration phase.
- For a proposed new commercial product, a better understanding of the potential market, expected market share, competitors, expected product development costs, and product pricing are key activities for the Valuation phase.

The key guideline for Valuation tailoring should be the following question: What does it take to provide sufficient answers to the Valuation questions listed earlier to make a reasonable business decision to proceed or to discontinue the project?

7.5 Role of Principles in Valuation Activities

To summarize the Valuation phase, we turn again to the four ICSM principles. It is in this phase that alternatives are more rigorously evaluated against prioritized needs and requirements and the risks and limitations of each alternative are better understood. In addition, risk mitigation plans are in place and ready to be implemented if the need arises. At the culmination of these activities, the organizational decision makers are called upon to commit to the Foundations phase with the current concept and alternatives, investigate one or more alternatives further with respect to valuation, adjust the project's scope and priorities before proceeding, or discontinue the project. Table 7-1 summarizes the role of the ICSM principles in the Exploration phase in this decision.

TABLE 7-1 ICSM Principles as Applied to the Valuation Phase

Principle	Application in Valuation Phase
Stakeholder value-based guidance	Identification of any new stakeholders (or personnel changes in stakeholder organizations) Reassessment of success-critical stakeholders priorities Stakeholders' negotiation of a mutually satisfactory solution space
Concurrent multidiscipline engineering	Re-evaluation of cyber, physical, and human factor aspects of each alternative for meeting the identified needs based upon more rigorous feasibility evidence Testing and interoperability assessments of candidate products to be used in top alternatives Prototyping and evaluation of new technologies or innovations Identification of development approaches for each strong alternative, to include reuse candidates and new development Estimation of cost and schedule for each alternative to include initial development costs, total cost of ownership, and potential return on investment Update of risk assessments for each alternative
Evidence- and risk-based decisions	Evaluation of Valuation evidence for the viability of the top alternatives and associated risk assessments in making the next incremental commitment
Incremental commitment and accountability	One of the following decisions: • Commitment to proceed to the Foundations phase with an appropriate budget and schedule • Conduct additional valuation activities to consider additional alternatives, further investigate key technologies, or develop better risk mitigation plans • Adjust scope and priorities before proceeding to the Foundations phase with an appropriate budget and schedule • Discontinue the project

7.6 Valuation for the MedFRS Initiative

At the end of the Exploration phase, two alternatives were identified for MedFRS devices and systems, each with different implications for both short- and long-term costs. A key activity planned for the Valuation phase was further investigations into the two alternatives and a better understanding of total life-cycle costs. In addition, it was decided that efforts should begin immediately to identify and gain consensus among all key trauma facilities for a standard electronic health record (EHR). Lastly, it was decided to conduct benchmark tests on candidate networks and communications systems to confirm published specifications and capabilities as well as total life-cycle costs for each alternative.

MedFRS Medical Devices. During the assessment of medical devices currently on the first responder vehicles, it was noted that there was a similarity among the messages and alarms from various devices/systems, but it is not easy to distinguish which device/system is issuing the alarm or message. As a result, if Alternative 1 (stay with existing medical devices for now) is selected, it will be necessary to provide a better user interface for device alarms and messages through custom software.

Further investigations into new medical devices for the first responder vehicles identified a third, more cost-effective solution: an integrated cardiac monitor, blood pressure monitor, defibrillator, and pulse oximeter. In addition, these integrated systems include wireless capabilities, allowing them to easily connect to the first responder computer and eventually to the telemedicine system. Quotes from several vendors indicate that the vehicle medical devices could be upgraded for about $20,000 to $25,000 each, depending on the vendor selected. New IV infusion pump monitors with the capability of wireless connection to the first responder computer were also investigated and costs for these ranged from $700 to $2000.

The software development needed to integrate medical devices with the first responder computer was estimated. It was predicted that the software development cost to integrate the new combination cardiac monitor/defibrillator/blood pressure monitor and pulse oximeter along with the wireless infusion pump would be one third of the cost to integrate the existing medical devices.

Common Electronic Health Care Records. Initial discussions with the regional hospitals showed that there were three different EHR systems across the four hospitals. However, it was pointed out that with the new national health care mandates, there would probably be a standard EHR in the near future to which all of the systems would be migrating. If the hospitals were forced to change to a common software system right away, the best option would be for two hospitals to adopt the system already shared by two hospitals. However, it would cost almost $1 million for each of the two hospitals to get out of its current maintenance contracts, purchase the new system, tailor them, migrate its current data to the new system, and train users on the new system. This also assumes that no hardware upgrades would be required to support the new EHR systems.

Telemedicine System. Initial estimates for telemedicine systems indicated that the cost per unit for each ambulance would be $4000 to $5000 and that the cost for each hospital would be $4000 to $8000, depending on the version selected. The total equipment costs would be $56,000 to $82,000. There would be additional costs if the telemedicine system were to be integrated with the medical devices on the ambulances and with the EHR system at the hospitals. In addition, there would be multiple telemedicine–EHR integration costs if there was no common EHR system.

During further discussions with the physicians in the hospital trauma centers that would be using the telemedicine systems, it was learned that the most valuable information from a telemedicine system is the patient-monitoring data and videos of the patient. If patient-monitoring data could be sent directly from the ambulance laptop to the trauma center and a wireless camera added to the laptop that could stream videos to the trauma centers, the more expensive telemedicine system would not be needed. Further investigations of wireless laptop cameras indicated that they could be purchased for $100 to $400 each, depending on the quality of images desired.

As a result of the initial Valuation-phase studies and evaluations, the estimated life-cycle costs for MedFRS were updated, along with the development of a schedule showing the rollout of MedFRS capabilities over time. If all of the initially desired capabilities were to be provided as part of this upgrade effort, it would cost $3.5 million to $5 million. Therefore, plans were adjusted to defer migration to a standard EHR system and to replace the telemedicine system with a wireless video camera that could be used to communicate with physicians at the trauma center. This change was expected to keep initial costs well under the $2 million constraint while retaining a budget to incorporate a standard EHR in the future.

A summary of the feasibility analysis for the Valuation phase is provided in Table 7-2. Table 7-3 summarizes the MedFRS Valuation phase.

TABLE 7-2 Feasibility Analysis Summary for the Valuation Phase

Valuation Activity	Summary of Findings
Evaluation of candidate first responder medical devices	The initial evaluation focused on staying with current devices or upgrading to devices that are more capable. Each of these options would require some integration of device outputs. Valuation investigations also identified a third alternative that provided the desired devices already integrated into a single unit. Further analyses of these alternatives determined that several vendors could supply the desired devices and that they were all within cost targets. When software development costs for each alternative were included in the analysis, it became clear that the pre-integrated set of devices would be more cost-effective.

TABLE 7-2 Feasibility Analysis Summary for the Valuation Phase (*Continued*)

Valuation Activity	Summary of Findings
Common electronic health record (EHR) system	Evaluation of current EHR systems showed that two of the four hospitals were already compatible. However, the cost to migrate the other two hospitals was beyond the available funds. It was also noted that there would probably be some additional changes required in the not-too-distant future to comply with expected national healthcare standards. It was decided to defer this capability until more was understood with respect to the national healthcare standards.
Evaluation of telemedicine systems	Several candidate systems were evaluated as part of a cost analysis of providing systems in all of the trauma centers and first responder vehicles. If telemedicine units were to be purchased and installed, the users would like them integrated with the medical devices so that all of the patient information could be viewed together using a common EHR system. Because the EHR system was being deferred, the users were consulted to better refine the telemedicine requirements. As a result, the telemedicine system was also deferred and the decision made to provide users with a high-quality camera that could be used to support patient care.
Communication system benchmarks	This evaluation confirmed vendor specifications for the 4G communications systems using devices from multiple vendors.

TABLE 7-3 Summary of MedFRS Valuation Phase

Objectives and business case	No change: Improve major trauma health care provided by first responders from site of incident to trauma center Improve emergency patient outcomes overall Reduce emergency patient recovery times and costs
Constraints	No change: Cost for system upgrades: $2 million Cost for additional personnel: $1 million/year No down time for existing capabilities during transition to new capabilities provided by MedFRS Interoperability with Ensayo trauma centers and hospitals
Alternatives	Devices and systems: Decision made to migrate to a standard set of devices and systems that include the integrated cardiac monitor/defibrillator/blood pressure monitor/pulse oximeter. Final decision on standard vendor to be determined in Foundations phase. Networks and communications: Decision made to start 4G upgrades immediately.
Risks	Obtaining consensus from regional hospitals and trauma centers for common electronic health record and telemedicine capabilities Providing power needed to support all of the devices and systems on the various platforms Providing necessary communications from the field to the trauma center for multiple first responders Availability of key personnel with both medical and systems engineering experience Target cost of $2 million for upgrades and $1 million for additional medical/first responder personnel/training

(*Continues*)

TABLE 7-3 Summary of MedFRS Valuation Phase (*Continued*)

Risk mitigation	Defer the electronic health record evaluation and consensus building until more is known about the national EHR standard under development as part of the national healthcare initiative
	Based on previous Tucson and East Baton Rouge experiences, begin upgrades by developing a prototype of the new integrated patient-monitoring systems and 4G communications on a single first responder vehicle and one Level 1 trauma center, adjusting the design as necessary before installing it on other platforms and in other trauma centers
	With the integrated cardiac monitor/defibrillator/blood pressure monitor/pulse oximeter, the need for multiple power supplies is significantly reduced
	Develop recruiting plans for key personnel with both medical and systems engineering experience
Risk-resolution results	Obtained preliminary information from a large cellphone company showing that communications from the field to the trauma center should not be a significant problem for even large catastrophes, as the cellphone company has the ability to add mobile towers to an area of interest fairly quickly. However, if the catastrophe is extensive in a region, available resources might become saturated.
Plan for next phase	Refine and elaborate alternatives
	Continue evaluation of integrated cardiac monitor/defibrillator/blood pressure monitor/pulse oximeter systems, IV infusion pump monitors, and ruggedized laptops and select vendors
	Develop a prototype of the new integrated devices on a single first responder vehicle and test upgraded communications with one Level 1 trauma center in the Ensayo region
	Update cost and schedule estimates for MedFRS based on more detailed information gained from the prototype phase
Commitment	Fund next phase

8

Foundations Phase

> "... a wise man ... built his house on the rock. The rain came down, the streams rose, and the winds blew and beat against that house; yet it did not fall, because it had its foundation on the rock."
>
> "... a foolish man ... built his house on sand. The rain came down, the streams rose, and the winds blew and beat against that house, and it fell with a great crash."
>
> —Matthew 7:24–27

The objective of the Foundations phase is to ensure that the proposed approach for a system or capability has the solid technical and management foundations needed to ensure successful development. These foundations include a sound system architecture and associated feasibility evidence, a set of requirements at the system level and for each architecture component, development plans, and cost and schedule estimates sufficient to convince key decision makers to proceed with the Development phase. It is the "goodness" of the system foundations that ensures the "goodness" of the system (or system capability). It has been shown time and time again that insufficiently understood, inflexible, weak, and poor foundations are the cause of many development problems or early system retirements.

8.1 What Is the Foundations Phase?

In the Foundations phase, management and technical foundations are developed for the selected option/alternative. At this point in the life cycle, there may still be more than one option or alternative under development. However, by the end of this phase, there is typically only one alternative going forward into the Development phase.

Technical foundations include a fully developed system architecture, prototypes of critical foundational aspects or components, and evidence of technology maturity for those newer technologies that are key to the selected option/alternative. Figure 8-1 provides an overview of the Foundations phase, showing the inputs and entry criteria that trigger the phase, the high-level activities performed in this phase, and the outputs and exit criteria that determine the conclusion of this phase.

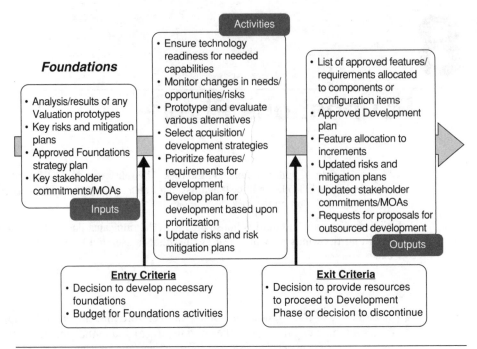

FIGURE 8-1 Foundations Process Overview

The following types of questions are used to guide the activities in this phase:

- Have needs or requirements changed?
- What is the context for the new need—for example, what are interfacing systems/components, data sources, and output destinations?
- What is the status of desired innovations or new technologies? Have they been sufficiently matured, or should alternatives be considered?
- What are the expected performance parameters for the capability (timing/speed, throughput, number of concurrent users, precision/accuracy), and have they been adequately demonstrated or evaluated?
- Are there any critical operating temperature, power, or space requirements or other constraints, and have these tolerances and thresholds been adequately evaluated?
- Is the new capability being provided as a system of systems capability?
- Does the new capability require the development of any new systems or components? If so, what are the candidate approaches and foundations for the new systems and components? Are the systems' and components' interfaces compatible with the interfacing systems and components? If not, how will these "connections" be handled? Will "connectors" impact the overall system performance parameters or constraints?

- For software-intensive devices and platforms:
  - How will software be used to control the interoperation of the components?
  - How will software contribute to the required capabilities/features?
  - What impact will software and software processors have on overall weight, fuel, power, or heat dissipation requirements?
- What are the minimum essential components?
- What is the desired versus expected performance of the system or capability?
- What are the tolerance levels for key performance parameters?
- Will less extreme performance/capability suffice? If so, what are the various levels of acceptability?
- If COTS products are in the candidate solution space, reevaluate the COTS Valuation questions before making a final commitment:
  - How much tailoring (e.g., adaptation, customization, initialization) will be required?
  - What will this tailoring effort entail?
  - Will this tailoring need to be reimplemented each time the product is upgraded?
  - How flexible is the product?
  - How scalable is the product?
  - How interoperable is it with other planned COTS products and systems?
  - How stable is the vendor?
  - How many customers are using the current version of the COTS product?
  - How satisfied are these customers?
- How will systems and components interoperate with each other to provide the desired capabilities?
- How will the system users interact with the system? How many users will be required to effectively or safely operate the system?
- How many users can concurrently use the system without significant degradation of capabilities? How does this compare to the expected number of concurrent users?
- How has the expected performance been demonstrated or estimated?
- How has compliance with constraints and tolerances been demonstrated?
- Which system features are "must haves," which are "needed to some extent, but not at full performance levels initially," and which are "nice to haves"?
- Are there any new stakeholders? If so, what are their win conditions?

By addressing these questions, the foundations for the new capability or system are designed, evaluated, and evolved until the solution architecture has been shown to be sufficiently robust, flexible, and cost-effective for subsequent development and longer-term enhancement. The Foundations phase is not just about process and tradespace considerations, but actually includes the development of the foundations necessary for successful development in Stage II. The final question to ask at the end of the Foundations phase is, "Have the Foundations been sufficiently defined to allow multiple teams to proceed with development in parallel?"

8.2 What Are the Potential Pitfalls during Foundations?

Many of the potential Foundations pitfalls that can lead to significant technical debt or a discontinued project late in the development life cycle after a considerable investment are more focused on overly optimistic plans and assumptions, insufficient understanding of necessary technologies and components, and lack of attention to shifting stakeholder goals and needs. It is important to revisit earlier assessments and assumptions as well as stakeholder priorities as larger commitments are made in the solution space. The potential pitfalls in this phase include the following:

- Inadequate Foundations budgets and schedules
- Overly complex or complicated design
- Insufficient foundations or design
- Neglecting success-critical stakeholders
- Prototyping shortfalls
- Over-reliance on immature or unproven technology
- Lack of success-critical stakeholder commitments and agreements
- Inadequate staffing and team building
- Inattention to changing needs and priorities over time
- Unprioritized features
- An inflexible system architecture that will not be able to adapt as needs change
- Inadequate Development plans, budgets, and schedules

8.3 Major Risks to Watch for at the End of Foundations

Again, after some amount of Foundations effort, an organization needs to make a "go/no go" decision with respect to the next phase. Not all of the Foundations questions will have solid answers. However, if indicators point toward funding the Development phase, it is critical to clearly identify key risks at this point and establish risk mitigation plans for them. Some key risks to watch for at this point include:

- Key technologies that are not yet mature enough
- Alternatives that depend on other systems or COTS products or services that are not well aligned with current needs and requirements and may not evolve in the desired direction over time
- Candidate COTS products or services that are provided by an unstable vendor or a vendor that has a record of support problems
- Reliance on older legacy systems that are close to the end of their life
- Success-critical stakeholders that have either not been consulted or are not in agreement with the need or candidate approaches
- Potential for changing stakeholder needs and requirements going forward
- Overly risk-embracing decision makers eager to commit to the next phase with insufficient understanding of the needs and information about candidate approaches and a philosophy that "we can always fix it later if it is not quite right"
- Overly optimistic plans, schedules, and estimates for the next phase commitments

Ways to identify, analyze, mitigate, track, and manage risks are discussed in Chapter 15.

8.4 How Foundations Effort Scales from Small to Large, Complex Systems

The level of Foundations effort typically depends on how well the problem and solution spaces are understood; the expected level of system performance such as scalability, timing/response time, precision, accuracy, security, and safety and the ability of the alternative(s) to meet these requirements; and the size, complexity, precedence, and cost of the anticipated solution. The goal is to define a solid foundation upon which the system can be developed and to understand the risks and issues going forward into Development. For example:

- For a new capability that can be developed through modifications and enhancements to existing systems, the Foundations phase may be combined with the Stage I Exploration and Valuation phases. Understanding of the impacts of the proposed changes to each system as well as an understanding of each constituent system's future evolutionary plans may be sufficient evidence for the capability foundations. The existing systems can provide a well-understood solution space and mature foundations upon which changes and enhancements can be made to implement the new capabilities.

- For a small app that is designed for a well-defined device (such as a cellphone) or set of new webpages that is developed to extend or update an existing website, the existing device or website provides the foundations for the new capabilities.

- For a new system that is to be part of a product line or is a variant of an existing system, analysis of impacts to the product line or differences from similar systems may be sufficient feasibility evidence for the new system foundations.

- For a new set of capabilities that may require an innovative solution, the development of one or more new systems, or the maturation of new technologies, a more rigorous approach is needed in the Foundations phase to develop a robust, flexible architecture that will be relatively stable and predictable with respect to expected performance and known constraints during initial development and sustainable over the expected life of the system.

Another aspect to Foundations scaling is related to the composition of the new capability or system:

- Custom software or modifications to existing software
- Integration of COTS software products with existing software or other COTS products
- Integration of off-the-shelf hardware components and custom hardware components
- Development of new hardware or hardware components

Large or small, precedented or not, the Foundations phase must clearly identify the top-level components of the system; the interfaces, protocols, or connectors between the components; and strategies for handling interoperability incompatibilities. For hardware–software systems and hardware-only systems, hardware prototypes or mockups are generally developed, evaluated, and refined until there is sufficient evidence to proceed with implementation and production. A good case study for platform foundations is found in Chapter 6 of *The Toyota Way* by Jeffrey Liker [1].

The goal is to provide enough design information so that if the decision is made to proceed with development, then various development teams or companies can be given the design information and associated system and component constraints and have confidence that they will integrate with other components and perform as needed.

8.5 Role of Principles in Foundations Activities

To summarize the Foundations phase, we again turn to the four ICSM principles. It is in this phase that an alternative is selected through additional assessment of options with respect to known needs, requirements, and constraints and the foundations for the selected solution sufficiently matured to support incremental development of software and construction of requisite hardware components, devices, or platforms. In addition, risk mitigation plans are in place and ready to be implemented if the need arises.

At the culmination of these activities, the organizational decision makers are called upon to commit to the Development phase based on the technical and management foundations, to adjust scope and priorities before proceeding, or to discontinue the project. Table 8-1 summarizes the role of the ICSM principles in the Foundations phase in this decision.

TABLE 8-1 ICSM Principles as Applied to the Foundations Phase

Principle	Application in Foundations Phase
Stakeholder value-based guidance	Identification of any new stakeholders (or personnel changes in stakeholder organizations) Reassessment of success-critical stakeholders priorities Stakeholders' negotiation of a mutually satisfactory set of Development and Life Cycle capabilities and plans
Concurrent multidiscipline engineering	Development/evolution of system architecture from the cyber-physical-human aspects, and covering both the current increment and best estimates of downstream capabilities Continued prototyping and evaluation of risky technologies or innovations planned for current and future increments Updated estimates for current increment development cost and schedule, total cost of ownership, and potential return on investment Updated risk assessments
Evidence- and risk-based decisions	Evaluation of Foundations evidence for the viability of the top alternatives and associated risk assessments in making the next incremental commitment
Incremental commitment and accountability	One of the following decisions: • Commitment to proceed to the Development phase with an appropriate budget and schedule • Conduct additional Foundations activities to ensure sufficiency of system architecture, further investigate key technologies, or develop better risk mitigation plans • Adjust scope and priorities before proceeding to the Development phase with an appropriate budget and schedule • Discontinue the project

8.6 Foundations for the MedFRS System of Systems

With the Foundations Commitment Review decision to proceed, trade studies to evaluate the integrated cardiac monitors (which included a defibrillator, blood pressure monitor, and pulse oximeter) and IV infusion pump monitors were initiated using the COTS evaluation criteria listed in the Foundations questions earlier. As a result, a single vendor was selected and purchase orders approved to purchase a single version of the cardiac monitor and IV infusion pump monitor. A ruggedized laptop that was compatible with the chosen devices was also selected to host the integrated prototype on the first responder platform. Table 8-2 summarizes the feasibility analysis activities conducted in the Foundations phase.

Next, plans were developed for the installation of the systems and the training of the personnel who would be using the systems. The plan was that the single vehicle would be taken out of service for one week; while the new systems were being installed and tested, the first responders would attend training at the vendor site on the configuration options, use, and troubleshooting processes. In the prototype version, there was to be minimal integration with the first responder laptop and the users would need to manually create messages to send information to the trauma centers. Once the systems were received, the installation and training plans were implemented.

In parallel, the Ensayo Information Technology (IT) group was tasked to begin designing custom software for the user interface on the laptop system that would integrate the devices with the laptop and provide images and reports integrated with patient identification information that could be sent as needed over 4G communications to the trauma centers. Table 8-3 summarizes the MedFRS Foundations phase.

TABLE 8-2 Feasibility Analysis Summary for the Foundations Phase

Foundation Activity	Summary of Findings
Integrated cardiac monitor trade study	Various products from different vendors were evaluated with respect to initial cost, total cost of ownership, usability (product demonstrations with hospital staff and paramedics), vendor stability and support with respect to the product, and vendor client assessments from clients that have been using the product for at least six months. Trade study analysis supported the decision to go with the vendor that currently supplies other medical equipment and supplies for the hospital.
Ruggedized laptop trade study	Various laptops from different vendors were evaluated with respect to initial cost, total cost of ownership, ease of integration with medical devices, ability to integrate additional medical devices in the future, compatibility with communications systems and handheld devices, ease of use, ease of installation, software development environment capabilities, vendor stability and support with respect to the product, and vendor client assessments from clients that have been using the laptop for at least six months.

TABLE 8-3 Summary of MedFRS Foundations Phase

Objectives and business case	No change: Improve major trauma health care provided by first responders from site of incident to trauma center Improve emergency patient outcomes overall Reduce emergency patient recovery times and costs
Constraints	No change: Cost for system upgrades: $2 million Cost for additional personnel: $1 million/year No down time for existing capabilities so as to transition to new capabilities provided by MedFRS Interoperability with Ensayo trauma centers and hospitals
Alternatives	Devices and systems: Vendor selected to provide an integrated cardiac monitor system and an IV infusion pump monitor for the first responder upgrade prototype. Vendor selected to provide ruggedized laptop for the prototype. Networks and communications: Migration to 4G communications to begin immediately for prototype.
Risks	Obtaining consensus from all trauma centers for common electronic health record and telemedicine capabilities Providing necessary communications from the field to the trauma center for multiple first responders Ability to afford full telemedicine capability on a long-term basis Availability of key personnel with both medical and systems engineering experience Target cost of $2 million for upgrades and $1 million for additional medical/first responder personnel
Risk mitigation	Evaluation of prototype Continued electronic health record evaluation and consensus building Identify sources of funding for desired telemedicine capability while continuing to assess the actual need for a full-up telemedicine capability versus a wireless camera to augment patient-monitoring device information Continued recruiting and training of first responder personnel with both medical and systems engineering experience
Risk-resolution results	Initial prototype results appear positive
Plan for next phase	Implement Increment 1: • Software to fully integrate information from the wireless devices (patient monitoring, IV infusion pump, and camera) with patient identification information onto the first responder laptop and transmit the integrated information to the designated trauma center using report formats developed in collaboration with the trauma care physicians • Improved voice communications between the first responder and the trauma center via 4G devices Assess impact of first responder prototype on patient outcomes Begin search for telemedicine capability funding planned for future increment while continuing to assess the need for full-up telemedicine capability Continue to monitor cost and schedule against the budget and update cost and schedule estimates for MedFRS based on more detailed information generated in Increment 1
Commitment	Fund next phase

8.7 Stage I Summary

As stated at the beginning of Part II of this book, the goal of Stage I in the ICSM is to converge on defining the system to be developed based on clear stakeholder needs, business value, technology maturity, and feasibility with respect to cost and schedule. Stage I consists of three phases:

- Exploration phase: Initial phase of Stage I. Concurrently identifies and clarifies system capability need(s), system constraints such as enterprise or systems of systems fit, and candidate solution options for providing the capabilities. Gathers and creates top-level evidence of candidate solution and life-cycle process option feasibility, and summarizes risks of proceeding forward into succeeding phases for stakeholder decision consideration.

- Valuation phase: Second phase of Stage I, which analyzes alternative solutions; determines the system's scope; evaluates feasibility evidence for alternatives under consideration, including a business case analysis; recommends a preferred alternative, possibly including a range of variants; and summarizes risks of proceeding forward into the Foundations phase for stakeholder decision consideration.

- Foundations phase: Final phase of Stage I. Develops management and technical foundations for the selected alternative, possibly identifying a range of variants. Technical foundations include a best-achievable system life-cycle architecture, prototypes, and evidence of technology maturity for those technologies that are key to the selected alternative. Management foundations include full-system and next-increment plans, budgets, and schedules; development approaches and methodologies (e.g., common cases) for the various components; and summaries of risks of proceeding forward into Stage II for stakeholder decision consideration.

Stage I phases may be combined (not skipped), depending on risk assessments, precedents in the solution space, and desired stakeholder involvement during the Stage I activities. The level of formality, rigor, and time spent in each phase depends on the size, complexity, urgency, and anticipated costs and risks of the system, system enhancement, or SoS enhancement under consideration.

Reference

[1] Liker, J. *The Toyota Way.* McGraw-Hill, 2004.

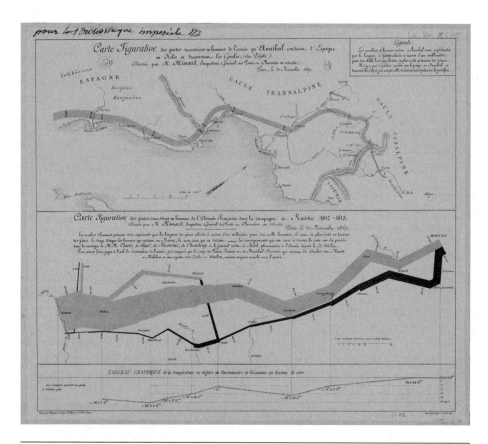

Charles Minard's 1869 chart showing the number of men in Napoleon's 1812 Russian campaign army, their movements, and the temperatures they encountered on the return path

Part III

Stage II: Incremental Development and Evolution

"The art of life lies in a constant readjustment to our surroundings."

—Okakura Kakuzō (1862–1913), author of *The Book of Tea*

"To improve is to change; to be perfect is to change often."

—Winston Churchill

As Minard's illustration so elegantly depicts, while there must be solid planning up front (something Napoleon did poorly on this occasion), there must also be monitoring, understanding, and reaction to the real environment and stakeholders as you move forward. This is as true for system development and business plans as it is for armies and battle plans. Part III addresses Stage II of the ICSM: the continuous, incremental evolution of a system from its initial development through its iterative and incremental production, operation, and refinement, until its final decommissioning or replacement.

Stage II begins with the Development Commitment Review (DCR) decision to proceed and is where the Stage I foundational plans are implemented. Stage II consists of two phases—the Development phase and the Production and Operations phase—and includes the following activities:

- The development or procurement of hardware and software components
- The integration and testing of these components in an iterative manner until a usable version of the system is created
- Acceptance testing of the system
- Production of copies or versions of the system, and associated supply-chain management activities

- Planning for sustainment and maintenance of the system including logistics activities to provide for any required spare parts
- Transition to users, including the development and production of user manuals, online help, and training to support the transition to operations
- Provisions for phase-out of the system or its components.

As is true for Stage I, the phases of Stage II are not a waterfall, but rather a choreographed and individualized dance in which the risks and opportunities determine the appropriate steps to take. In most systems, the evolutionary development and production and operations are continuous, overlapping activities. The breadth and depth of these activities depend upon the type, size, and scope of the system of interest.

Section 2.4 in Chapter 2 presented five primary alternative Stage II models, summarizing each in terms of examples, strengths, and weaknesses. It may be useful to revisit that section and consider those models as you read through the chapters in this section.

- Chapter 9 describes the development, integration, and testing of hardware and software components in the Development phase.
- Chapter 10 completes the discussion of Stage II by considering the Production and Operations phase.

9

Development Phase

"You can't just ask the customers what they want and then try to give that to them. By the time you get it built, they'll want something new."

—Steve Jobs

"But Mousie, thou art no thy lane,
In proving foresight may be vain:
The best-laid schemes o' mice an' men
Gang aft agley,
An' lea'e us nought but grief an' pain,
For promis'd joy!"

—Robert Burns, "To a Mouse, on Turning Her up in Her Nest with the Plough"

Stage I, when successfully executed, provides a solid foundation for development along with a development strategy and plan. At this point, "concurrent engineering" transitions to "concurrent development" of components, integration, and testing. The result of this phase is a system that can go forward into production and operations.

This chapter presents a general overview of the development process. Chapter 11 provides additional guidance with respect to a set of "common cases" that characterize various types of common systems that are developed and evolved today.

9.1 What Is the Development Phase?

Once solid system foundations have been established and the DCR decision made to proceed, development begins. Key decisions made at the DCR are used to guide the development activities: development priorities (what to build first) and the context for the development, such as a new system or set of systems (some of which may be COTS products), a new capability based on modifications to existing systems or prototypes, or a combination of new system development and modifications to existing systems. In addition, there is typically a development plan that has been put in place to guide the development of the first few increments of the desired system or capability.

[handwritten margin notes: how to interactive foundations Stage a lot to hush out details]

Even with solid foundations, there is still much lower-level design (detailed design) to do. As a result, the development of hardware–software systems often requires a significant amount of "back and forth" between foundations, detailed design, and implementation. This process is very iterative in nature, often requiring additional analyses, investigations of alternatives, and synthesis of lower-level designs in response to the maturation of the solution space as well as discovered changes in the target system environment or stakeholder needs.

Complicated systems and systems that require solutions for discovered wicked problems require considerably more "back and forth" to converge on an acceptable detailed design and solution. In addition, as development proceeds and components are integrated, unanticipated emergent behaviors may be identified. Most of the complicated and "wicked" aspects of the system should have been identified and addressed in Stage I. However, emergent behaviors between components and unexpected complexities can remain hidden until Stage II and need up-front attention, possibly involving modifications to the system foundations.

System component size, level of complexity, and required levels of precision, integrity, security, or assurance of correct function determine how each system component will be developed and with what level of rigor. That said, the development approach and level of rigor for a given component may change over time as new aspects and nuances to the system under development are discovered. For example, a new COTS product may be identified that can be used instead of developing new software. These changes often lead to changes in iteration and increment plans and potentially to the overall development schedule.

With the majority of the systems of interest being relatively complex, development is typically done using an incremental process in which multiple teams work concurrently and iteratively to develop or update components that can then be integrated and released to testers and early users as a system or capability increment. This incremental process allows for release of early initial capabilities to the users as well as the ability to learn from users, monitor potentially changing needs, and adjust requirements as necessary. It also allows the developers to continually evaluate the suitability of the foundations and adjust them if necessary or transition to a better technology or approach.

The length of the increments to be used in the system's development and evolution varies based on the system's characteristics and priorities. A small agile software project might use two- to four-week iterations with increments every two to four months. By comparison, a relatively large system development project such as a command-and-control system with independently evolving interfaces or external systems may need an initial increment of up to two years (with several internal integration sub-increments) to develop and integrate an initial operational capability. Some very large hardware systems or platforms (e.g., aircraft, watercraft, or automobiles) take even longer to develop their initial increments, and are often scheduled to synchronize their deliveries with concurrently evolving infrastructure or software increments.

Figure 9-1 provides an overview of the Development phase, showing inputs and entry criteria that trigger the phase, the high-level activities performed in this phase, and the outputs and exit criteria that determine the conclusion of this phase.

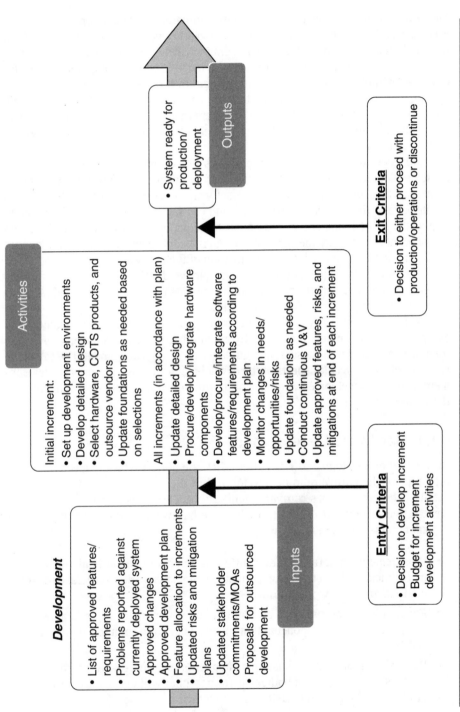

FIGURE 9-1 Development Process Overview

Development

Inputs
- List of approved features/requirements
- Problems reported against currently deployed system
- Approved changes
- Approved development plan
- Feature allocation to increments
- Updated risks and mitigation plans
- Updated stakeholder commitments/MOAs
- Proposals for outsourced development

Entry Criteria
- Decision to develop increment
- Budget for increment development activities

Activities

Initial increment:
- Set up development environments
- Develop detailed design
- Select hardware, COTS products, and outsource vendors
- Update foundations as needed based on selections

All increments (in accordance with plan)
- Update detailed design
- Procure/develop/integrate hardware components
- Develop/procure/integrate software features/requirements according to development plan
- Monitor changes in needs/opportunities/risks
- Update foundations as needed
- Conduct continuous V&V
- Update approved features, risks, and mitigations at end of each increment

Outputs
- System ready for production/deployment

Exit Criteria
- Decision to either proceed with production/operations or discontinue

The development activities tend to be iterative in nature. Each development effort for each increment may iterate multiple times, exploring options at the detailed design level and then iteratively building the system increment. Increments are fieldable versions of the system. In addition, there may be multiple versions of an increment—for example, multiple versions of a software system that run in different environments, operating systems, or web browsers. In some cases, increments may not be fielded, but rather comprise early versions of the system that are used to support operational testing, beta testing, or training. The development phase is repeated for each increment of development.

Initial development for a new system starts with establishing or reserving the requisite development facilities and tools for both hardware and software development. Final selections for COTS hardware, COTS software, and software outsourcing vendors are made, and the associated purchasing and contracting activities are performed to acquire the desired components and establish commitments with any planned vendors and subcontractors. Once the hardware design is complete, procurement selections are made for various components and construction of the hardware begins.

After the initial increment has been completed, development takes on a different perspective. The goal for subsequent increments is typically to expand capabilities as well as to improve existing capabilities.

Tables 2-4 and 2-5 (in Part I) describes several models of incremental and evolutionary development for both software and hardware development, as well as their strengths and weaknesses, and guidance for using each model. The following sections address specific aspects of the development process for hardware development, software development, and use of continuous integration, test, synchronization, and stabilization.

9.1.1 Hardware Development

At the start of development (right after DCR), the project typically has at least one prototype of the hardware to be developed, but the scope, capability, and level of detail of these prototypes can vary significantly. The types of hardware development activities performed also depend on the hardware approach for the system. Typical options include the following:

- Procurement, integration, and configuration of commercially available mechanical and electrical components such as networks, servers, computer devices, and user workstations
- Procurement, programming, and integration of commercially tailorable components (e.g., components that include field programmable gate arrays [FPGAs])
- Development of multiple custom components (e.g., hardware boards, cables, cases, shelters, platform bodies, airframes) that will eventually need to be produced through some custom manufacturing process
- Some combination of the above

The goal of the Development phase with respect to hardware is to develop the "first article" or unit that can then be tested. The first unit will also contain all of the software required to support the planned first-article testing. However, depending on the results of first-article testing, major changes may be required for the hardware (e.g., unanticipated metal fatigue that cannot be detected and resolved until a certain number of flight hours as experienced on the Joint Strike Fighter [JSF] in early 2013). The intravenous infusion pump described in Section 1.2 would generally follow a similar path, albeit on a much smaller scale with limited operations to ensure ease of use and evaluate safety aspects with actual users.

For some hardware development projects, the development of many components may be outsourced. Key to the management of these vendors are clear design and interface specifications, performance and tolerance specifications, due dates, on-site monitoring, and quality assurance audits, often with intermediate synchronization points. As components are completed, they are assembled into larger units until the system first article (or unit) is complete.

The following questions can be used to help guide the hardware detailed design and development activities in this phase:

- What are the size constraints for the hardware?
- What are the weight constraints for the hardware?
- What are the power constraints for the hardware?
- What are the heating/cooling constraints for the hardware?
- What are the security constraints/goals for the hardware system (or components) and how will they be implemented and tested?
- What are the safety constraints/goals for the hardware system (or components) and how will they be implemented and tested?
- What are the performance requirements for the hardware device?
- Which COTS components will be used?
- Which components will be custom-made?
- What is the lead time for custom-made components?
- Which functions will be performed by hardware and which will be performed by embedded software/firmware?
- Who is responsible for the development and control of embedded software/firmware (e.g., systems engineering, hardware engineering, software engineering)?
- What are the manufacturing goals and constraints for both custom components and the overall system hardware?
- What is the target cost per unit?
- Can the hardware design be adjusted to mitigate key risks?
- How can the hardware design be refined or simplified to better meet these constraints?

Depending on how many units will be developed during the Production phase, manufacturability may become a major area of interest. Indeed, manufacturing engineers are often involved in the design process. Initial units are often "handcrafted" with systems, hardware, mechanical, and production engineering personnel working side-by-side in the development of this unit. This encourages the transfer of key tacit knowledge between these engineering groups to support design trades. It also allows the assembly instructions and procedures to be developed and subjected to a dry-run before formal production starts.

Once the first article or unit is complete and has been tested to the extent possible, test results, any foundations/hardware changes, and expected costs per unit go through a Production Commitment Review before proceeding further. If test results or costs per unit are not acceptable, additional development work is scheduled and production delayed. Otherwise, production begins for the next units and the first unit continues to be evaluated using more extensive and rigorous operational tests. Depending on the nature of the planned tests, there may be several "first units" to support testing, especially if some of the tests are potentially destructive in nature—for example, mechanical tests to determine robustness and safety levels of the system or "shake and bake" tests using vibration, impact, or temperature.

9.1.2 Software Development

The role of software is to provide flexible and easily adaptable system capabilities. These capabilities can range from small features to complex capabilities that require the interaction of multiple software-intensive systems. Traditionally, software development started with a clean sheet of paper and was often developed in a top-down manner—that is, by decomposing larger components into smaller units and functions. As software systems became larger and more complex, the traditional top-down development approach became too expensive and took too long. Software visionaries realized that some types of software were being redeveloped time and again within various organizations and that there might be a market for standard types of tailorable business applications. Out of this vision came commercial off-the-shelf (COTS) software products. Some of the earliest COTS software products were database management systems and business applications such as billing, accounting, and inventory management. In the scientific, real-time software domain, the earliest COTS software products were scientific packages and libraries that contained a variety of complex mathematical functions of varying levels of precision as well as graphical display packages to support the development of user interfaces. Fast-forward to more recent times, and users can also purchase software services that can be integrated into a wide variety of systems. Some popular examples of software services include the Global Positioning System (GPS) for location and various weather services that provide current weather and weather forecasts for almost any location.

In general, software for a given system typically includes multiple software components that may or may not be integrated with each other. In addition, software within a system can take on many forms. The most widely used forms include the following:

- Custom application software components: These software components typically start with a "clean sheet of paper." The top-level design is decomposed into a set of lower-level components with well-defined interfaces that can then be developed in parallel.

- Software components tightly coupled with hardware: These programmable hardware components can be easily tailored for various types of systems. They may also include custom system software components that manage various aspects of the hardware, such as interface handlers, device drivers, network management, or software reconfiguration based on hardware configurations.

- COTS software integration: One or more COTS products may be integrated with each other and often with custom software. In some software modernization efforts, COTS products may gradually replace older legacy software. This software solution provides tailorable software that is maintained and updated by a commercial vendor. However, there are typically costs associated with the initial software licenses, annual maintenance fees, and some custom software development to integrate COTS products with each other and to develop needed extensions to provide features not provided by the COTS products.

- Integration of software services: Software services are available over the Internet that can be accessed from a software system. Some services may be free, whereas others have a fee associated with them. Using a standard service application program interface (API), web services are easy to use and integrate. However, these generally available services can change over time, requiring the software systems that use them to make quick changes to maintain access to the desired services. These services may also be referred to as web applications, software-as-a-service, or online applications.

- Incorporation of reusable custom software or open-source software: This includes software that has been previously developed so that it could be reused, typically in a product line, and software source code that is generally available to the public. These software components provide basic functions and allow developers to tailor or use them at their own risk.

Generally, the software top-level design or architecture identifies the major software components and indicates how the software will be provided: custom components, programmable hardware components, COTS, software services, or reused/open-source software. Some components may include a combination of these types of software. As with hardware development, the development of software includes further lower-level design prior to actual implementation. The lower-level design may be structural in nature, focusing on the complete design of software units, or it may consist of use cases that focus on providing capability features that require the interaction of multiple software units/services.

Iterations, Increments, and Versions in the ICSM

The concepts of iteration and increment are malleable ones. Each organization should try to define and standardize its particular understanding. This means discovering the natural cadence of the organization's work in terms of development, integration, delivery, and evolution. In the ICSM, there is no requirement that cadences be coupled, so delivery and development cadences can proceed independently. We generally find that "iteration to increment to version" is the natural progression and use the following definitions of these units.

Iterations are multiple cycles of an activity or set of activities, in a revolving or recursive way. Iterations may be of fixed length or variable length. Within an iteration, teams may go back and forth (or up and down) to explore options and refine an approach or design. Iterations may also go through many levels of detail, with "back and forth" activities going deeper and deeper within the system hierarchy. The iterative process generally results in a given increment of design or development, such that one or more iterations is performed within an increment of work. An iteration is never longer than an increment.

Increments are interim releasable (or fieldable) updates to a given system between major releases (or versions) of a system. While increments are releasable/fieldable, they are not always released to the user community as a whole. Increments may be used as prototypes to gain more information for future releases; they may be used to handle a special, urgent need in a limited capacity; or they may be used to support operational testing. Increments are typically configuration managed and identified as updates to a major version or release using "dot" release identifiers; for example, if the major release is "n", then the "dot" releases would be "n.1, n.2, ... n.m."

A **version** of a system is a major release of a new system. In addition, a version may have many instantiations for different platforms, operating systems, web browsers, or other environments, each with its own identifier and each with its own set of incremental upgrades.

Whatever approach is selected, software features or units are prioritized and allocated to software increments. Within each increment, the features or units are further prioritized to support early integration and test strategies. Software increments can also be organized to enable what has variously been called timeboxing, time-certain development, or "schedule as independent variable"

(SAIV), in which borderline-priority features are added or dropped to keep the increment on schedule. Increments can also be organized to accommodate foreseeable changes, such as user interfaces or transaction formats. For larger developments with multiple development teams, the incremental process also includes a continuous verification and validation (V&V) team whose members analyze, review, and test the evolving product to find defects early and minimize the buildup of rework.

Whether the total software size is large or small, the focus is on short iterations, leading to larger fieldable increments. To support this development approach, there is an integration environment where new modules and components can be installed and tested as they are developed. This integration environment can also be used to conduct experiments and evaluate alternatives before committing to a specific approach or design.

Integration for a new software system can be organized as top-down, bottom-up, or "neighborhoods" where small units are integrated to form larger components that can then be integrated with other components or "neighborhoods." Integration for modifications and extensions to an existing software system focuses on adding new software to an integration environment that contains current versions of the software system being updated. More than one version of the software may exist in the development integration environment to support multiple software configurations or multiple target environments. Whatever integration strategy is selected, the most important objectives are to support continuous integration and test, and to provide the ability to identify problems early so as to minimize extensive rework.

Key to achieving high productivity in the development environment and low technical debt in the software product are tools that are tailored to the development processes and with which the development team is experienced. These tools, which support efficient development and monitoring of the status of development activities and known problems, include software configuration management tools, change and problem reporting tools, automated standards checking, software modeling and code generation tools, and test automation and status-monitoring tools. Software configuration management tools should not just be used for source code management, but rather should encompass development tools such as compilers, test procedures and data, and integration and test software builds. Formal configuration management needs to include all versions of the software that are currently in use and supported by the development team, along with the tools that were used to create the software, both source code and executable code. Without this type of instrumented development environment, manual processes will be slow and error-prone. In addition, it will be difficult to respond to problems reported in fielded software.

The ICSM three-team evolutionary concurrent approach elaborated in Figure 9-2 can apply to complex systems with multiple development organizations and SoS capability development as well as single-system developments:

- In the complex system case, the top-level agile rebaselining team and V&V team is the lead or prime development organization, and the

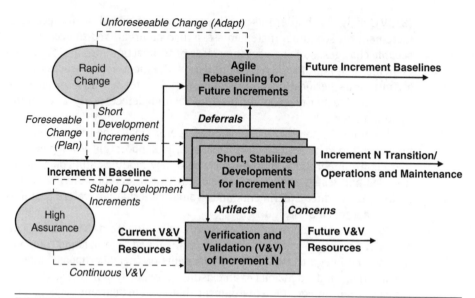

FIGURE 9-2 ICSM Three-Team Model for Multiple Development Teams and SoS

development teams are the organizations responsible for the major system components.

- In the SoS case, the agile rebaselining team and V&V team is the SoS engineering (SoSE) team and the development teams are the constituent system development teams. However, the SoS constituent system development teams often view the SoSE team as another stakeholder whose needs must be integrated with those from other stakeholders. In addition, each constituent system has its own development organization that balances single-system needs with SoS needs. A good source for further information on system of systems engineering is the U.S. Department of Defense's *Systems Engineering Guide for Systems of Systems* [1].

The following questions can be used to help guide the software development activities in this phase:

- How many developers will be developing software for the system and at which locations/sites?
- How will development facilities be managed to ensure adequate tools and resources are available for all of the developers?
- What is the plan for software tools? Who is responsible for getting the tools installed and tailored for the software teams? By which date?
- Which components will be new? Modified reusable code? Reused "as-is"?
- What are contingency plans for reusable software that is found not to be as reusable as initially planned?

- How will development, integration, and testing be accomplished before actual hardware is available?
- What are critical differences between the development integration and test environment and the actual target environment (e.g., single core versus multicore, different operating system versions)? How will the differences be addressed during integration and testing?
- What are the various environments, platforms, and operating systems in which the software must operate?
- What is the development and integration strategy to provide early increments or early capabilities?
- What are the dependencies with externally developed software?
- What are the dependencies with legacy systems that are already operational?
- What are the data standards and formats for data that is shared within the software system as well as with external systems?
- How will components and subsystems interoperate with each other?
- What are the interoperability challenges with external or legacy systems?
- Who (which system or development team) is responsible for ensuring interoperability with external or legacy systems?
- Which software capabilities are based on unknown interfaces or external constraints and subject to change?
- Which software components or algorithms have extreme performance requirements (e.g., real-time constraints, number of transactions per unit of time, large number of concurrent users, hardware constraints)? What are the plans to ensure adequate performance?

9.1.3 Continuous Integration and Testing, Then Synchronization and Stabilization

As mentioned earlier, the key to successful development is the ability to continually integrate and test new features and components. There comes a time, though, when development activities need to converge on a final system that can go through a final acceptance or preproduction test. This is the time to synchronize and stabilize the final configuration for the system planned for production and operation.

The nature of system acceptance or preproduction tests depends on the type of system and the importance or criticality of the capabilities provided by the system. The goal is to have the key system capabilities functional and operating correctly, reliably, and safely. System tests must also be designed to support system certifications or accreditations that are required before operations. Finally, system tests are the point at which everything comes together and offer yet another opportunity to look for unanticipated emergent behaviors (good and bad). Depending on the type of system, undesirable emergent behaviors may need to be addressed before the system can proceed to the Production and Operations phase. Good emergent behaviors, even though identified late in the development process, may lead to ways to streamline design and simplify or reduce production or operation costs.

Software acceptance tests are developed in parallel with the software and focus on the software requirements, key scenarios, or use cases. These tests should address all new capabilities provided by the software plus provide for regression testing of any capabilities carried forward from previous software releases. They test the fully integrated software system and may include interface simulators for external systems that the system under test is expected to interoperate with. (Note that interface simulators should have their own development plan, development team, processes, and schedule.) The software may be tested using general-purpose hardware or using custom hardware as part of a device or platform, depending on the nature of the system and its intended target environments. For software developed for custom hardware, testing may begin in a test environment that includes hardware emulators.

Hardware acceptance and preproduction tests can be extremely varied depending on the type of system. Typically critical custom components undergo their own acceptance tests. These components may have been outsourced and, therefore, have their own acceptance criteria. Once all of the components have been assembled (including software required to operate the hardware), yet another level of acceptance testing is performed. Again, the types of tests performed are based on the requirements and performance parameters for the system. In addition, some of the tests that must be performed may be destructive in nature, such that several units must be produced to support the necessary tests.

The following questions can be used to help guide the integration, testing, synchronization, and stabilization activities in this phase:

- What are the "must have" capabilities for the system?
- What are the "nice to have" capabilities for the system that will significantly increase system value?
- What can be deferred to the next release?
- What are the planned hardware upgrades or obsolescence?
- What are the planned upgrades for COTS software within the system (e.g., operating systems, database management systems, web browsers, application COTS) or external systems with which the system must interoperate (e.g., web browsers, services, legacy systems)?
- If recent COTS software upgrades have not yet been incorporated, should they be incorporated or is there risk of destabilizing the system?
- Will the hardware or COTS software upgrades require a change in system requirements or the ability to meet current requirements?

- Will near-term updates to external systems affect the operation of the system under test/ready for production or require a change in system requirements?
- What are the key performance requirements for the system?
- Which capabilities must be certified or accredited through the development and testing processes?
- What is the cost of testing versus the risk of not testing some system features or capabilities?
- Where (e.g., in-house, external, contracted) will testing take place?
- Which specialized test equipment is required and which resources are needed for these tests (e.g., crash or drop tests, "shake and bake," environmental temperature or weather extremes, security)?
- How many physical environments must the system be tested in?
- Which facilities are required to support tests?
- In how many platform environments must the system be tested (e.g., hardware platforms such as automobiles, aircraft, ships; manned or unmanned; software environments such as computers, operating systems, web browsers)?
- Which simulators and emulators will be required to support testing?
- How many of the tests are destructive?
- Can any of the test units be reused if not affected by earlier tests?
- Can the tests be ordered in a way that minimizes the costs of destructive testing?
- If destructive tests are performed last, what will be the impact to schedule if any of these tests fail?
- Is cumulative damage testing required?
- What is the repair plan for test units?
- How many units will be required to support testing in the worst case and the best case?
- What are the lead time and associated costs to produce another unit to support testing?

9.2 Ready to Release?

The decision to release a new system or a new increment or version of an existing system is based on the current state of the system and feasibility evidence that it performs sufficiently well. Seldom are there no known problems with a given system after testing. Consequently, the decision needs to be made as to whether the system is "good enough" to go into the Production and Operations phase. This assessment typically depends on the known problems and their severity levels as well as the list of features that did not make it into the system increment. Figure 9-3 shows an example where system testing is in the last week of testing, but a considerable number of reported problems have not yet been resolved or closed. If the open problems are minor or cosmetic, a decision to release the system is often made. However, if the open problems are severe or critical, the system release may be deferred until the problems have been sufficiently resolved. In some cases, it may be possible to release a partial version of the system (the part that works sufficiently well), work on the problem areas, and then release the rest of the system as a subsequent increment. The partial release process works well with software-intensive systems or SoS where not all new/updated components are required for the operation of the system.

For commercial products, the decision to release a new product may also depend on the current status of product marketing and what the competition has just released or is getting ready to release. In the case of business products, business value and market share are key drivers.

For software releases, the decision to release may also depend on the status of site preparations:

- Have all of the new (or updated) required hardware, networks, and user devices been installed and configured for the system?

- Is any data conversion required to migrate to the new system or system release? If so, have data conversion procedures and tools been sufficiently tested? Is the "time to convert" within acceptable limits for the planned upgrade?

- Is user training ready for delivery? Has training been scheduled for (or delivered to) the trainers (e.g., train-the-trainers)? Has training been scheduled for the users? At all sites?

- If alternative ways of doing business are to be employed during the installation and transition to the new system, are there procedures or mechanisms to update the system with the interim business transactions?

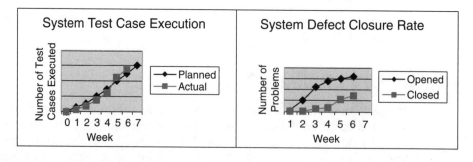

FIGURE 9-3 Assessing Readiness for Production and Operations

9.3 What Are the Potential Pitfalls during Development?

Many of the potential Development-phase pitfalls that can lead to significant technical debt or a discontinued project late in the development life cycle are related to overly optimistic plans and assumptions, insufficient understanding of necessary technologies and components, and lack of attention to shifting stakeholder goals and needs. Common pitfalls that can occur in this phase include the following:

- Inadequate budgets and schedules
- Neglecting success-critical stakeholders
- Neglecting to take the time to fix architecture/foundations problems when problems hinder development
- Inadequate risk identification in earlier phases
- Inadequate risk mitigation of earlier risks
- Starting development by implementing the easiest capabilities first without solutions in place for high-risk elements to guide the development, potentially leading to:
  - Considerable rework once solutions for high-risk elements have been determined
  - Discontinued project due to lack of a viable solution
- Inadequate development monitoring and rescoping as development challenges are discovered
- Inadequate testing
- Inadequate change monitoring and response
- Unvalidated and unprioritized next-increment capabilities
- Inadequate Production and Operation plans, budgets, or schedules

9.4 Major Risks to Watch for during Development

Previous-phase risks either disappear in the Development phase or turn into actual issues or problems. However, there may still be risks associated with the Development and Production/Operations phases that can be monitored or mitigated during development. The following list identifies some key risks to watch for during Development:

- Overly optimistic plans, schedules, and estimates for development increments
- Key technologies that are not yet mature enough

- COTS products that do not meet expectations with respect to provided capabilities, thus requiring additional tailoring or customization
- Reuse items that are not as "reusable" as initially planned
- Critical engineering staff shortfalls
- Weak critical links in the vendor support/supply chains
- Weak manufacturing process or quality controls

Ways to identify, analyze, mitigate, track, and manage risks are discussed in Chapter 15.

9.5 How Development Scales from Small to Large, Complex Systems

If the system Foundations have been sufficiently defined, including interfaces between major components, the Development phase is where multiple teams can work concurrently to develop different components of the system that can be integrated to create an increment for testing and transition to production and operations. Scaling in the development phase focuses on iterative, incremental development using one or more development teams. The larger and more complex the system, the more extensive the teams and often the more numerous the engineering specialists who must collaborate to continue to balance the system objectives while making lower-level design decisions.

The levels of rigor and agility are typically determined at the component level and depend on the size, scope, criticality, level of foundation or system environment maturity, and precedence of the component under development. The following describes development scaling for some common types of systems:

- Small systems: Such systems are typically developed in a single increment with one or more teams using an organization similar to that shown at the highest level in Figure 9-4.
- Larger systems: Basic functions are developed in the first increment, and then additional functions and features are added in subsequent increments. Multiple teams, often from multiple organizations and disciplines, work on each increment. In many cases, each component team or organization will have its own three-tiered agile rebaselining team, development teams, and continuous V&V teams (as illustrated by the multiple levels in Figure 9-4). For more complex systems or SoS, each component, subsystem, or constituent system engineering organization may also have its own three-tiered set of teams.
- Large platforms: The first increment is the basic platform, and subsequent increments then add features and integrate additional systems and

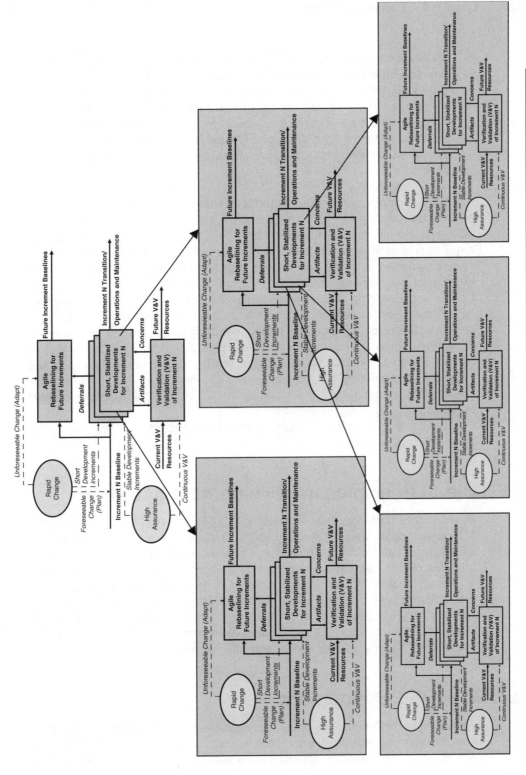

FIGURE 9-4 Multi-level Three-Tiered Organizations for Larger System and Platform Development

devices on the platform. As with the larger systems, the lead development organization will have a top-level three-tiered team and may have multiple lower-level three-tiered teams. The teams responsible for the development of systems and devices to be installed on the platform will have their own three-tiered teams as described previously for small and larger systems. For larger platforms, there are typically more levels of three-tiered teams that must interact to concurrently develop the platform and its systems and devices.

Again, Figure 9-4 illustrates a multilevel three-tiered organization for larger system and large platform development. At the highest level (Level 1), the agile baseline/rebaselining team develops the system foundations and allocates requirements to plan-driven teams that are responsible for the development of system components. These components may be hardware, software, or a combination of hardware and software. The plan-driven teams may be part of the Level 1 organization responsible for the development of the system, or they may be subcontractors or vendors to whom work has been outsourced. As the subsystem agile teams further refine component designs, lower-level requirements or features are allocated to the subsystem plan-driven teams. The number of levels for a given system can be a few or can be many levels deep, depending upon the size and complexity of the Level 1 system. Figure 9-4 also illustrates the fact that continual V&V is happening at each level within the development organization.

Additional information on software development scaling can be found in the Chapter 11 common cases.

9.6 Role of Principles in Development Activities

To summarize the Development phase, we again turn to the four ICSM principles. It is in this phase that the development teams are organized and tasked with developing either the first increment or a new increment of a system. At the culmination of these activities, the organizational decision makers are called upon to commit to moving into the Production and Operations phase based on the first article or unit, continuing with the Development phase to resolve issues or incorporate newly discovered needs that are a "must have" for the version to be released into production, or discontinuing the project. Table 9-1 summarizes the role of the ICSM principles in the Development phase in this decision.

9.7 MedFRS Development

At the end of the Foundations phase, the agile baseline team had selected an integrated cardiac monitor, an IV infusion pump, and a ruggedized laptop to upgrade one of the 10 first-responder ambulances. In addition, three wireless cameras were

TABLE 9-1 ICSM Principles as Applied to the Development Phase

Principle	Application in Development Phase
Stakeholder value-based guidance	Identification of any new stakeholders (or personnel changes in stakeholder organizations)
	Reassessment of success-critical stakeholders priorities
	Stakeholders' continued negotiation of a mutually satisfactory set of Development and Life Cycle capabilities and plans
Concurrent multidiscipline engineering	Systems engineering continues in the detailed design of system components to be developed and then transitions to "concurrent development of system components"
	Continued prototyping and evaluation of risky technologies or innovations planned for future increments
	Updated estimates for initial development cost and schedule, total cost of ownership, and potential return on investment
	Update of risk assessments
Evidence- and risk-based decisions	Earlier "evidence" is replaced with actual development
	Most risks either disappear as the system is developed or they become actual problems or issues to be resolved. However, risks that require continuous monitoring, mitigation, and resolution include those associated with Productions and Operations. Feasibility evidence related to Production and manufacturing is often developed during system assembly when production engineers work side-by-side with systems engineers. Feasibility evidence related to Operations is typically developed during operational tests.
	As new capabilities are identified and considered for incorporation, evidence is used to evaluate alternatives and decide on solutions
Incremental commitment and accountability	One of the following decisions: • Commitment to proceed to the Production and Operations phase with an appropriate budget and schedule • Conduct additional Development activities to resolved system problems or add newly identified features and capabilities needed in current increment • Discontinue the project

selected for evaluation as part of the prototype evaluation. The plan for the Med-FRS Development phase is as follows:

- Install the selected monitor and camera drivers on the laptop; test the integrated equipment; and, once testing is complete, install the system on the ambulance
- Train the users on the new equipment while the equipment is being integrated and installed on the ambulance
- Begin operation of the prototype
- While the prototype is under evaluation, begin development of the first increment of the integrated system, which includes custom software for the user interface on laptop system

- The user interface for the first increment should:
  - Integrate the devices with the laptop and provide images and reports integrated with patient identification information—thereby ensuring that there will be no confusion between patients when multiple sessions are in progress with a trauma center or hospital
  - Provide the ability to send integrated patient information as needed over 4G communications to the trauma centers
  - Incorporate feedback from both the first responders and the trauma center physicians who are evaluating the prototype

As Increment 1 development proceeded, feedback from the prototype indicated that adjustments were needed to layout of equipment in the ambulance and that tighter controls were needed on the software interface to ensure patient privacy and the security of data transmissions to the trauma center. These were high-priority changes for Increment 1. However, the first responders and the trauma centers did not want to delay the rollout of Increment 1. Therefore, two complex reports planned for Increment 1 were delayed until Increment 2 to keep Increment 1 on schedule.

In addition, during the development of Increment 1, a change request was received from one of the Ensayo area hospital administrators and a local city councilwoman to add a plug-compatible multipurpose breath-analyzer produced by a local company to the MedFRS complement of devices. The rebaselining team analyzed this request. Even though they determined that the device (1) is certified, (2) is being successfully used by the police department, and (3) would add good diagnostic value, they decide to defer it to a future increment to keep Increment 1 on schedule and to obtain more information on the legal aspects of performing breath analysis on people who may not be able to give consent to such a test.

The Development-phase feasibility analysis activities associated with the ambulance and hospital prototypes, the late request for a breath-analyzer, and final testing are summarized in Table 9-2.

While the plan-driven development team is developing the first increment and the V&V team is evaluating Increment 1 functionality, the agile rebaselining team continues to work on Increments 2 and 3. The following key features are under consideration for these increments:

- Additional power to support additional wireless devices and telemedicine units.
- Feasibility of incorporating a breath-analyzer to the suite of trauma care devices.
- Electronic health record compatible with evolving national standards and the local trauma units.
- Telemedicine capability between first responders and the Level 1 trauma centers. It was determined that the Level 3 and Level 4 trauma centers

TABLE 9-2 Feasibility Analysis Summary for the Development Phase

Development Activity	Summary of Findings
Installation of MedFRS medical equipment and laptop in a single ambulance as a prototype to determine feasibility of planned layout in the ambulance and feedback from medical first responders on use of systems in the actual environment	Prototype discovered problems with the layout of equipment in the ambulance and adjustments were made based on the user recommendations.
Installation of a single hospital MedFRS unit to interact with the users of the ambulance prototype equipment and obtain information on suitability of design and system interactions	Hospital trauma staff indicated that tighter controls were needed on the software interface to ensure patient privacy and better security for data transmissions to the trauma center.
Evaluation of request to incorporate breath-analyzer as part of MedFRS medical equipment	Feasibility assessment indicated that this was technically feasible, but there were several issues tied to the legal aspects of using this device on people who may not be able to give proper consent.
Testing of MedFRS new equipment integrated with the Increment 1 user interface to ensure readiness for Production and Operations phase	Late changes to the user interface software based on findings of the hospital prototype delayed the start of testing. However, because the prototype had identified issues during development (instead of during testing), the overall testing schedule did not need to change. A few additional low-priority problems were identified, but they were quickly resolved and retested.

seldom have the need for a telemedicine capability since the most seriously injured people are taken to one of the Level 1 trauma centers. In addition, it was observed that each of the two Level 1 trauma centers could handle up to 5 telemedicine sessions (for a total of 10 sessions) and that there were only 10 ambulances that would be able to initiate a telemedicine session. Therefore, telemedicine capabilities between just the Level 1 trauma centers and the first responders are sufficient for the near term.

As Increment 1 comes to completion and final test results become available, an Operations Commitment Review (OCR) is scheduled. The OCR focuses on the results of the prototype and the test results of Increment 1. Since there are no serious issues, the commitment is made to proceed to production and operations for Increment 1 and to begin development of Increment 2.

Table 9-3 summarizes the MedFRS goals, constraints, trades, risks, next-phase plans, and commitments at the end of the Development phase. Note that Chapter 11 provides additional information on the development of the MedFRS components through the ICSM common cases.

TABLE 9-3 Summary of MedFRS Development Phase

Objectives and business case	No change:
	Improve major trauma health care provided by first responders from site of incident to trauma center
	Improve emergency patient outcomes overall
	Reduce emergency patient recovery times and costs
Constraints	No change:
	Cost for system upgrades: $2 million
	Cost for additional personnel: $1 million/year
	No down time for existing capabilities to transition to new capabilities provided by MedFRS
	Interoperability with Ensayo trauma centers and hospitals
Alternatives	Alternative analyses focused on the options for Increments 2 and 3: additional power, EHR capabilities, and telemedicine capabilities.
Risks	Consensus on a common electronic health record has been reduced significantly by the efforts to define a national standard in the near term
	Ability to afford full telemedicine capability on a long-term basis
	Availability of key personnel with both medical and systems engineering experience
	Target cost of $2 million for upgrades and $1 million for additional medical/first responder personnel
Risk mitigation	Evaluation of prototype
	EHR evaluations focus on national standards that should be compatible with various hospital systems
	Identify sources of funding for desired telemedicine capability while continuing to assess the actual need for a full-up telemedicine capability versus a wireless camera to augment patient-monitoring device information. In addition, number of telemedicine centers reduced from four to two.
	Continued recruiting and training of first responder personnel with both medical and systems engineering experience
Risk-resolution results	Prototype results positive, with minor adjustments needed
	Prototype experience identified some shortfalls in training that will be modified for future first-responder vehicle upgrades
Plan for next phase	Implement Increment 2 and update plans for Increments 3 and 4; Increment 2 to include reports that were dropped from Increment 1
	Continue search for telemedicine capability funding planned for future increments while continuing to assess need for full-up telemedicine capability
	Continue to monitor cost and schedule against budget and update budgets in response to future increment plans
Commitment	Fund next phase

Reference

[1] Office of the Under Secretary of Defense for Acquisition and Technology (OUSD A&T), Systems and Software Engineering. *Systems Engineering Guide for Systems of Systems*, Version 1.0. Washington, DC: ODUSD(A&T)SSE, 2008. http://www.acq.osd.mil/se/docs/SE-Guide-for-SoS.pdf.

10

System Production and Operations

"By the year 2026, the US defense budget will be able to produce one airplane."

—Norman Augustine, *Augustine's Laws*

"Typical operations and support costs range from 60% to 84% for ground, sea, and air vehicles."

—Quentin Redman

System production and operations is where the system is manufactured and pulled together (or "packaged") for delivery to the users. It also includes the activities required to support the users as they operate or use the system. Production and operations are often described together because a very iterative process may be used as the system evolves or is upgraded in response to problems or limitations detected during operations. This chapter first describes the Production phase and then the Operations phase. It concludes by providing an example using the MedFRS system.

10.1 What Is "Production"?

"Production" is the activity associated with pulling together all the pieces and packaging them for the user or for mass distribution. For software, it may be as simple as creating the executable software and packaging it with any user documentation. Commercial software is typically distributed to users via commercial outlets or online. Custom software developed either under contract or by an internal development organization (e.g., an IT group) is typically installed for the users according to a detailed installation plan as part of the Operations phase. For new devices and platforms, production includes a manufacturing/assembly process along with the installation of the system software. For upgrades to devices and platforms, it might take the form of replacement kits that are later installed during system maintenance activities. Figure 10-1 provides an overview of the Production

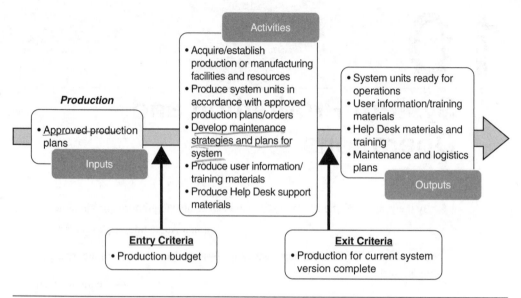

FIGURE 10-1 Production Overview

phase, showing inputs and entry criteria that trigger the phase, high-level activities performed in this phase, and the outputs and exit criteria that determine the conclusion of this phase.

To produce and operate multiple units, the types of components, desired product characteristics, and desired economies of scale will determine the appropriate levels of precision and automation for manufacturing, materials used, and numbers of components to produce. In some cases, it is much more cost-effective to produce spare parts when the initial parts are manufactured. This ensures adequate and comparable spares are available during the expected life of the system or system component and minimizes manufacturing setup costs.

10.2 What Are the Potential Pitfalls during Production?

Many of the pitfalls during the Production phase are related to poor configuration management of system components or poor quality controls during the manufacturing or assembly processes. Common pitfalls that can occur in this phase include the following:

- Weak manufacturing processes and quality controls
- Inadequate source code control or configuration management, leading to wrong component versions being included in a software release

- Inadequate configuration management of system software and hardware components, leading to assembly or installation of the wrong version of the system or wrong parts in a given version of a system
- Inadequate phase budgets and schedules
- Neglecting success-critical stakeholders

10.3 Major Risks to Watch for during Production

The following list identifies some key risks to watch for during Production:

- Overly optimistic plans, schedules, and estimates for the development of the manufacturing facilities
- System parts or components that are not received as scheduled for assembly
- Breakdown of manufacturing equipment or lack of spares for manufacturing equipment
- Inadequate manufacturing plans or procedures
- Component quality/defective parts
- Assembly quality
- Inadequate transition plans and preparations

Ways to identify, analyze, mitigate, track, and manage risks are discussed in Chapter 15.

10.4 What Is the Systems Operations Phase?

The goals of the Operations phase are sustainment and maintenance of the fielded system. The Operations phase begins with the rollout of a new system or new system increment. It includes the installation of the system (or system update), any activities required to move system and user data forward to the new system/system update, training information for the system users, and initial operational testing of the system to ensure that it is operating correctly. It often also includes continuing user support through a system Help Desk or website. The system Help Desk or website allows users to report problems and provides solutions to user problems, whether they are problems caused by the user not knowing how to operate the system/perform a given function or known problems for which a workaround or fix is available. Problems related to the performance of the system or new needs flow back to the development team for further analysis and resolution.

To proactively sustain and maintain a system, it can be useful to view a system as part of one or more SoS, as systems seldom operate in a stand-alone environment. Viewing the system as part of a SoS allows the operations personnel to better assess performance, look at how users use the system, and incrementally optimize user capabilities within the system environment(s) based on problems/issues the users and other stakeholders encounter. It also allows the operations personnel to better anticipate future system needs.

System operations and upgrades continue until the system has reached a point where it is no longer feasible to maintain or evolve it to meet new needs. At this point, it is time to plan for a major modernization or replacement of the system if there is still a need for it. Otherwise, it is time to plan for the retirement of the system and disposal of any components or parts that have special disposal requirements (e.g., electronics, nuclear materials).

Figure 10-2 provides an overview of the Operations phase, showing inputs and entry criteria that trigger the phase, the high-level activities performed in this phase, and the outputs and exit criteria that determine the conclusion of this phase. Note that this phase is repeated for every version of a system that is fielded and that the operations team might be supporting multiple versions of a given system at any point in time.

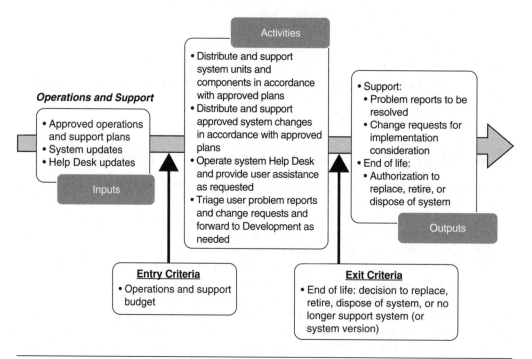

FIGURE 10-2 Operations Overview

10.5 What Are the Potential Pitfalls during Operations?

Common pitfalls that can occur in this phase include the following:

- Inadequate transition plans and preparations for initial system release as well as new increments or upgrades
  - Initialization of system data including user accounts and privileges
  - Migration/conversion of system data from previous version to new version
  - Training/support for users related to system changes and new capabilities
- Inadequate budgets and schedules for sustainment activities
- Neglecting key system stakeholders (primarily the users)—if the system does not perform adequately, they will not use it
- Inadequate plans or budget for ongoing user support
- Inadequate user support and change management
- Little or slow response to reported problems
- Inadequate logistics support and spares provisioning
- Inadequate plans or budget to deploy upgrades

10.6 Major Risks to Watch for during Operations

Testing is seldom comprehensive and, therefore, newly deployed capabilities and systems must be closely monitored to ensure continued correct performance. In addition, users and operations support personnel should watch for emergent behaviors, both good and bad, so that good emergent behaviors can be supported and evolved and undesirable emergent behaviors can be eliminated or mitigated. The following list identifies some key risks to watch for during the Operations phase:

- Inadequate attention to how users are using the system
- Lack of attention to user suggestions and complaints
- Lack of attention to product recalls for embedded components or products
- Lack of attention to changing external systems and services that may impact operation of the current version in use

Ways to identify, analyze, mitigate, track, and manage risks are discussed in Chapter 15.

10.7 Production and Operations for the MedFRS Initiative

Once the OCR process gives the go-ahead for production and operations, plans are implemented to upgrade the prototype systems in the first ambulance and trauma center. After an initial checkout of Increment 1, the rest of the ambulances and hospitals are scheduled for installation. Components are ordered for all of the sites/platforms as well as systems needed to support training. This order includes 10 sets of components for the ambulances, 4 sets of components for the hospitals, 4 additional ambulance sets to support training, and 2 additional hospital sets to support training—a total of 14 ambulance sets of components and 6 hospital sets of components.

Once the components have been received, they are individually checked to ensure that they operate correctly in accordance with the vendor specifications. Then, the components for each site/platform are integrated and tested in the integrated configuration. If the integrated configuration test passes, the components are installed in the platform. "Installation" on the ambulance platform means that the components are installed in racks and locked down in these racks to prevent injuries from falling equipment as well as to prevent theft. Installation also includes hookups to the platform power and wireless communications systems. After installation is complete, one more round of testing is performed to confirm that all of the equipment is properly functioning before turning it over to the first responders. A similar process is used for the hospital systems, although the hospital versions are not installed in locked racks.

While installation is being done for a given ambulance or hospital, ambulance and hospital personnel are sent to training. Several group training sessions are scheduled to minimize the impact to first responder and trauma care personnel duties. In addition, it is planned to have both hospital trauma personnel and first responders participate in each session so that they can practice using the system and better communicating with each other using the new features provided by MedFRS. The goal is that as each group completes training, they begin to use the new system immediately to reinforce their training.

The final aspect of the Productions and Operations phase for this first increment is the establishment of the MedFRS Help Desk support. For the first increment, development team members will be on call via pagers to handle calls related to the custom user interface, laptop, barcode system, camera, and communications between the ambulance and the hospital. Medical device vendors have been funded to initially provide Help Desk support for the integrated cardiac monitor and IV infusion pump until the hospital staff becomes more familiar with the new equipment. The planned Help Desk personnel are scheduled to attend user training sessions to help them better anticipate the types of questions that the users have and update their Help Desk information for later transition to full-time Help Desk personnel.

Table 10-1 summarizes the MedFRS goals, constraints, trades, risks, next-phase plans, and commitments for the Production and Operations phase.

TABLE 10-1 Summary of MedFRS Production and Operations Phase

Objectives	Continue to improve health care provided by first responders from site of incident to trauma center.
Constraints	Cost. No down time for existing capabilities. Interoperability with all Ensayo trauma centers.
Alternatives	Major alternatives for the first increment of the system were decided in the Foundations phase and lower-level alternatives in the Development phase. Alternatives investigated in the Production and Operations phase focused on installing the systems on the ambulances and in the trauma centers as well as training users on the operation of the systems without impacting trauma care. As a result, multiple training sessions were scheduled and a transition plan was put into place where users could continue to use existing systems until the new one was installed and they had been sufficiently trained on it.
Risks	Trauma care is impacted due to platform down time for installation or due to unfamiliarity with the new system. Trauma care is impacted due to equipment failures.
Risk mitigation	1. To mitigate the potential impact to trauma care due to the new system installation or user unfamiliarity with the system, it was decided to keep the old communications system in place until all users were familiar with the new system and the expected system performance had been confirmed. 2. To mitigate the potential impact to trauma care due to equipment failures, 4 ambulance systems and 2 hospital systems will be installed in the training facility and made available as spares if needed.
Risk-resolution results	1. While the risk mitigation required more equipment for the users, the backup communications improved patient safety during the transition period. 2. The additional spare systems continue to support training as needed as well as provide backup equipment for any failures in the field or at the hospital.
Plan for next phase	Plan production and operations activities for the next system increment.
Commitment	Fund production and operations planning for the next system increment.

10.8 Stage II Summary

In Stage II, the focus is on iterative and incremental development and how things cycle through for the life of the system until it is time for major modernization, replacement, or disposal. Once the initial version of the system is operational, the developers continue with iterative, incremental development activities to evolve the system to meet changing needs and to refresh technology as newer versions of components become available. As a system matures, its maintenance and upgrade cycles tend to develop a cadence where users can expect upgrades on a periodic basis. This continues until end-of-life for the system is reached, at which point the system goes through a major modernization or replacement. In some cases, a system loses its value over time and is permanently retired. System retirement may be prompted by obsolete technology, shifting business areas, business mergers and acquisitions, political priorities, or market interests.

In this stage, the ICSM principles are integrated with systems thinking, always looking back to identify what is not working well and looking forward to find new opportunities and needs to guide the evolution of the system. The ICSM provides guidance on what to consider in each phase as well as when to revisit earlier decisions when they are creating more problems than they are solving.

Finally, key to the ICSM is its focus on risk throughout the full system life cycle. How the ICSM phases are structured will differ for each type of system—it is not a one-size-fits-all process. Rather, the phases depend on the size and scope of the system, along with how well risks, technology maturity, level of innovation, and cost/schedule constraints have been addressed in Stage I. The process also depends on the development approaches selected for Stage II along with the associated Stage II commitments. This topic is discussed further in Chapter 11, where several examples and ICSM patterns are presented.

Teaching Alchemy 101

Part IV

Applying ICSM to Your Organization

"One of my primary objects is to form the tools so the tools themselves shall fashion the work and give to every part its just proportion."

—Eli Whitney

Now that you have the principles ingrained in your thought processes and the stages, phases, and diagrams well learned, it is time to think about applying ICSM to create change in your processes. We understand that at this point you may believe this is some impossible alchemical transmutation of lead into gold. However, it always helps to have an example and a few specific pointers to follow, so in Part IV we introduce tools and strategies for implementing ICSM in your organization. We illustrate their use in the development of several example systems, including the Medical First Responder System (MedFRS) case study.

- Chapter 11 introduces the use of ICSM phase-combining patterns, describes the common cases, and provides examples of their use.
- Chapter 12 describes how ICSM enhances assets that you already have and how ICSM adoption impacts your organization.

Implementing ICSM requires some adaptation of the way you do your work. For that reason, it makes sense for us to provide additional information in three management and technical skill areas that do require a bit of adaptation from their traditional execution.

- Chapter 13 discusses implementing evidence gathering within an evidence-based life cycle—that is, how to determine the evidence needed, plan for its development, and apply it in a commitment review context.

- Chapter 14 looks at the estimation activities that support ICSM phases, stages, and increments and considers how much more critical they are in achieving value-based decisions.
- As a spiral model process generator, the ICSM is driven by risk. Chapter 15 discusses how risk and opportunity management work together to support the four ICSM principles.

Finally, the Afterword provides a look at how we intend to evolve the ICSM to meet the changing development environment while remaining true to the four principles in our own plan.

11

ICSM Patterns and Common Cases

"Hoare's Law of Large Problems: Inside every large problem is a small problem struggling to get out."

—Sir Charles Antony Richard (Tony) Hoare, 1934–

The key to a successful project is having the right people, the right processes, and the right tools. ICSM is a process generator that can help you define the right processes to support the right people and integrate well with the right tools. Once you understand the stages and phases, you can begin to tailor them to suit the needs of your system development project. To begin, system developers should view the system development process as a set of activities that are tailored based on the type and size of system to be developed, the types of components or subsystems to be developed and integrated, and the associated unknowns and risks at both the system and subsystem/component levels. In addition, there are many development methodologies, techniques, and tools available to support development at both the system and subsystem/component levels, all of which are compatible with the ICSM when they fit the problem. The various methodologies, techniques, and tools should be viewed as the contents of a toolbox, from which the appropriate ones are selected to perform the various activities.

The selection of the various methodologies, techniques, and tools should be based on the characteristics of the system or system capability under development as well as the experience base of the engineers. Tools should be selected that are compatible with each other, useful to the engineers, and tailored to support the development activities. Technical tools that often support or automate development activities include prototyping, modeling, computer-aided design and manufacturing, software development environment and code generation, performance assessment, and test automation tools. Management tools include scheduling and task network analysis, requirements/backlog management, configuration management, and status monitoring tools. These tools are not discussed in detail in this chapter, but rather are mentioned here simply to acknowledge that they are important in planning the project, tailoring processes, and ensuring an efficient process for developing a quality system.

The rest of this chapter discusses the ICSM patterns and common cases, provides some high-level examples of each, and concludes with a more detailed example for the Medical First Responder System (MedFRS) case study.

11.1 ICSM Patterns

It has been mentioned several times that when risks are negligible, the ICSM encourages phases to be combined into a more streamlined process. Before starting a detailed discussion of some ICSM common cases, it is a good idea to understand the situations in which one might consider combining phases. The "combination of phases" has led to the development of four ICSM patterns, illustrated in Figure 11-1.

The first three patterns in Figure 11-1 are typically used to develop a new system. These three patterns begin with an Exploration Commitment Review that initiates the first "phase." The scope of this first phase depends on the size, scope, criticality, existing resources that contribute to the desired capability/system, level of innovation required, needed feasibility assessments related to key aspects of the alternatives, identified risks and uncertainty, and level of funding

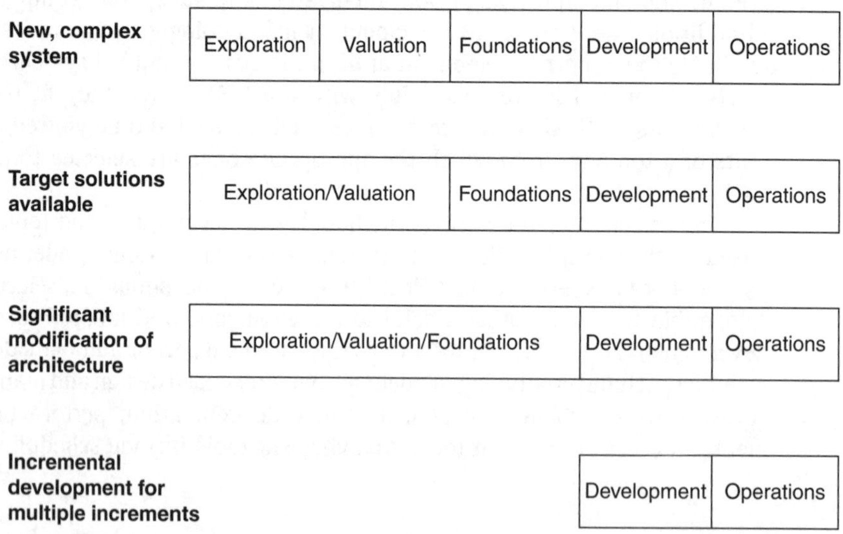

New, complex system	Exploration	Valuation	Foundations	Development	Operations

Target solutions available	Exploration/Valuation		Foundations	Development	Operations

Significant modification of architecture	Exploration/Valuation/Foundations			Development	Operations

Incremental development for multiple increments				Development	Operations

FIGURE 11-1 ICSM Patterns Involving Combined Phases

available. The following describes the "home grounds" for each of the first three ICSM patterns:

- ICSM Pattern **"New, complex system"** is the pattern typically used when the new desired capability or system is thought to be large, complex, or otherwise relatively risky. It might require considerable innovation or it might be a complex new capability that requires the development of one or more new systems and modifications to other systems with which the new systems must interoperate. It is also the pattern that would typically be used to guide the modernization of an obsolete or fragile system or system of systems. With this pattern, there is a Commitment Review at the end of each phase during which alternatives are reviewed, feasibility evidence and risks assessed, and a decision made on how to proceed: conduct further engineering and analysis in the current phase, continue forward, or discontinue.

- ICSM Pattern **"Target solutions available"** is the pattern in which key alternatives for the desired new capability or system are relatively well understood early in the Exploration phase and the Exploration and Valuation activities can be combined into a single phase with minimal risks. However, to go forward with any of the key alternatives, significant Foundations work is required. This might be major modifications to or refactoring of an existing architecture or the development of new foundations. With this pattern, the alternatives, expected costs, feasibility evidence, and risks are first reviewed in a formal commitment review at the end of Valuation activities and an explicit commitment made to go forward with the Foundations work.

- ICSM Pattern **"Well-understood modification of architecture"** is the pattern typically used to develop a new system where some significant level of foundations or architecture exists that can be used as a starting point. For example, this might be a new product that is part of a product line or family of systems. The same pattern can be used when a combined Exploration and Valuation phase converges on a solution that has high and well-understood reuse from an existing system.

The last ICSM Pattern, **"Incremental development for multiple increments,"** is used in the development of multiple increments that have been previously approved as a group of features or capabilities to be fielded over multiple increments. Small shifts of features from one increment to another may occur over time, but the overall system foundations are relatively stable. However, if an increment requires major new components (especially significant hardware upgrades) or the restructuring of an underlying database or repository, then the ICSM Pattern **"Significant modification of architecture"** should be used instead, as these types of upgrades will require additional installation activities and coordination with the user organizations to field the increment.

Finally, while the patterns are relatively simple, they can be combined to characterize the development large, complex systems in a multi-developer environment as well as the development and integration of multiple systems in a system of systems or the development of multiple components within a product line or family of systems. In addition, each pattern allows for iteration between phases if new risks or problems are identified that can be better addressed in a previous phase. For example, if during development it becomes evident that it will be difficult to achieve the desired system performance or to scale up to the anticipated number of users, it is often better to go back to the Foundations phase to fix the architecture issues and then resume development rather than continue development by "patching" the problem areas and hoping for the best.

11.2 ICSM Common Cases

Because of the perceived complexity of some of the ICSM views, a set of ICSM common cases have been developed to show users how to use the framework to create a development process appropriate for their system of interest. These cases cover the very small to the very large as well as the use of COTS products and services in the development of a large, complex custom system, or integrated sets of software applications. Each of these situations presents risks at the various stages of development, with some risks being more critical than others. The goal of the ICSM is to identify these risks and then tailor the process to include rigor where necessary to investigate and manage the risks and to streamline the process when risks are negligible, allowing the development team to be more agile when possible. The seven common cases are as follows:

- Software application or system
- Software-intensive device
- Hardware platform
- Family of systems or product line
- System of systems (SoS) or enterprise-wide system
- Brownfield modernization

Table 11-1 briefly describes when to use each common case and provides some examples of each. Note that larger systems may be composed of multiple subsystems, with each subsystem developed using its own best-fit common case. In some cases, several subsystems might be developed by outsource vendors. Small systems may be developed using primarily one common case. However, if a custom device contains significant software features and graphical user interfaces, those software features would be developed using the *software application or system* common case. For other systems with embedded software, the software may be part of field-programmable gate arrays (FPGAs) or firmware components and be developed by systems or hardware engineers.

TABLE 11-1 ICSM Common Cases

System (or Subsystem) Is...	Use...	Examples
Software application/system that executes on one or more commercial hardware platforms. It can be a stand-alone software system or a constituent within one or more systems of systems (SoS).	Software application or system	Cellphone app, business application or system, military command-and-control software system, pharmacy systems, inventory management systems, computer operating system software, database management system
An object, machine, or piece of equipment that is developed for a special purpose and has significant features provided by software.	Software-intensive device	Computer peripherals, weapons, entertainment devices, health care devices (including small robotics used in surgeries or to assist injured people), GPS navigation device, manufacturing tools
Vehicle (land, sea, air, or space)	Hardware platform	Small unmanned ground or air vehicle, automobile, military jeep, tank, ship, airplane, space shuttle, space station, Mars rover
Computer.	Hardware platform	Supercomputer, mainframe, server, laptop, tablet, cellphone
Part of a set of systems that are either similar to each other or interoperate with each other	Family of systems or product line	Car models that share many core components; interoperating back-office systems such as billing, accounting, customer care, pricing, and sales force automation systems that share a common underlying repository with standard data definitions/formats for the business domain and are provided by a single vendor
A new capability that will be performed by more than one interoperating system	System of system or enterprise-wide systems	Multiple interoperating systems that are owned and managed by different organizations—for example, navigation systems that include airborne and land systems that also interoperate with GPS
Refactoring or re-implementation of an older legacy system or set of systems	Brownfield modernization	Incremental replacement of old, fragile business systems with COTS products or technology refreshment/upgrading of existing systems

One can typically determine candidate common cases for a new capability (or set of capabilities) during the Valuation phase. These cases are then often refined during the Foundations activities, setting the stage for the Development phase. As mentioned earlier, for larger capabilities or systems, several common cases might be used. For example, one subsystem might be best addressed by a COTS product or service, while another subsystem may require the development of a new hardware component. The following sections briefly describe each of the common cases.

Software Application or System

ware application or system case is appropriate for software that is devel-
d evolved over time to operate as a software system. It can be installed and
d in one or more software environments and computer platforms. It could
ʋͼ ͼ ͻ ͻalth care application, a business application, or a command-and-control/
sensor processing system, anywhere from quite small to very large. Several strategies can be used to create the software, as described in Table 11-2.

Once you know that part of your solution contains software and you have
determined which functions the software must perform, the next question you ask
is whether there exist some COTS products or services that will provide a sufficient
solution. As part of the Valuation activities, you will investigate these COTS alternatives as well as the option of developing your own custom software.

If you choose to pursue custom software development options, you need to
determine the level of required software innovation, the criticality of the software
to be developed (e.g., is it a "nice to have" feature or is it safety-critical?), the
need for the software to operate in a regulated environment or meet regulatory
standards, and the size and complexity of the software. These answers will provide guidance as to the number and experience levels of the software developers,
the number of teams that will work in parallel, and the feasibility of outsourcing
development. The answers to these questions will also let you decide how agile
or formal you need to be in the development of this custom software. Figure 11-2
illustrates the key options for software development processes. Note that different
processes may be used for different components within the same system.

Whatever strategy is selected, with software development, features are identified and prioritized, prioritizations updated as needed, and then the backlog worked

TABLE 11-2 ICSM Software Strategies

Name	Description
Architected agile	Initial agile iteration focuses on software foundations and architecture issues, then transitions to a purely agile process for development of software capabilities
Agile	Software developed using purely agile methods with short-duration iterations, used after initial architected agile iteration or in cases where the environment for the new software application is well defined—for example, a cellphone app with well-defined interfaces
Plan-driven	Traditional software development process guided by detailed plans and schedules, typically employing incremental or evolutionary methods
Formal methods	Critical software system or subsystem, often containing security- or safety-relevant software or critical/high-precision algorithms that must be rigorously developed, tested, and often certified
COTS/services	Software functionality provided through the integration of one or more commercial off-the-shelf software components or software services

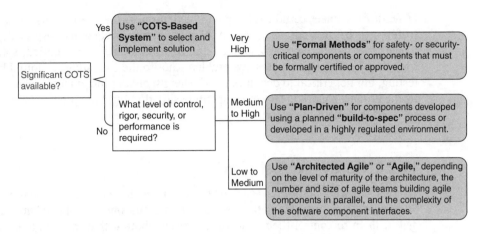

FIGURE 11-2 Selecting a Software Strategy

off in an iterative and incremental manner, focusing on the higher-priority features in the backlog. Software for software-intensive systems will often be upgraded (new increments or versions) on a regular basis over the life of the system. Many of these upgrades are responses to changing stakeholder needs or technology refresh. It is also often the case that over time, lower-priority features in the backlog maybe discarded due to obsolescence or replaced by newer technologies or COTS software products.

11.2.2 Software-Intensive Device

The *software-intensive device* case includes the development of both hardware and software features. Often it includes embedded software that controls the hardware as well as user interface software. Embedded software can be executable software that is actually loaded and can be easily updated on the platform as well as firmware or FPGAs that are part of the platform/device. User interface software allows the user to interact with the system, select features, and control how the features operate. The software can also operate "soft" switches and dials. Key for this case is early and continuing concurrent engineering and collaboration between systems engineering, hardware engineering, human factors, software development, manufacturing/production, and other engineering specialists. In this case, hardware and software are tightly coupled and key performance, user satisfaction, and cost/unit aspects are tied to appropriate trades in the Valuation and Foundation tradespaces as well as to detailed design during the Development phase.

After the first units are produced and tested, work often begins on variants of the device: larger, smaller, more features, or different configurations of features to meet certain price points. Oftentimes, there are plans to upgrade features or to incorporate new technologies in future versions—especially with today's cellphones, laptop computers, and tablet computers. In addition, software fixes may be developed to resolve problems not found in testing (or found late in testing, but not critical to operations). The length of later increments will be driven by the product's marketplace or competitive situation until the product is retired or replaced by something better.

11.2.3 Hardware Platform

Today's hardware platforms—such as various types of vehicles, both manned and unmanned, and computer platforms—have enormous amounts of software embedded in them to control their functions. Articles abound that indicate today's aircraft and automobiles have several million lines of code in them [1]. Therefore, hardware platforms are no longer "all hardware." Many powertrain, flight control, and navigational functions and capabilities within platforms are now provided by software. In addition, mission-support software systems are often on military aircraft, watercraft, and tanks. This trend means that the *hardware platform* case is more like the *software-intensive device* case on steroids. The software that controls or supports the operation of the platform is developed concurrently with the hardware, much like the *software-intensive device* case. However, many of the mission systems or entertainment systems that are not required for the operation of the platform are developed somewhat independently, then installed on the platform right before the platform is ready to go into operation. Consequently, the selection of systems such as automobile GPS navigation systems and entertainment systems can be deferred until the automobile is ready for production, for example, and the version installed will be close to "state-of-the-art" for that system and may even be an optional feature on the platform. This is also true for mission-support systems that are installed on military platforms.

What this means with respect to the ICSM is that several systems and subsystems will be in development at a given point in time, with each development activity tailoring the ICSM to fit the circumstances and characteristics of the system or subsystem. In this scenario, the basic platform body or shell design and development may take a considerable amount of iteration, the operational hardware-software components are developed in parallel, and the mission-support systems may be primarily software or software-intensive devices. Some of the subsystems are unique to the platform and may be outsourced as part of the platform development. Other subsystems may be COTS products and can be selected and integrated later in the development of the platform.

When a platform is developed using this case, it is often developed as a product line with several variations to meet different user needs or desires. It can also evolve several times, incorporating newer technologies or different features, before it becomes obsolete and retired.

11.2.4 Family of Systems/Product Line

The *family of systems* or *product line* case is where an organization makes an investment in the development of a core foundation upon which several products can be developed.* Key for this case is building a sustainable foundation for a product line along with reusable/evolvable components. The common "foundations" are used to design various related products and the reusable components are shared between two or more products. The goals is to develop a set of products that meet the following criteria:

- Can be quickly configured and integrated to meet a somewhat common need. A software example is a set of COTS products that can support back-office operations such as accounting, order entry, sales force automation, customer care, and billing, all supported by a common repository that allows a single point of entry for common information (such as customer-related information). By developing such a set of interoperating systems, vendors can market their software products to organizations pursuing a COTS-based strategy for their *software systems* needs.

- Can be used to provide a variety of products with common features. A hardware example is an automobile product line with various-size engines, two-door or four-door bodies, and optional features such as navigation systems and backup cameras.

In some respects, the *family of systems* case is similar to the *system of systems* case presented next. However, a key difference between these two cases is that the family of systems is typically owned and evolved by a single organization or vendor. In turn, the owning organization has much more control over the evolution of the components of the family of systems, thus possibly reducing some risks, especially in the area of system interoperability. As a result, an organization pursing a *family of systems* solution rather than a *system of systems* solution may be able to streamline the ICSM process because of the reduced risks and the reduced amount of work required to integrate the components.

11.2.5 System of Systems

In the *system of systems* case, cross-cutting capabilities are developed by composing new capabilities using features of existing systems, changes to existing systems, additions to existing systems, and sometimes the addition of a new system.

---

*Another view of the family of systems case is where there is a standard specification for the development of a product and many vendors can develop a product that will be interchangeable with other vendors' products, such as a car battery or sound system. This case is not discussed here; it would be more appropriate for one of the other cases, depending on the type of interchangeable product that is being developed.

Key to the success of SoS software capabilities are coordination and collaboration across multiple development teams, a development approach that allows the fielding of incomplete features that do not adversely impact system/SoS operation, and a feature prioritization scheme that addresses SoS capabilities (i.e., low priority for a given system, but high priority at the SoS level) as well as single-system capabilities/needs.

In this situation, the goal is to integrate a set of existing systems (or guide and evolve the integration of a set of existing systems). These systems are primarily developed, owned, and maintained by an organization other than the one that is attempting to manage and guide the set of systems as a system of systems. Because of the independence of these constituent systems, the SoS organization has little or no formal control over the processes used to maintain and evolve the constituent systems. The SoS may be an enterprise-wide business SoS, with the constituents being primarily COTS products along with some legacy applications. Alternatively, it may be Department of Defense (DoD) warfighting SoS, where the constituent legacy systems are integrated to increase capabilities on the battlefield [2].

Traditional systems engineering activities are typically tailored for the *system of systems* case to define an SoS architecture, better coordinate the activities of multiple systems in migrating to the SoS architecture, and provide synchronization points for the SoS. Pilot studies have shown that many DoD SoS have reorganized the traditional systems engineering activities into a set of seven core elements: (1) translating capability objectives; (2) understanding systems and relationships; (3) assessing performance relative to capability objectives; (4) developing, evolving, and maintaining SoS design; (5) monitoring and assessing changes; (6) addressing new requirements and options; and (7) orchestrating updates to SoS [3]. Further analysis shows that these elements map fairly well at the SoS level to the ICSM three-team model discussed in Chapter 9.

What makes this case different from *family of systems* case is that each of the constituent systems uses its own processes, schedules, and increment and version releases without much, if any, coordination with other constituent system schedules. Therefore, it is important for constituent systems to be able to interoperate with other systems that have not yet been upgraded to support the new capabilities, requiring some systems to remain backward compatible with other systems while evolving their own new capabilities and features.

11.2.6 Brownfield Modernization

The goal of *brownfield modernization* is to upgrade legacy system features and capabilities in an incremental way—rather than in one big bang. It includes technology refresh as well as reengineering and replacement of poorly performing legacy software. Typically modernization starts with an analysis of the existing software system to identify critical business/application features and functions. The system may then be restructured to support incremental replacement with new hardware, COTS products, and/or new software applications and components. This restructuring is often the first increment (or first few increments for more complex restructuring activities) in the *brownfield modernization* case.

For hardware upgrades, it may be necessary to upgrade system software such as operating systems and database management systems at the same time. It may also be the case that the brownfield system contains COTS software products that are no longer supported (or, even worse, whose vendors have gone out of business). In these cases, one may need to plan for these COTS software upgrades or replacements before making the transition to the new hardware.

Legacy software can present a different set of challenges. This software has often been developed and evolved by many generations of developers and the current incarnation of the system could best be described as "spaghetti code" with no clear functional boundaries. In addition, many of the original software developers may no longer be with the organization. Software restructuring activities make it possible to replace restructured components with COTS products or new custom software components as they become available. The identification or development of replacement components is accomplished through *software application or system* strategies, and it is good to have an idea of which COTS products will be used to replace legacy software so that the restructuring aligns well with the selected COTS software products.

If it becomes too difficult to make upgrades incrementally due to hardware, COTS, and custom software operating system/database management system dependencies, it may be better to handle the modernization as a replacement system using the *software application or system* case. If it is decided to develop a replacement system, the legacy system continues to operate in its current condition until the replacement system is ready to go operational. The decision to go with either brownfield modernization or a replacement software system is made in the initial brownfield assessment that is part of the Exploration and Valuation phases.

11.3 Common Case Examples

To better explain the common cases, we provide several examples in Table 11-3. This table summarizes the key characteristics and criteria associated with each example. The first few columns of the table describe the characteristics of the case (or application category) with respect to size and complexity; expected change rate during the development process; the overall criticality of the application, typically as it applies to human life, security/protection of information, or financial liability; and the type of NDI/COTS support one might expect for an application in this category. (In the table, commercial off-the-shelf [COTS] is used as a shorthand for other types of non-developmental items [NDIs] such as government off-the-shelf [GOTS] components, open source components, and cloud services.) The last column indicates the organizational and personal capabilities that are required to be successful at building this type of application. These summary examples are followed by a more detailed example based on the MedFRS case study.

TABLE 11-3 Common Case Examples

Example	Common Case	Size/Complexity	Typical Change Rate for Increment	Criticality to Business or User	NDI Support	Organization Personnel Capability
Accounting application	COTS software package	Small/low	Low	High	COTS candidates available	COTS experience medium to high
Simple custom business application	Architected agile software development	Small/low	Medium to high	Medium	No COTS available; development and target environment well defined	Agile-ready, domain experience high
Cellphone feature	Agile software development	Medium/medium	Medium to high	Low	Development and target environment (hardware, operating system) well defined	Agile-ready, domain experience high
Security kernel	Formal methods software development	Small/low	Low	Extra high	No COTS available; development and target environment well defined	Strong formal methods experience
Electronic health record system	Plan-driven software development	Medium/high	Low to medium	High	No compatible COTS; development and target environment (hardware, operating system) well defined—must be integrated with rest of health care system	Domain experience medium to high
Multi-sensor control device	Hardware device	Small/high	Mixed parts	Very high	Development environment well defined	Domain experience medium to high
Unmanned air vehicle	Hardware platform	Medium/high	Mixed parts	Very high	Some in place	Domain experience medium to high
Crisis management	System of systems	Large/very high	Mixed parts	Very high	Many COTS; some in place	COTS and domain experience medium to high
Medical device product line	Family of systems	Medium/very high	Product core once stabilized: low; device unique: medium to high	Very high	Development environment well defined	Domain experience medium to high
Incremental legacy phase-out	Brownfield modernization	Large/high	Medium for business features, low for COTS products	High	COTS as legacy replacement	Legacy reengineering experience, COTS experience, some domain experience

11.3.1 MedFRS Example

In Chapters 6–10, we followed the MedFRS upgrade process throughout the ICSM phases. Here, we look at how this process can be described in terms of the ICSM patterns and common cases. Because there was already an existing capability for first responders that needed to be upgraded, we would characterize the overall effort as a "brownfield modernization" project. As described, the project spent time in each ICSM phase, as illustrated in Figure 11-3: needs were explored, options were evaluated, and then a high-level solution was selected in the Foundations phase. It was decided that the selected solution would be further evaluated as a prototype on a single platform (ambulance) engaging experts at a single Level 1 trauma center before a final commitment was made for the full development of the first increment.

From feedback received from the prototype activity, adjustments were made and development activities began. Figure 11-3 summarizes the capabilities that were to be provided by Increment 1 on the ambulances and at the Level 1 trauma centers. In the Development phase, work began in parallel to procure devices and other hardware and to develop the software needed to integrate the devices and provide a single user interface for each user group for communications between

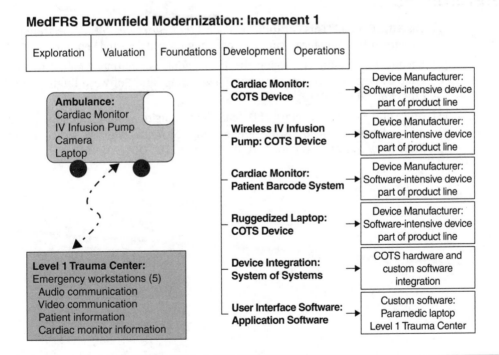

MedFRS Brownfield Modernization: Increment 1

FIGURE 11-3 MedFRS Common Cases

the ambulance and the trauma center. Figure 11-3 also highlights the fact that each of the device vendors used the *product line* common case to develop the software-intensive device selected for the MedFRS project.

The last observation with respect to the common cases and MedFRS is that once the systems from the different vendors are integrated on the ambulance, the ambulance systems should be viewed and managed as a SoS. In addition, when the ambulance systems are integrated with the trauma center, it will become a higher-level SoS that must also be managed as a SoS to ensure that single-system changes do not adversely affect the MedFRS capabilities.

11.4 Summary: The ICSM Common Cases Overview

In this chapter, we have described how the ICSM can be applied to many types of systems. However, these "common cases" do not encompass all types of systems. What we have provided is high-level guidance for several frequently encountered types of system development, from the very small to the very large and complex. The thought processes illustrated through these common cases can be used to further tailor and adapt the ICSM to other situations not explicitly covered here.

References

[1] Charette, Robert. "This Car Runs on Code." *IEEE Spectrum.* http://spectrum.ieee .org/green-tech/advanced-cars/this-car-runs-on-code, posted February 1, 2009.

[2] Boehm, B., & Lane, J. "Using the Incremental Commitment Model to Integrate System Acquisition, Systems Engineering, and Software Engineering." *CrossTalk.* 2007;20(10).

[3] Office of the Under Secretary of Defense for Acquisition and Technology (OUSD A&T), Systems and Software Engineering. *Systems Engineering Guide for Systems of Systems*, Version 1.0. Washington, DC: ODUSD(A&T)SSE, 2008.

12

ICSM and Your Organization

"We don't make the products you buy; we make the products you buy better."

—Tagline from BASF television commercial

To this point, we have continually stated that the ICSM is a process *generator*, not a process. There are two reasons that we continue to hammer this thought home. First, it is true (q.e.d.)—that is the way the original spiral model was defined, although rarely how it was used. And therein lies the second reason—the way to use the ICSM is as a process generator.

In Chapter 11, we described patterns and common cases, and provided examples for the way ICSM can be applied to specific projects. This is important because we have also stated that the ICSM is not a one-size-fits-all process (remember Motel Procrustes). However, focusing on a specific project's process can obscure some of the benefits of ICSM at a larger level.

In this chapter, we will talk more about why ICSM needs to be approached as an organizational asset rather than as a project asset. Certainly, it is important to tailor the ICSM usage to your organization's activities. However, it is just as important to use ICSM to take maximum advantage of the organizational investments you have already made in processes, practices, skill building, team building, and the whole array of organizational improvement activities.

12.1 Leveraging Your Current Process Investments

Your organization most likely has invested in any number of organizational improvement assets. Along the way, you probably have acquired tools to support your development activities. Configuration management, simulation and modeling infrastructure, computer-aided design/computer-aided manufacturing (CAD-CAM), software development environments, and scheduling and task network analysis tools are examples that, depending on your organizational domain, you may already have and employ.

Perhaps less concrete are the investments in standards, process improvement philosophies, or development approaches. Table 12-1 illustrates only a few examples of the approaches that require investments for adoption. Training

TABLE 12-1 Examples of Existing Assets That Can Be Applied within ICSM

Approach	Thumbnail (Authors)	Synergies with ICSM Practices
Total Quality Management (TQM)	Continuous process improvement framework based on plan–do–check–act cycle (Feigenbaum, Ishikawa, Deming, U.S. Navy)	Understanding needs, envisioning opportunities, reflection in action
Lean manufacturing	Comprehensive manufacturing approach based on the Toyota Production Process (Womack)	Stakeholder value-based guidance: focus on value-adding activities
Six Sigma	Application of quality methods and statistical process control concepts to business processes (Smith, Motorola)	Prioritizing defects by value increases return on investment (ROI) from quality methods
ISO-9000	International quality standard	Quality as satisfaction of stakeholder value propositions
IEEE/IEC-15288	International systems engineering process standard	Explicit characterization of common-case process configurations
Model Based Systems Engineering	Approach to systems engineering in which each step in the process is represented by progressively more detailed models (Freidenthal, LMCO, INCOSE)	Value/risk-based model elaboration: deeper modeling of higher-value/risk elements
Systems Modeling Language (SysML)	A systems-level version of the software-based Unified Modeling Language (OMG)	Use of SysML parametric diagrams for generating evidence
DoD Architecture Framework	A systems architectural diagram hierarchy deployed by the U.S. Department of Defense (DoD)	Value-based prioritization of multiple views
Capability Maturity Model Integration (CMMI)	A DoD-sponsored integration effort to resolve conflicts between software, systems engineering, and integrated product development process improvement models and provide a common, extensible process improvement framework (DoD, CMU)	Mapping in appendix; improvements toward use of agile methods
Capability Maturity Model for Software (CMM)	The first attempt by the Software Engineering Institute to implement a process improvement framework for software based on IBM research concepts (Radice, Humphries, CMU)	Lower levels are highly one-size-fits-all; Level 5 is more flexible
Cleanroom	A formal method used to develop software for safety-critical and defense systems that employs iteration and statistics-based testing (Mills, IBM)	Criteria for when to use as an ICSM common case
Scrum	An agile management method involving short iterations (sprints), prioritized requirements, and a small, tight team structure (Takeuchi/Nonaka, Schwaber/Sutherland)	Criteria for when to use as an ICSM common case

eXtreme Programming (XP)	An agile software development approach that includes technical and management best practices taken to the "extreme" (Beck/Cunningham)	Criteria for when to use as an ICSM common case
Dynamic Systems Development Method (DSDM)	A European-developed product development framework based on agile software principles and rapid application development (DSDM Consortium)	Criteria for when to use as an ICSM common case
Information Technology Infrastructure Library (ITIL)	A U.K.-developed library of IT service management best practices, including implementation infrastructure, and providing the basis for the ISO/IEC 20000 standard (U.K. Office of Government Commerce)	Aid in envisioning opportunities; criteria for use of COTS/NDI/services
Test-Driven Development (TDD)	A primarily software development approach in which requirements are captured by tests that are written before the software is designed or implemented; implies automated testing support and provides consistent unit testing, integration testing, and regression testing (Beck)	Earlier use via evidence-based decision guidance
Behavior-Driven Development (BDD)	An extension of TDD to include the concepts in domain-driven design and business analysis; rather than focusing entirely on technical requirements, BDD captures and drives tests of system behaviors and allows these to be linked and traced in the same way as formal requirements traceability (North)	Aid in earlier use via evidence-based decision guidance
DevOps	A concept in which developers and operations staff are integrated to allow more rapid deployment of software to the enterprise (Kim)	Synergetic with Stage II three-team approach
Unified Modeling Language (UML)	An object-oriented modeling language that resulted from Rational bringing together the three top object-oriented software development methodologists to create a unified approach and notation (Booch, Jacobson, Rumbaugh, OMG)	Value-based prioritization of multiple views
Scaled Architecture Framework (SAFe)	A framework to scale agile software development technology to large-system and enterprise-level development (Leffingwell)	Criteria for use as the architected agile common case
Kanban	Value-based scheduling and process improvement approach based on theory of constraints, lean manufacturing, and queuing theory (Anderson, Reinertsen)	Value-based activity prioritization; synergy with agile software engineering team triage
Participatory Design	Scandinavian method of stakeholder-collaborative system design	Stakeholder value-based guidance; concurrent engineering of hardware, software, and human factors
Cognitive Task Analysis, Contextual Design: Personas	Additional human–system integration methods	Concurrent hardware–software, human factors engineering

executives, managers, and practitioners in these approaches, coaching and consulting expenses, and the cost of creating and maintaining the information required to support assessments and appraisals can be significant. It is important that you understand that ICSM is not about replacing or discontinuing your current process improvement structure or your process assets. Instead, it focuses much more on understanding how to determine when and where to gain the greatest leverage for your investments.

While almost every process, standard, or approach provides a means of tailoring or adjusting its implementation, very few provide a sufficient decision framework regarding such tailoring. ICSM is a framework for making those decisions (along with project specific decisions discussed earlier). By applying the ICSM principles, phase patterns, and life-cycle framework, you are constantly evaluating the risks of applying one or more of your process assets to a given project, capturing evidence of the effectiveness of those assets, and applying the risk-driven decision process across the entire portfolio of your organization.

12.2 Maximizing the Value of Your Organizational Knowledge

Using ICSM across an organization is probably less difficult than implementing many process improvement or technical development approaches. In truth, it means adopting the principles and meta-principles as a significant guide to your decision making. The stages and phases of the ICSM represent a set of knowledge levels about a project, program, portfolio, or enterprise. The fact that there is an evolutionary component applies as well across the enterprise of a large, successful company concerned about maximizing shareholder value, as it does to a company in its infancy applying the rules of lean start-up.

Chapters 6–10 provided examples of the risk-based decision techniques involved in the various phases of the ICSM life-cycle framework as it applies to a product or system. Applying those at an enterprise level is not significantly different. The questions are the same, but the targets of the decisions operate at a higher level. While developing a product can cross technical boundaries, enterprise-level initiatives can cross organizational and even corporate boundaries. The risks assessed are very different, as are the stakeholders. However, the fundamental principles still apply, as defined in Table 12-2.

12.3 Where the Impact Is

The evidence collected from multiple projects and systems is an extremely valuable asset in its own right in helping to understand the real cost of work as well as the proven capacity of organizational components. This evidence can be applied

TABLE 12-2 ICSM Principles Applied at the Enterprise Level

Principle	Application
Stakeholder value-based guidance	Identification of success-critical stakeholders, understanding their value propositions, negotiating mutually satisfactory win-win objectives and approaches, and using evidence to monitor and control maintenance of a win-win equilibrium works as well at the enterprise level as it does at the project level.
Incremental commitment and accountability	Similarly, development and nurturing of strategic partnerships at the cross-enterprise level works best if defined and applied incrementally, along with mutual commitments to honor agreements.
Concurrent multidiscipline engineering	Successful mergers, acquisitions, and strategic partnerships involving enterprises operating in multiple domains similarly need to invest in mutual understanding, win-win negotiation, and full-life-cycle planning, execution, and controlling.
Evidence- and risk-based decisions	Enterprise-level decisions similarly need to invest in competitive analysis, technology maturity analysis, business case analysis, and other sources of buying evidence to reduce risk.

to internal operational planning, external proposal development and bidding, and evaluation of suppliers.

12.3.1 An Experience Factory

In the late 1980s, the goal–question–metric approach [1] to measurement was connected to a concept called the Experience Factory [2]. The core idea was to form a group within a development organization that created refined models based on carefully designed measurement programs and experimented with ways to improve the outcomes associated with specific organizational goals. The NASA Software Engineering Lab used this approach for 25 years with significant success, but it was finally disbanded due to funding priorities, reorganizations, and new leadership [3]. In the 2000s, under a grant from the National Science Foundation, USC and the Frauhofer Center at the University of Maryland created the Center for Empirically-Based Software Engineering (CeBASE). CeBASE revised and refined the concept as an enterprise improvement process [4]. The idea of a central group to analyze, model, and experiment with organizational processes is still valid and has continued to evolve in different versions. The latest version, developed by Vic Basili and the Fraunhofer Center, is called GQM + Strategies [5,6]. The reason for presenting this seemingly unrelated history here is that when using the ICSM, the evidence that is captured and presented as a first-class deliverable provides a fertile collection of organization-wide data to support this type of strategic activity.

12.3.2 Reducing the Cost of Failure

As we mentioned in Chapter 0, the record of complex system development success, particularly where large software components are involved, is disheartening. However, an additional benefit of applying the ICSM across multiple projects is the flexibility and agility provided by the off-ramps on individual projects provided in the Commitment Reviews. Not only can this keep your organization from throwing away good money on a death march project—or, even worse, on a successful project that has missed its market window—but it can also keep you out of the chaos study statistics and (one hopes) improve rather than interrupt your career.

There is also an impact on personnel. The honest evaluation of project risk provides a sense of relief to the developers, who know the project is doomed and would much rather be working on something that provides value to the organization or the community. Additional benefits of ICSM to the personnel include the opportunities to cross-train when implementing the evolutionary three-level model, or to join a successful project in an increment and experience the process. ICSM can thus build more realistic resource allocation estimates, support human capital development through breadth of experience, and provide for development of a more flexible staff with broader experience when economic or technical droughts occur.

References

[1] Basili, V. R., & Weiss, D. M. "A Methodology for Collecting Valid Software Engineering Data." *IEEE Transactions on Software Engineering*. 1984;SE-10(6): 728–738.

[2] Basili, V. R. "The Experience Factory and Its Relationship to Other Improvement Paradigms." In *Proceedings of the Fourth European Software Engineering Conference (ESEC)*, Garmisch-Partenkirchen, Germany, 1993. The *Proceedings* appeared as "Lecture Notes" in *Computer Science* 717.

[3] Basili, V., Caldiera, G., McGarry, F., Pajerski, R., Page, G., & Waligora, S. "The Software Engineering Laboratory: An Operational Software Experience Factory." In *Proceedings of the Fourteenth International Conference on Software Engineering*, May 1992.

[4] Boehm, B., Port, D., Jain, A., & Basili, V. "Achieving CMMI Level 5 Improvements with MBASE and the CeBASE Method." *CrossTalk*. Hill Air Force Base, Utah: U.S. Air Force Software Technology Support Center, May 2002: 9–16.

[5] Basili, V. R., Lindvall, M., Regardie, M., Seaman, C., Heidrich, J., Munch, J., Rombach, H. D., & Trendowicz, A. "Linking Software Development and Business Strategy through Measurement." *IEEE Computer*. 2010;43(4):57–65.

[6] Basili, V. R., et al. *Aligning Organizations through Measurement: The GQM + Strategies Approach*. Elsevier, in preparation.

13

Evidence-Based Life-Cycle Management

"Trust, but verify."

—Russian proverb, adopted by Ronald Reagan

The fourth principle of the ICSM requires evidence-based management. Evidence-based life-cycle management is an extension of product life-cycle management that emphasizes the use of analysis and models to produce evidence that the system architecture and design describe a feasible system. Evidence like this is generally desired, but rarely produced. The primary reason for its absence is simple: it is not identified as a project deliverable or first-class documentation. Developing products and systems without proven solutions frequently leads to late and over-budget projects.

Based on our experience in developing and using evidence across a variety of large and small projects, this chapter describes a process for feasibility evidence evaluation at major milestones, establishes a Feasibility Evidence Description (FED), and provides a risk-based process for ensuring that evidence requirements are developed within agile and lean documentation value principles.

13.1 Motivation and Context

Chapter 4 provided case studies of representative results when projects do and don't implement evidence- and risk-based decision making, providing a rationale for *why* this step is success-critical. It also discussed *what* feasibility evidence is and isn't, and provided top-level guidance on *how much* evidence is enough. But it touched only lightly on *how* this type of decision making is done and managed, *who* was responsible for producing it and reviewing it, and *when* this step would be done.

This chapter defines a process by which management reviews not only the system definition and developed evidence, but also the results of independent experts' evaluation of the evidence and developers' response to the evaluation comments. As any shortfall in evidence is an uncertainty or probability of loss, the response should include a risk management plan for reducing either the probability or the impact of any loss, or both. It then provides a process framework by which system definers can cost-effectively develop feasibility evidence with respect to satisfying the success-critical stakeholders' value propositions.

The strength of the evidence and the risk management plans will provide the stakeholders with a much better basis for deciding whether to proceed into the next phase or to take one of the other three risk-driven options. Evidence-based approaches have a deep pedigree; ours draws on two premier evidence-based methods developed in the 1980s: the AT&T Architecture Review Board [1,2] and the TRW Ada Process Model used in the successful CCPDS-R project [3] described in Chapter 4 and generalized in "Anchoring the Software Process [4]."

Many projects begin with good intentions for providing feasibility evidence, but fail to maintain sufficient emphasis on this step when faced with hardships. For example, when budgets are tight and when traditional contract provisions relegate feasibility evidence to optional appendices (with no reward for completion and no penalty for omission), it is not surprising the evidence-gathering work somehow gets "overlooked" in the daily grind.*

Having feasibility evidence listed on the contract as a first-class deliverable means customers and developers must ensure feasibility evidence is consistently planned for, estimated, budgeted for, scheduled, developed, tracked, and reviewed. Success in developing and using such an approach on a very large project, as well as many smaller ones, has shown its value [5,6].

13.2 Commitment Review Process Overview

To understand the type and level of evidence needed for successful systems development, it is useful to review how that evidence is used. Figure 13-1 illustrates the activities performed when preparing for a commitment review, during the review, and after the review has been completed. The entry criteria include ensuring that the feasibility evidence preparation has been successfully tracking its earned value milestones. The inputs include preparing domain extensions to the core review questions, identifying committed expert reviewers for each of the review questions, and familiarizing them with the review process.

The review meeting will include not only the developer systems engineers and expert reviewers, but also the stakeholder upper-management decision makers, who will need some context setting before the developer responses to reviewer issues are discussed. The review exit criteria and tasks include key stakeholder concurrence on the way forward and commitment to support the next phase, as well as action plans and risk mitigation plans for the issues identified.

---

*Of course, the systems engineering function is the first to be impacted by a conspiracy-of-optimism budget, management "redistribution of resources," or the customer's reconsideration.

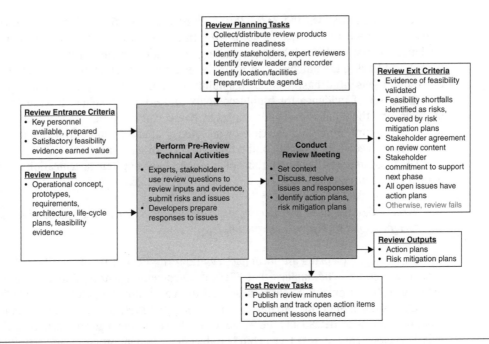

FIGURE 13-1 Overview of Commitment Review Process

13.3 Feasibility Evidence Description Development Process

The FED contains evidence provided by the developer and validated by independent experts that if the system is built to the specified architecture, it will do the following:

- Satisfy the requirements: capabilities, interfaces, levels of service, project constraints, and evolution directions
- Support the operational concept
- Be buildable within the budgets and schedules in the plan
- Generate a viable return on investment
- Generate satisfactory outcomes for all of the success-critical stakeholders
- Resolve all major risks by treating shortfalls in evidence as risks and covering them through risk management plans
- Serve as basis for stakeholders' commitment to proceed

Such evidence may come from prototypes, models and simulations, benchmarks, safety cases, or other forms of analysis, or, where possible, by simply pointing to the results from equally or more complex systems that the proposed team has developed.

FED content follows the *Meta-Principle of Balance: Balancing the risk of doing too little and the risk of doing too much*, by having the content of the evidence be risk balanced between having too little evidence (often the case today) and having too much evidence (analysis paralysis). Thus, the FED includes a minimum-essential base case of feasibility evidence for simple systems, and a detailed set of evidence for highly complex and critical systems. Intermediate systems, and the simpler parts of complex systems, can use a risk-based approach for "tailoring up" from the base case by selectively applying appropriate elements of evidence needed for complex and critical projects or elements.

The most important characteristic of evidence-based system specifications and plans is quite simple:

If the evidence does not accompany the specifications and plans, the specifications and plans are incomplete.

Since the designs or plans are incomplete without the FED, it becomes a first-class project deliverable. This implies that FED's development is managed and its value determined based on the potential risk exposure costs, not the perceived available budget. Besides monitoring progress on developing the system, the project needs to monitor progress on developing the feasibility evidence, taking corrective action if evidence development progress lags behind product development progress, and adapting the feasibility evidence work to changes in project objectives and plans. If evidence generation will be complex, it is generally a good idea to perform pilot assessments.

This does not mean that the project needs to spend large amounts of effort in documenting evidence of the feasibility of a simple system. The appropriate level of detail for evidence is based on the perceived risks and criticality of the system to be developed. This is *not* a "one size fits all" process, but rather a framework to help developers and stakeholders determine the appropriate level of analysis and evaluation. As with any development artifact, such as specifications and plans, evidence can be appropriately reused. If a more complex system than the one being reviewed has been successfully developed by the same team, a pointer to the previous project's evidence and results will be sufficient.

Table 13-1 outlines a process that can be used for developing realistic, risk-driven feasibility evidence requirements [7]. The process clearly depends on having defined the appropriate work products and activities for the phase (Step A). As part of the engineering work, high-priority feasibility assurance issues are identified that are critical to the success of the system development program (Step B). These are the issues for which options are explored, and potentially viable options further investigated (Step C). We have used letters rather than numbers to show clearly that these and later steps are not sequential, but rather are performed concurrently. An example is provided in Section 13.5.

This process follows a more efficient method for tailoring the evidence requirements. Such tailoring is traditionally performed by "tailoring down"—that is, by removing individual pieces of extensive guidance that were created for the riskiest,

TABLE 13-1 Steps for Defining Evidence Requirements

Step	Description	Examples/Detail
A	Develop phase work products/ artifacts	Understand the goals of the next phase, and identify which artifacts or activities are expected. For a Development Commitment Review (DCR), this would include the system's operational concept, prototypes, requirements, architecture, life-cycle plans, and associated assumptions.
B	Determine most critical feasibility assurance issues	In which artifacts or activities will lack of feasibility evidence be program-critical? Key performance requirements, significant infrastructure capabilities, and the degree of efficiency gained from legacy or reuse components are examples of areas often program-critical. The Evidence Evaluation Framework can also provide insight into critical areas.
C	Evaluate feasibility assessment options	How can evidence be established? Cost-effectiveness of evidence gathering options; necessary tool, data, scenario availability.
D	Select options, develop feasibility collection and assessment plans or mechanisms	The list of options in step C is the obvious place to start.
E	Prepare FED assessment plans and earned value or other milestones	The plans include the enablers in step G.
F	Begin monitoring progress with respect to plans	Also monitor changes to the project, technology, and objectives, and adapt plans.
G	Prepare evidence-generation enablers	Assessment criteria; parametric models, parameter values, bases of estimate; COTS assessment criteria and plans; benchmarking candidates, test cases; prototypes/simulations, evaluation plans, subjects, and scenarios; instrumentation, data analysis capabilities.
H	Perform pilot assessments; evaluate and iterate plans and enablers	Short bottom-line summaries and pointers to evidence files are generally sufficient; perform interim and final evaluations using the Evidence Evaluation Framework.
I	Assess readiness for Commitment Review	Shortfalls identified as risks and covered by risk mitigation plans; proceed to Commitment Review if ready.
J	Hold Commitment Review when ready; adjust plans based on review outcomes	See Commitment Review process overview.

Note: "Steps" are denoted by letters rather than numbers to indicate that many are done concurrently.

most complex, worst-case scenario system imaginable by the powers that be. Unfortunately, this creates a situation where the project manager's path of least resistance (and least personal risk) is to forgo tailoring completely and include everything possible. Flying in the face of lean and agile principles, this approach usually wastes effort on unneeded non-value-adding items and creates a huge burden on the project (except in the rare cases where the project *is* the riskiest, most complex, worst-case scenario system imaginable). The FED starts with the simplest version, adding depth as risk and context suggest: if it's risky to exclude something, put it in; if it's not risky to exclude something, leave it out. This establishes a sufficient level of guidance for any system imaginable.

Table 13-2 provides guidance to help determine whether a project is simple (S), complex (C), or intermediate (I; often with simple and/or complex parts). Because the FED content is based on this determination, it is a required part of the documentation and supported by general project information, which can be "tailored up" for more complex projects (Figure 13-2). The information might be expanded with less-simple projects for many reasons. For example, if different

TABLE 13-2 Criteria for Simple, Intermediate, and Complex (Parts of) Projects

Criterion	Size	Complexity	Criticality	Capability
Criterion content	Number of personnel	Novelty; technical risk; stakeholder conflicts; external constraints	Loss due to defects	Personnel; organization: relative to complexity and criticality
Simple level	1–10	Low	Comfort; discretionary funds	High to very high
Intermediate level	10–100	Mixed	Serious funds; quality of life factors	Mixed
Complex level	More than 100	All high to very high	Essential funds; loss of human life	Low

Project Name: _____

Project Primary Objective: _____

Success-Critical Stakeholders: _____

_____

(Includes Role, Organization, Authorized Representatives and Contact Info for each stakeholder)

Life-Cycle Process: ☐ Agile ☐ Architected Agile ☐ IC Spiral ☐ RUP ☐ Vee ☐ Other _____

Decision Milestone: _____

Key FED Dates:

    Review Version Complete _____

    Review Complete _____

    Decision Meeting and Outcome Decided _____

FIGURE 13-2 FED General Information for Simple Projects

parts have different success-critical stakeholders and schedules, they may require contract information, formatting instructions, version indicators, tables of contents, lists of figures and tables, and pointers to subsidiary information such as applicable policies, formal expert review reports, risk mitigation plans, or other action items.

13.4 Evaluation Framework for the FED

The FED and its review by independent experts form the basis for informed risk-based commitment decision making by the project's success-critical stakeholders. They are organized to apply to all of a project's commitment milestones. The specific FED content depends on the project or system under development and will vary from milestone to milestone, with a risk-driven level of detail. As described in Table 13-1, the ICSM approaches developing life-cycle guidance for FED creators through a "tailoring up" framework and process.

ICSM contains an Evidence Evaluation Framework that is summarized in Table 13-3. It is organized into a hierarchy of Goals, Critical Success Factors (CSFs), and Questions. The hierarchy of review questions enables projects to define higher or lower *Impact* and *Evidence of Feasibility* levels for each Question, enabling the

TABLE 13-3 Evaluation Framework Goals and Critical Success Factors

Goal 1: Concurrent definition of system requirements and solutions
CSF 1.1 Understanding of stakeholder needs: capabilities, operational concept, key performance parameters, enterprise fit (legacy)
CSF 1.2 Concurrent exploration of solution opportunities; analysis of alternatives (AoA) for cost-effectiveness and risk (measures of effectiveness)
CSF 1.3 System scoping and requirements definition (external interfaces; memoranda of agreement [MoA])
CSF 1.4 Prioritization of requirements and allocation to increments
Goal 2: System life-cycle organization, planning, and staffing
CSF 2.1 Establishment of stakeholder life-cycle responsibilities, authorities, and accountabilities (RAAs) (for system definition and system development)
CSF 2.2 Establishment of integrated product team (IPT) RAAs, cross-IPT coordination needs
CSF 2.3 Establishment of necessary plans and resources for meeting objectives
CSF 2.4 Establishment of appropriate source selection, contracting, and incentive structures
CSF 2.5 Establishment of necessary personnel competencies
Goal 3: Technology maturing, architecting
CSF 3.1 COTS/non-development item (NDI)/services evaluation, selection, validation for maturity and compatibility

(Continues)

TABLE 13-3 Evaluation Framework Goals and Critical Success Factors (*Continued*)

CSF 3.2 Life-cycle architecture definition and validation
CSF 3.3 Use of prototypes, exercises, models, and simulations to determine technological solution maturity
CSF 3.4 Validated system engineering, development, manufacturing, operations, and maintenance budgets and schedules
Goal 4: Evidence-based progress monitoring and commitment reviews
CSF 4.1 Monitoring of system definition, development, and testing progress versus plans
CSF 4.2 Monitoring of feasibility evidence development progress versus plans
CSF 4.3 Monitoring, assessment, and replanning for changes in needs, opportunities, and resources
CSF 4.4 Use of milestone reviews to ensure stakeholder commitment to proceed?

assessment of its likely project risk. Thus, assigning a Little or No Impact level to Questions can cause unimportant aspects to be dropped. This framework is a very useful tool to help tailor the feasibility evidence. The complete set of Goals, CSFs, and Questions can be found in Appendix A.

The Evaluation Framework was developed as part of a U.S. Department of Defense (DoD) Systems Engineering Research Center (SERC) research project to develop an evidence-based systems engineering risk assessment instrument for application to DoD systems [8]. Nevertheless, it can be helpful even when a system is simple or of intermediate complexity.

An Excel-based tool is available on the ICSM website that supports this process through pull-down menus and automated calculations. The Impact levels are quantitative ranges of likely extra project cost to remedy each aspect's shortfall (0–2%; 2–20%; 20–40%; 40–100%), and the Evidence of Feasibility levels are quantitative levels of probability of occurrence of the aspect deficiency (0–0.02; 0.02–0.2; 0.2–0.4; 0.4–1.0). These levels enable the tool to determine a quantitative project risk exposure level for each aspect.

The framework can also be used as a measure of readiness for a Commitment Review or to determine progress within any particular phase. By conducting an evaluation, it becomes possible to determine which specific risks have been addressed with feasibility evidence, and where more work is necessary.

13.5 Example of Use

Quantitative Methods, Inc. (QMI), is a leader in developing environmental impact report (EIR) generator packages for use by systems developers and government agencies. QMI has successfully developed EIR generators for the states of California, Colorado, Florida, Maine, Massachusetts, Oregon, Texas, and Washington. QMI has recently been awarded a contract for developing an EIR generation package for the state of Georgia, which has put the use of the FED deliverable into the contract. QMI and State of Georgia personnel are collaboratively tailoring the FED contents to the project.

QMI has provided evidence that its EIR generator results for California, Florida, and Texas were more comprehensive than those needed for Georgia, except for Georgia's request to include some recent advanced environmental pollution analysis algorithms for the Atlanta metropolitan area. The parties have agreed that QMI needs to include only evidence of successful definition and development of these algorithms. The contract initially identified point-solution goals for the key performance parameters (KPPs) of analysis throughput, response time, and accuracy. However, due to the uncertainties in the algorithms' performance against complex operational scenarios, the contract was modified to identify ranges of acceptable and desired KPP values.

The resulting tailoring activity enabled the parties to identify not only the evidence needs, but also the key technical activities and data needs involved in this aspect of the project. For CSF 1.1 of the Evidence Evaluation Framework, the definition of KPP ranges has taken care of Question (a), but Question (c) on verification of feasibility via modeling and simulation is tailored in. To address CSF 1.2 on Analysis of Alternatives, QMI plans to perform benchmark tests of algorithm performance on several high-performance-computing platforms to provide evidence of achievable throughput, response time, and accuracy vs cost. These activities will take care of Question 1.2 (a), and the resulting evidence will be reviewed by tailoring in Question 1.2 (d).

These preparations for the assessment and selection of alternative solutions are sufficient to address the questions in CSF 1.3 on system scoping, but an additional concern arises with respect to Question 1.4 (b), which covers the ability of the solutions to scale up to future growth (Table 13-4). A proposed future growth option for the Atlanta metropolitan area is to expand the environmental monitoring systems via a smart sensor network with more than 1000 times as many sensors. It is unclear whether any of the currently available solutions could scale up by a factor of 1000, but it is also unclear how rapidly the future sensor network solution technology will scale up to such levels. The issue is addressed by tailoring in Question 1.4 (b), and identifying this issue as a potential risk to be analyzed by an integrated product team (IPT) of relevant experts, and assessed at the project's Development Commitment Review (DCR).

The tailoring of Question 1.4 (b) covers Question 2.1 (b) with respect to pre-DCR plans and Question 2.2 (a) with respect to the use of IPTs (Table 13-5). Questions 2.2 (b) and (c) are tailored in to review evidence that the IPTs are appropriately staffed with experts, and that they do not over-optimize on scalability at the expense of other KPPs. Question 2.5 (d) could be added, but it is redundant in this case and is not necessary.

The remainder of the tailoring-in activities are straightforward. With respect to CSF 3.1 on COTS evaluation and selection, tailoring in a focus on evaluating COTS products for future scalability would be worthwhile. If solution scalability is identified at the DCR as a future risk, Question 4.1 (d) on risk management could be tailored in, and followed up by Question 4.3 (c) on preparation for milestone risk reviews (Table 13-6).

TABLE 13-4 Evidence Evaluation for QMI Example Goal 1

CSF 1.1 Understanding of stakeholder needs: capabilities, operational concept, key performance parameters, enterprise fit (legacy)	
(a) At the FCR, have the key performance parameters (KPPs) been identified in clear, comprehensive, concise terms that are understandable to the users of the system?	Out: handled by KPP definition
(c) Has the ability of the system to meet mission-effectiveness goals been verified through the use of modeling and simulation?	In
CSF 1.2 Concurrent exploration of solution opportunities; analysis of alternatives for cost-effectiveness and risk (measures of effectiveness)	
(a) Have at least two alternative approaches been explored and evaluated?	Perform benchmark tests of algorithm performance
(d) Have the claimed quality of service guarantees been validated?	Results of benchmark tests of algorithm performance
CSF 1.3 System scoping and requirements definition (external interfaces; memoranda of agreement [MoA])	
(a) Have external interface complexities been identified and addressed via MoA or their equivalent? Is there a plan to mitigate their risks?	Handled by 1.2 (d)
(b) At the DCR, are the major system-level requirements (including all KPPs) defined sufficiently to provide a stable basis for the development through initial operational capability (IOC)?	Handled by 1.2 (d)
(c) By the FCR, is there a plan to have information exchange protocols established for the whole system and its segments by the DCR?	Handled by 1.2 (d)
(d) Have the key stakeholders agreed on the system boundary and assumptions about its environment?	Handled by 1.2 (d)
(e) At the DCR, do the requirements and proposed solutions take into account likely future mission growth over the program life cycle?	In: potential risk to be analyzed by an IPT of relevant experts, and assessed at DCR

TABLE 13-5 Evidence Evaluation for QMI Example Goal 2

CSF 2.1 Establishment of stakeholder life-cycle responsibilities, authorities, and accountabilities (RAAs) (for system definition and system development)	
(b) At the FCR, are there validated plans, budgets, and schedules defining how the pre-DCR activity will be done, and by whom?	See Question 1.4 (b)
CSF 2.2 Establishment of integrated product team (IPT) RAAs, cross-IPT coordination needs	
(b) Are the IPTs staffed by highly qualified personnel?	Tailored to ensure IPT expertise
(c) For IPTs addressing strongly coupled objectives, are there super-IPTs for resolving conflicts among the objectives?	Tailored to ensure broad view and avoid over-optimization

TABLE 13-6 Evidence Evaluation for QMI Example Goals 3 and 4

CSF 3.1 COTS/Non-development item (NDI)/services evaluation, selection, validation for maturity and compatibility	
(a) Have COTS/NDI/services opportunities been evaluated prior to baselining requirements?	Focus on scalability
(b) Have COTS/NDI/services scalability, compatibility, quality of service, and life-cycle support risks been thoroughly addressed?	Focus on scalability
(c) Has a COTS/NDI/services life-cycle refresh strategy been developed and validated?	Focus on scalability
CSF 4.1 Monitoring of system definition, development, and testing progress versus plans	
(c) Is the project adequately identifying and managing its risks?	If scalability is risk at DCR
CSF 4.4 Use of milestone reviews to ensure stakeholder commitment to proceed?	
(d) Are developer responses to identified risks prepared prior to review events?	Follow up to 4.1

Having the FED as a first-class citizen provides an alternative to the current situation where the path of least resistance is a set of deliverables in which evidence preparation and review are optional, and which often leads to uninformed milestone decisions and subsequent project crises. A document tailored up from a simple version avoids this problem. Treating evidence as a first-class deliverable implies that the evidence to be generated needs to be assessed for useful value, planned for, tracked with respect to plans, reviewed by independent experts, and used as a basis for milestone decisions. The case study shows that the process of tailoring is about more than efficiency—it also enables the project stakeholders to collaborate, understand, and plan for key issues in achieving success.

13.6 Applicability Outside ICSM

If desired, this tailoring up framework can be used outside the ICSM. While the CSFs and Questions often refer to ICSM decision milestones, they can be mapped fairly straightforwardly onto other domain terms. For example, they correspond fairly closely to the U.S. Department of Defense (DoD) Milestones A and B [9]; to the completion of the Exploratory and Concept stages of ISO/IEC 15288 [10] on Systems Engineering Processes; and to the concurrent-engineering version of the Vee model [11]. They also correspond to the Life Cycle Objectives and Life Cycle Architecture milestones for the Rational Unified Process [12] and to the Discovery and Architecture milestones of the AT&T Architecture Review Board [13] process.

References

[1] AT&T. *Best Current Practices: Software Architecture Validation*. Lucent/AT&T, 1993.

[2] Maranzano, J., et al. "Architecture Reviews: Practice and Experience." *IEEE Software*. 2005;22(2):34–43.

[3] Royce, W. *Software Project Management: A Unified Framework*. Reading, MA: Addison-Wesley Professional, 1998.

[4] Boehm, B., "Anchoring the Software Process." *IEEE Software*. 1996;13(4):73–82.

[5] Blanchette, Stephen Jr., Crosson, Steven, & Boehm, Barry. *Evaluating the Software Design of a Complex System of Systems* (CMU/SEI-2009-TR-023). Software Engineering Institute, Carnegie Mellon University, 2010.

[6] Crosson, S., & Boehm, B. "Adjusting Software Life Cycle Anchorpoints: Lessons Learned in a System of Systems Context." *Proceedings of the Systems and Software Technology Conference*. Salt Lake City, UT, April 20–23, 2009.

[7] Boehm, B., & Lane, J. A. "Evidence-Based Software Processes." *New Modeling Concepts for Today's Software Processes Lecture Notes in Computer Science*. 2010;6195:62–73.

[8] Boehm, B., et al. *Early Identification of SE-Related Program Risks*. Tech Report USC-CSSE-009-518. SERC, September 30, 2009.

[9] Interim DoD Instruction 5000.02, "Operation of the Defense Acquisition System." November 25, 2013. http://www.dtic.mil/whs/directives/corres/pdf/500002_interim.pdf.

[10] International Standardisation Organization/International Electrotechnical Commissions/Institute for Electrical and Electronics Engineers. ISO/IEC/IEEE 15288:2008.

[11] Forsberg, K., Mooz, H., & Cotterman, H. *Visualizing Project Management*, 3rd ed. New York, NY: John Wiley & Sons, 2005.

[12] Kruchten, P. *The Rational Unified Process: An Introduction*, 3rd ed. Boston, MA: Addison-Wesley Professional, 2003.

[13] AT&T, op. cit.

14

Cost and Schedule Evidence Development

Prediction is difficult, especially about the future.

—Niels Bohr

The ICSM decision milestones require evidence that the desired capabilities can be developed within the budget and schedules available or planned. This is not an easy task, and evidence must be more than an educated guess or a politically acceptable wink and a nod. Estimation is a broad and deep subject, and there are myriad ways to approach it. In this chapter we provide some fundamental guidance on the type of estimation you might need in various instances, and on strategies for dealing with the inevitable estimation uncertainties.

The two Cones of Uncertainty discussed in Chapter 2 and reproduced as Figure 14-1 illustrate the challenges of providing accurate evidence of a project's ability to complete within its given budgets and schedules—or even on deciding what the given budgets and schedules should be.

The width of system, hardware, or software cones will vary as a function of Shenhar and Dvir's diamond of system complexity, technology, pace, and the degree of novelty [1].

Dimensions of Shenhar and Dvir (2007) Diamond Model

- **Complexity:** Measures the intricacy of the product, the task, and the project organization. There are three associated values: assembly, system, and array.

- **Technology:** Measures technological uncertainties and the amount of/level to which new technology is required. There are four associated values: low-tech, medium-tech, high-tech, and super-high-tech.

- **Novelty:** Measures the uncertainty of the product's goal and the clarity and understanding of requirements by customers, users, and other stakeholders. There are three associated values: derivative, platform, and breakthrough.   ← uncertainty of products goal and understanding ofreqs.

- **Pace:** Measures the program schedule based on the urgency of the project. It has four associated values: regular, fast/competitive, time-critical, and blitz.   ← urgency of project

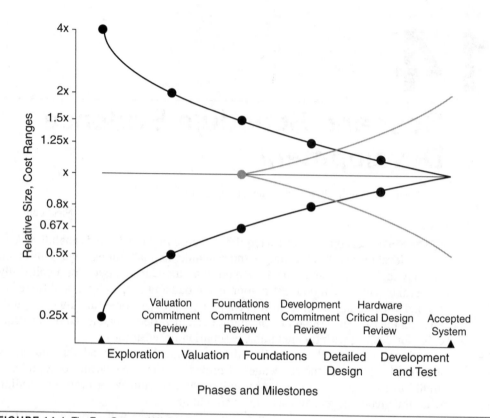

FIGURE 14-1 The Two Cones of Uncertainty

Using information on the size and percentage of functionality of prototypes, or on the actual versus estimated degree of reuse or requirements volatility, can often reduce the width of the first Cone of Uncertainty [2]. To prevent a reasonable estimate from getting rapidly worse due to the second Cone of Uncertainty, you need to be sure that the estimate is revised as proposed changes are evaluated and adopted.

Clearly, cost and schedule evidence development activities involve significant uncertainties and risks, making the guidance in Chapter 15 particularly relevant. Some key implications of Chapter 15 for cost and schedule evidence development are listed here:

- The uncertainties and risks favor the use of evolutionary over single-step development.

- The uncertainties and risks indicate that multiple methods of cost and schedule estimation should be used to help calibrate the degrees of uncertainty. A summary of the primary methods of cost and schedule estimation is provided in this chapter.

- Costs and schedules should be expressed as much as possible in terms of uncertainty ranges versus single numbers. Given that organizational plans require specific budgets and delivery dates, these should include a risk reserve proportional to the degree of uncertainty.

- Buying information via prototyping, analysis, expert judgment, or some other means to identify and reduce major sources of risk should be pursued.

- Results of the agile change evaluation team's triage process described in Chapter 2 should be used to reflect the impact of the changes on cost and schedule estimates and uncertainty ranges.

- Where fixed budgets and schedules are necessary and become the independent variables, system functionality should become a dependent variable. This can be done by prioritizing the system features and dropping or adding borderline-priority features to meet the fixed budget or schedule. Ways to do this are described later in this chapter.

- Organizations should accumulate experience bases to help improve estimation models and methods, as well as identify the major sources of cost and schedule uncertainty and risk for future projects.

14.1 A Review of Primary Methods for Cost and Schedule Estimation

The cardinal rules of all estimation efforts are to use several methods for each estimate, to rationalize any significant differences through an affordability case, and to always provide a range of estimates commensurate with the accuracy (not the precision) of your information. Indicating there is not enough information for an estimate and that more research is necessary is much less dangerous than an off-the-cuff guess—and it will never come back to haunt you at a later review or delivery.

As stated earlier, multiple methods of cost and schedule estimation are available. Table 14-1 summarizes the major strengths and weaknesses of the various techniques.

Algorithmic models are based on cost estimating relationship (CER) or schedule estimating relationship (SER) algorithms. These estimate a system's definition, development, or evolution cost or schedule as functions of cost- or schedule-driver parameters, whose values are determined by some combination of statistical analysis and expert judgment. A fairly general model, COSYSMO [3], is available for system engineering cost estimation. For physical system development and evolution cost estimation, many organizations or communities have specialized domain-specific

TABLE 14-1 Estimation Method Comparison

Method	Strengths	Weaknesses
Algorithmic model	Objective, repeatable, analyzable formula Efficient, good for sensitivity analysis Objectively calibrated to experience	Subjective inputs Assessment of exceptional circumstances Calibrated to past not future
Expert judgment	Assessment of representativeness, interactions, exceptional circumstances	No better than participants Biases, incomplete recall
Analogy	Based on representative experience	Representativeness of experience
Top-down	System-level focus Efficient	Less detailed basis Less stable
Bottom-up	More detailed basis More stable Fosters individual commitment	May overlook system-level costs Requires more effort, less efficient
Unit cost	Cost of purchased or leased facilities, equipment, or supplies	Does not include costing of activity-based services
Activity-based	Cost of labor	Does not include costing of unit-priced services
Price-to-win	Often gets the contract	Generally produces large overruns

cost estimation models, along with two fairly general commercial models, TruePlanning [4] and SEER-H [5]. Fairly general software definition, development, and evolution cost and schedule estimation models include COCOMO II [6], SEER-SEM [7], SLIM [8], and True Planning-Software [9]. In addition, there are cost models for some of the other ICSM common cases, such as extensions to COSYSMO for SoS engineering and complex systems engineering [10] and the COCOTS [11] model to estimate the effort associated with tailoring, customizing, and integrating COTS products.

Expert judgment is often attempted by cost specialists who may not understand the technical area or by technical experts who may not understand the cost area. This approach is risky; it is better to include representatives of both specialties in making expert-judgment estimates. Various group-consensus techniques can be used to converge on estimates; the most prevalent are the Wideband Delphi method [12] and Planning Poker [13,14], Both involve group members simultaneously providing their initial estimate followed by discussion of why some estimates were higher or lower, followed by re-estimating, and iterating the process until a satisfactory degree of convergence is reached.

Algorithmic models and expert judgment methods complement each other well. The strengths of expert judgment in assessment of new or exceptional circumstances complement the weaknesses of algorithmic models in those areas, and the strengths of algorithmic models in objectivity and efficiency complement the weaknesses of expert judgment in those areas. Thus it is generally a good idea to use both and to investigate situations where their estimates significantly diverge.

Analogy methods involve reasoning by comparison to similar completed projects. Agile methods frequently use "yesterday's weather" (based on the fact that about 70% of the time, today's weather can be predicted to be the same as yesterday's) to estimate effort on a similar project. Often, the estimate will be adjusted to reflect known differences from the previous project, such as adding costs for new types of functionality or subtracting costs due to learning curve or reuse effects. The main strength of the methods is that they are based on actual representative project costs. The main weakness may be that the previous project was in the same domain and had similar functionality, but may have been unrepresentative in other respects, such as needing to work on a different underlying platform or to experience higher levels of change traffic. A version of the COCOMO II model called Agile COCOMO II provides a way to adjust the analogy estimate by determining which of its 23 parameters will be changing and by how much, enabling a more accurate estimate to be made with one or two parameters rather than all 23 [15].

Analogy methods are a particular special case of *top-down estimating*, which can also include reasoning from other general information such as productivity rates for projects in given domains. The overall cost is then allocated to project functions based on work breakdown structure percentages for projects in the domain. Again, these have the strength of being based on complete projects, but have the potential weakness of neglecting special features of the new project, such as perhaps its need to operate as a node in a Net-centric system of systems.

Bottom-up estimating is the complement of top-down estimating, in which component estimates are made by the responsible performers, and then summed up into a full-system cost estimate. Its strengths complement the weaknesses of top-down estimating, such as building in performers' commitment to fulfill their estimates and being based on detailed knowledge of the job to be done. Its weaknesses, such as focusing on component costs and potentially missing system-wide costs such as system integration, configuration management, and project management, are complemented by the strengths of top-down estimating.

Again, this complementary nature suggests that applying multiple estimation methods will be stronger than just using one method. A good approach is to pick one or more options from top-down estimating, analogy, and expert judgment, and then one or more options from bottom-up estimating and a choice of algorithmic models.

Unit cost approaches determine the cost of one unit of what is being acquired (cellphones, MedFRS boxes, first-aid kits, ambulances, gallons of gasoline) and multiply the unit cost by the number of units acquired. Often, there will be learning curve effects or volume discounts providing economies of scale. For software, however, acquiring several equal-size incremental capabilities generally will experience diseconomies of scale, as the learning curve effects will be dominated by the costs of evolving the earlier increments, in what is called the incremental development productivity decline [16].

Some services are priced as *units*, such as monthly charges for Internet services or medical insurance, for which the unit cost approach works well. However, other services are priced based on activity level, such as legal or training services.

These are better addressed by activity-based costing, which is primarily used to estimate labor costs. Such efforts generally involve estimating how many people of each labor grade will be involved and for how long a time (e.g., for people preparing the training material, people providing the training, and people taking the training), multiplying the number of people in each labor grade by their number of hours involved times their labor rate, and adding up the results.

In competitive bidding situations, bidders will often succumb to the temptation to submit cost proposals based not on algorithmic models, expert judgment, analogy, or activity levels, but rather on marketing intelligence about the *price to win*. As shown in Figure 1-2 in Chapter 1, this creates a win-lose situation for the "winning" bidder, who will either lose by having to pay for overrunning the contract budget, or will need to collude with the customer to deliver a poor-quality project that the losing user will reject, or will need to collude with the user on a cost-plus contract to add features and costs until the customer loses by running out of funds. Either way, the win-lose situation will turn into a lose-lose situation. The whole purpose of evidence-based decision making is to avoid such outcomes, by requiring bidders to provide an objective, independently validated basis for estimating their proposed cost that can be used to reject bids having no evidence of feasibility.

One benefit of the iterative approach to development activities is that as functions or features are developed, the development experience can be incorporated into the process and can continuously improve the estimation. Techniques that track measures—such as "yesterday's weather," where one assumes that the productivity in terms of similar features will generally hold from day to day given the same staff level and difficulty of the tasks—can support tuning the estimates on a regular basis. Metrics from flow-based scheduling systems such as Kanban can provide statistically based lead times for task accomplishment. The key point is that good measurement programs can significantly improve estimation, and that all models used should be calibrated using the history of similar tasks performed by the development team—or some surrogate such as a benchmark or industry standard.

14.2 Estimations and the ICSM

The ICSM employs two significant techniques to mitigate risk and to support cost and schedule estimation in an environment of uncertainty. First, it requires that there be some effort to approach the task at hand from a systems perspective in the exploration and valuation phases. This provides an opportunity to prioritize the requirements and establish minimum feasible increments. It also promotes architecture flexibility to largely isolate areas where there are "known unknowns" to deal with—such as evolving interfaces, still-maturing technology, or organizational instability.

The second technique is incremental development, with the concept of timeboxing or schedule as independent variable (SAIV). This recognizes that if the development schedule is subject to the Cone of Uncertainty but the delivery date is fixed, the schedule is the project's independent variable; thus the delivered functionality must

functionally altered based on schedule.
Dependent on schedule

become a dependent variable that is adjusted to meet the schedule. This has been the most successful approach for dealing with uncertainty in software, and it has been effectively applied in hardware system development as well (although hardware systems often have fixed lower limits: one cannot deliver an aircraft without flight controls or landing gear). By limiting the scope (batch size, as the lean experts would say) of the development work to relatively short intervals, there is a nearly continuous opportunity to refine estimates and to adapt to changing environments.

The SAIV process model and its counterpart cost as independent variable (CAIV) process model are also applicable where there are severe constraints, such as mandates not to exceed budgets and drop dead delivery dates. The following section summarizes the SAIV/CAIV process model; further discussion and a case study are provided elsewhere [17] and on the book's website.

14.2.1 The SAIV Process Model

The key to successful SAIV practice is to strategically plan through all life-cycle areas to meet a delivery date. The ICSM provides the process guide for this planning. SAIV is defined as the following six process elements:

1. Manage expectations by establishing a stakeholders' shared vision of achievable objectives, including at least a minimum-essential core capability within the available schedule.
2. Prioritize system features.
3. Estimate subsets of features that can be developed with high confidence within the available schedule.
4. Establish a coherent set of core capabilities with borderline features to be added if possible, and a software/system architecture to easily accommodate adding or dropping borderline features.
5. Plan development increments, including a high-confidence core capability and next-priority subsets.
6. Execute development plans with careful change and progress monitoring and control processes. Changes requesting additional capabilities must identify which lower-priority capabilities should be dropped to maintain schedule.

The process model for CAIV is essentially the same except for the definition of the operative boundary. For SAIV projects, this is cumulative calendar time. For CAIV projects, the cumulative cost is used.

14.2.2 Estimating Size

Usually, the largest determinant of cost and schedule is the size of the system to be developed. In general, "larger" means "more expensive" and "longer," with some exceptions at the low end such as with nanomanufacturing. As seen from the data in Figure 14-2, both cost and size usually show equal ranges of uncertainty, at least for software (for hardware, the situation depends on the length of the production run). For other sources of knowledge work, such as systems engineering, the COSYSMO definition of size involves a complexity-weighted sum of functional requirements, interfaces, operational scenarios, and critical algorithms.

For many physical systems, weight is used as the primary determinant of size, again often modified by relative complexity. Software, however, doesn't weigh anything, and the usual measure of software size is the number of deliverable source lines of code (SLOC). Even this quantity is hard to standardize; the best set of options for defining it is provided by Park [18]. As SLOC is difficult to estimate during the early stages of system definition, various early proxies for software size have evolved, such as complexity-weighted numbers of requirements, use cases, or external attributes. An example of the latter is function points, a complexity-weighted combination of system inputs, output, queries, internal files, and external interfaces [19].

These approaches are generally useful, but can be misleading in several cases. One involves how much of the functionality will be taken care of by reuse of

[handwritten margin note: function points help estimate SLOC (size range)]

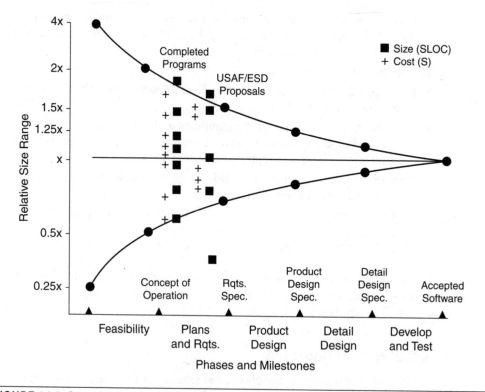

FIGURE 14-2 Cone of Uncertainty with Data Regarding Projects

non-developmental items, such as reusable components, COTS products, or services, at relatively little cost. Another is the effect of nonfunctional requirements, as in the Unaffordable Requirement case study in Chapter 4, in which the alteration of one character in a 2000-page requirements specification (changing the required response time from 1 second to 4 seconds) reduced the cost from $100 million to $30 million. Another is the effect of program objectives, such as in the Weinberg experiment summarized in Figure 1-1, in which the size of the program optimized on output clarity was five times as large as the program optimized for small size, although both had the same functionality and required the same amount of effort.

Particularly for smaller software projects, the high correlation between size, effort, and cost shown in Figure 14-2 has led project managers to say, "If we have to guess at the inputs, such as size, we might as well guess at the outputs, such as effort or cost," leading to such practices as yesterday's-weather analogies, Wideband Delphi, or Planning Poker effort estimation.

The many potential sources of variation suggest that it is generally best to represent sizes as ranges, particularly in the early phases of system definition, and to invest in reducing the size (and estimated effort, cost, and schedule) ranges as the system gets better defined. For example, the COCOMO II model has three versions: an early Application Point model with 5 early-estimable parameters and a factor of 2 uncertainty range, an Early Design model with 13 parameters and a factor of 1.5 uncertainty range, and a Post-Architecture model with 23 parameters and a factor of 1.25 uncertainty range.

14.2.3 Estimation Methods for Development Schedules

The primary techniques for estimating development schedules are similar to those for estimating development costs (e.g., algorithmic models, expert judgment, analogy), but with some differences between hardware and software development. For example, hardware development schedules can generally be reduced by adding more development personnel. However, software development (and other knowledge work such as systems engineering) generally is subject to Brooks' law: "Adding more people to a late software project will make it finish later [20]."

Up to about 1990, software projects were organized to minimize development costs, and software effort and schedule estimation methods converged on a schedule estimation model in which (generally)

$$\text{Schedule in calendar months} = 3 * \sqrt[3]{\text{(Effort in person months)}}.$$

Thus, a project requiring 27 person-months of effort would minimize its costs by using a development schedule of $3 * \sqrt[3]{27} = 9$ calendar months, with an efficient small staff of $27/9 = 3$ people [21].

However, in the 1990s and after, competitive pressures to meet market windows or rapidly respond to threats led to the use of more concurrent, lean, and agile development approaches that had more of a square-root relationship between effort and schedule. For such approaches, a 27 person-month project would use an average of 5.2 people for 5.2 months, and would finish 3.8 months before the 9-month cost-optimized project would finish. Further, agile-project organizations found that even larger schedule compressions could be achieved on smaller (10 or fewer persons) projects with cohesive, experienced agile teams. For example, experiments found that the use of pair programming resulted in 43% reductions in schedules at an added cost in effort of 14% to 15% [22,23]. Other studies summarized in the *Balancing Agility and Discipline* book [24] showed similar results.

The recent Rapid Application Development (RAD) CORADMO-Agile schedule compression estimation model [25] uses several product, process, people, project, and risk factors identified during interviews in a schedule-compression study to successfully estimate the schedule reductions for about a dozen small-to-medium architected-agile calibration projects. A description and a working Excel version of the model are provided on this book's website.

Alternative methods for estimating a project's schedule include critical-path analysis of the project's network of activity predecessors and successors [26]. However, complex projects with numerous subcontractors and high change traffic may find that defining and evolving such a project's activity network is extremely difficult and likely to degrade in accuracy. That said, project networks are invaluable in determining schedules with the following attributes:

- Where there are known development dependencies (e.g., certain development activities cannot start until certain other activities have been completed)
- Where there are long lead times to procure necessary parts or components
- When scheduling constituent systems in an SoS to implement changes for an SoS capability and the constituent system's near-term increments are "fully booked"

The lean concept of pull or on-demand scheduling has been adopted in many software development organizations where the work is generally homogeneous with respect to size and effort. Pull scheduling is designed to maximize flow and delivered value by pulling the most valuable work from a backlog as resources become available. Estimation in pull systems is generally based on the organization's "lead time"—that is, the most probable elapsed time from the acceptance of a development task from the requestor to the delivery of the finished software to the requestor. Lead time is statistically derived from flow measurements and is maintained over time. It may also be used as the basis for service-level agreements between a software development organization and the system development organization. Overall estimates can then be provided based on multiplying the number of tasks by the lead time and then adjusting the result to take into consideration the degree of variability in the task size. Recent work has expanded this concept to integrated scheduling networks to provide additional visibility for the continuous flow of work in operational enterprises and systems of systems as they evolve [27].

14.3 The Bottom Line

As always within the ICSM, the need for and the content of this type of evidence should be risk-driven; for a well-coordinated agile team, its track record should be sufficient. In general, evidence of the feasibility of the cost and schedule estimates should be provided in a Basis of Estimate summary and included in the Feasibility Evidence Description requirements. The Basis of Estimate document should include summaries of and/or pointers to the sources of evidence. For higher-risk estimates, ranges or cumulative probability distributions should be provided.

References

[1] Shenhar, Aaron, & Dvir, Dov. *Reinventing Project Management: The Diamond Approach to Successful Growth and Innovation*. Boston: Harvard Business School Press, 2007: 37–59.

[2] Aroonvatanaporn, Pongtip. *Shrinking the Cone of Uncertainty with Continuous Assessment for Software Team Dynamics in Design and Development*. USC PhD dissertation, 2012.

[3] Valerdi, R. *The Constructive Systems Engineering Cost Estimation Model (COSYSMO)*. USC PhD dissertation, 2005.

[4] Price Systems LLC. *Customers Overview*. Price Systems, 2008.

[5] http://www.galorath.com/index.php/library/hardware; 2013.

[6] Boehm, B., Abts, Chris, Brown, A. Winsor, Chulani, Sunita, Clark, Bradford K., Horowitz, Ellis, Madachy, Ray, Reifer, Donald J., & Steece, Bert. *Software Cost Estimation with COCOMO II*. Upper Saddle River, NJ: Prentice Hall, 2000.

[7] Galorath, D., & Evans, M. *Software Sizing, Estimation, and Risk Management*. Auerbach Publications, 2006.

[8] Putnam, L., and Myers, Ware. *Measures for Excellence: Reliable Software on Time, Within Budget*. Upper Saddle River, NJ: Prentice Hall, 1991.

[9] Price Systems, 2008.

[10] Lane, J. "Cost Model Extensions to Support Systems Engineering Cost Estimation for Complex Systems and Systems of Systems." *Proceedings of the Seventh Conference on Systems Engineering Research,* 2009.

[11] Abts, C., Boehm, B., & Clark, E. "COCOTS: A COTS Software Integration Lifecycle Cost Model: Model Overview and Preliminary Data Collection Findings." *Proceedings ESCOM-SCOPE 2000 Conference*, Munich, Germany, April 18–20, 2000, pp. 325–333.

[12] Boehm, B. *Software Engineering Economics*. Upper Saddle River, NJ: Prentice Hall, 1981.

[13] Cohn, M. *Agile Estimating and Planning.* Upper Saddle River, NJ: Prentice Hall, 2005.

[14] Grenning, J. *Planning Poker.* Renaissance Software Consulting, 2002.

[15] Boehm, B. "Safe and Simple Software Cost Analysis." *IEEE Software.* September/October 2000:14–17.

[16] Moazeni, R., Brown, A. W., & Boehm, B. "Productivity Decline in Directed System of Systems Software Development." *Proceedings, ISPA/SCEA 2009,* June 2009.

[17] Boehm, B., Port, D., Huang, L., & Brown, A. W. "Using the Spiral Model and MBASE to Generate New Acquisition Process Models: SAIV, CAIV, and SCQAIV." *CrossTalk.* January 2002:20–25.

[18] Park, R. *Software Size Measurement: A Framework for Counting Source Statements.* ESC-TR-92-020. Software Engineering Institute, Carnegie Mellon University, 1992.

[19] International Function Points User's Group. 2013. http://www.ifpug.org.

[20] Brooks, F. *The Mythical Man-Month: Essays on Software Engineering,* 2nd ed. Reading, MA: Addison-Wesley Professional, 1995.

[21] Putnam, Lawrence H. "A General Empirical Solution to the Macro Software Sizing and Estimating Problem." *IEEE Transactions on Software Engineering.* 1978;SE-4(4):345–361.

[22] Williams, L., Kessler, R., Cunningham, W., & Jeffries, R. "Strengthening the Case for Pair Programming." *IEEE Software.* August 2000:19–25.

[23] Baheti, P., Gehringer, E., & Stotts, D. "Exploring the Efficacy of Distributed Pair Programming." *Proceedings, XP/Agile Universe 2002.* Springer, 2002:208–220.

[24] Boehm, B., & Turner, R. *Balancing Agility and Discipline.* Addison Wesley, 2004.

[25] Ingold, D., Boehm, B., Koolmanojwong, S., & Lane, J. "A Model for Estimating Agile Project Process and Schedule Acceleration." *Proceedings, ICSSP,* 2013.

[26] Wiest, J., & Levy, F. *A Management Guide to PERT/CPM.* Prentice Hall, 1977.

[27] Turner, R. "A Lean Approach to Scheduling Systems Engineering Resources." *CrossTalk.* May/June, 2013.

15

Risk–Opportunity Assessment and Control

"If you don't actively attack the risks, they will actively attack you."

—Tom Gilb, *Principles of Software Engineering Management*,
Addison-Wesley, 1988

[handwritten: we look for risks & Opportunities]

In Chapter 4, we noted that when we use the term "risk," we include not only the negative uncertainties normally associated with risks, but also the positive uncertainties associated with opportunities. Thus, the ICSM is really risk and opportunity driven, in that whenever resources are expended in identifying and dealing with risks, they can also be expended in identifying and dealing with opportunities. In this chapter, we address both possibilities.

15.1 The Duality of Risks and Opportunities

As discussed in Chapter 4, the generally accepted quantity for reasoning about risk is risk exposure (RE):

*[handwritten: P(L) * (Size loss)]*

$$\text{Risk Exposure (RE)} = \text{Probability (Loss)}^* \text{Size(Loss)}$$

Opportunity can be considered as the opposite of risk, as a decision not to pursue an opportunity has a negative expected value equal to the probability of success for the opportunity times its size of gain if it succeeds. This could be called its risk exposure, but it is more positive to call it its opportunity:

$$\text{Opportunity Exposure} = \text{Probability(Gain)}^* \text{Size(Gain)}$$

Robert Charette defines such a holistic view as risk entrepreneurship [1]. It operates not only at the enterprise level, but also down to the task level, in evaluating choices of reusable components, COTS products, or cloud services. Its practitioners are not extreme thrill seekers; they are careful, judicial, value-aware decision makers. They understand the possible costs of risks as well as the return from the opportunities. However, where the business value is sufficiently large and the risk both understandable and within the bounds of the organization's capability to manage it if something goes awry, they have

Risk entrepeneurship: recognizing risks but also the return from opportunities

the ability and the courage to embrace the risk. Such risk entrepreneurs also have the courage to take the ICSM off-ramp to discontinue or adjust the scope of a project if it becomes clear that the project's risks are too high and unaddressable.

The ICSM provides an excellent framework for risk entrepreneurship through the intentional use of evidence-based decisions, anchor-point milestones, and its fundamental incremental approach. Acknowledging and managing uncertainty is woven throughout the fabric of the four key principles underlying the ICSM.

It should be noted that even when practitioners take a holistic approach in managing opportunities as well as risks, risks generally have a much stronger impact than pure opportunities (those not paired with a risk). The INCOSE/IEEE Systems Engineering Body of Knowledge [2] states that:

> In principle, opportunity management is the duality to risk management, ... Thus, both should be addressed in risk management planning and execution. In practice, however, a positive opportunity exposure will not match a negative risk exposure in utility space, since the positive utility magnitude of improving an expected outcome is considerably less than the negative utility magnitude of failing to meet an expected outcome [3,4].

In other words, the utility function usually applied to project and program managers is strongly weighted toward the negative; that is, making a $1 million loss has about the same negative utility as has the positive utility of making a $5 million gain. Edmund Conrow's excellent book *Effective Risk Management* has some further cautions about overenthusiastic opportunity management [5].

15.2 Fundamentals of Risk-Opportunity Management

impact risk > oppt. gain

Most of us by now have been introduced to the fundamentals of risk management. These don't change dramatically within the ICSM. However, because of the ICSM's focus on stakeholder value, its use of risk in making large and small decisions, and its use of evidence as a means of assessing risk and opportunity, there are more ways to look for opportunities and to better understand risk and risk mitigation. To illustrate these ways, we next provide ICSM enhancements of the fundamental risk management activities of risk assessment and risk control. We will use *risk* as the overarching term, but we will always consider the risk-opportunity dualism in the discussion.

15.2.1 Risk Assessment: Identification, Analysis, and Prioritization

Risk identification produces lists of the project-specific risks or opportunities likely to change a project's outcome. Typical identification techniques include checklists, decomposition, comparison with experience, and examination of decision drivers.

Using the ICSM is particularly helpful in risk identification in two ways. One involves identifying conflicts among the success-critical stakeholders' value propositions. The gray lines in Figure 2-2 of Chapter 2, showing instances of conflicts between the value propositions of the Bank of America MasterNet project's users, acquirers, developers, and maintainers, are good examples of identified risks. These and their counterparts in other projects need to be addressed early during the ICSM Exploration phase, rather than leaving them to be discovered as expensive rework later on.

The other ICSM contribution to risk identification is via its evidence-based decision criteria, in that shortfalls in evidence are uncertainties or probabilities of loss, which when multiplied by their size (loss) becomes risk exposure. Thus, an important risk identification strategy is to look for risks with the highest size of loss. A particularly useful checklist in this regard is a list of the top 10 sources of serious risk: a recent compilation is provided in the next subsection. On the positive side, bringing the stakeholders together to identify and discuss their value propositions often produces opportunities as well as risks, in that their combined experience may identify synergies or capabilities that can be addressed as opportunities to be evaluated for probabilities and sizes of gain for the project.

Risk analysis produces assessments of the gain/loss probability and gain/loss magnitude associated with each of the identified risks, and assessments of the compounding that may occur if risks interact to change probabilities or magnitudes when more than one happens to occur. Typical techniques include network analysis, decision trees, cost models, performance models, and statistical decision analysis.

Even for medium-size projects, risk identification may identify as many as 100 candidate risks to address. However, the maximum number of project-wide risks that a project should take on simultaneously is approximately 10. The overall objective of risk analysis in the ICSM is, therefore, to determine the relative risk exposure of each identified risk—initially just accurately enough to separate the "big rocks" from the "pebbles"—and subsequently to provide more insight on how best to reduce the big-rock probabilities and sizes of loss. If these quantities cannot be accurately determined, the project has two main choices. One is to assign relative values for Probability(Loss) and Size(Loss), generally on a scale of 0 to 10. The other is to buy information to reduce risk, via stakeholder interviews, surveys, prototypes, or high-level models. These forms of evidence generation are addressed in more detail in Chapter 13.

Risk prioritization produces a ranked ordering indicating which risks are to be subjected to budgeted risk mitigation and control, and which are to be monitored for opportunistic risk mitigation or growth to become a serious risk requiring budgeted risk mitigation. The emphasis on risk mitigation budgets reflects the reality that projects have limited budgets, and that the relative cost of risk mitigation is as important as the relative risk or opportunity exposure. This brings into play the second fundamental risk quantity, risk reduction leverage, basically the ratio of risk exposure reduction to the cost of achieving the reduction for a given risk reduction alternative:

$$\text{Risk Reduction Leverage} = (RE_{before} - RE_{after}) / \text{Risk Reduction Cost}$$

Thus, having a high risk exposure may not be a good criterion for choosing which risks will be mitigated. If an emerging technology is so immature that a very large budget or long schedule would be required to reduce its risks of performance, reliability, scalability, or maintainability, it would be best to defer consideration of its use until it reaches a higher level of maturity. Typical risk prioritization techniques include RRL analysis, particularly involving cost–benefit analysis, and Delphi or group-consensus techniques.

15.2.1.1   A Top-10 List of Serious Risk Sources

Following is a recent list of the 10 most serious sources of risk, based on a 2011 USC-CSSE Affiliates survey, recent Standish Group and National Defense Industry Association systems engineering risk surveys, and several other top-10 risk lists coming from a third survey by Arnuphaptrairong [6].

1. Inflated expectations
2. Success-critical stakeholder lack of involvement or value conflicts
3. Underdefined plans and requirements
4. Architecture/reuse/non-developmental item (NDI) conflicts
5. Personnel shortfalls
6. Immature or obsolete processes; unbridled requirements volatility
7. Human–system integration shortfalls
8. Legacy asset incompatibilities
9. Unbalanced nonfunctional requirements or -ilities
10. Immature technology

The following paragraphs explain what these risks are and how the ICSM supports their mitigation.

1. *Inflated Expectations.* When trying to obtain funding for a project, or when trying to win a competitive bidding process to develop a product, there will be strong temptation to overpromise on achievable capabilities while accepting optimistic estimates of budgets and schedules. As with the failed remotely piloted vehicle example in Chapter 3, these lead to a "conspiracy of optimism," in which budget and schedule commitments are initially set at the lower bound of the Cone of Uncertainty, and subsequently travel up the lower curve as realities are encountered. A good way to counter budget and schedule conspiracies of optimism is to require and analyze basis-of-evidence rationales,

showing productivity rates or defect rates from comparable previous projects as evidence of feasibility. Overly optimistic functional capabilities and -ility levels can best be addressed through the evidence development process presented in Chapter 13. Also, as discussed in Chapter 14, realistic cost estimates are necessary to provide realistic return on investment (ROI) business cases for proposed projects, and realistic schedule estimates are necessary to provide realistic market share expectations for the "return" part of the ROI.

2. *Success-Critical Stakeholder Lack of Involvement or Value Conflicts.* Failed projects often focus on a single stakeholder to the extent of disempowering other success-critical stakeholders. In the failed Bank of America Master Net project described in Chapter 2, the project focused too ardently on the voice of the customer, overloading the system with questionable features and making losers of the acquirers and top management with overruns, the developers with unrealistic expectations, and the maintainers with an unfamiliar, poorly performing system incompatible with their other applications. Another frequently encountered case is having the engineers and programmers invoke the Golden Rule ("Do unto others as you would have others do unto you") and create engineer-friendly or programmer-friendly user interfaces that turn off doctors, lawyers, fire dispatchers, and the general public. As noted in Chapter 1, once you create win-lose relationships among the success-critical stakeholders, the entire project will turn into a lose-lose situation not too much later. Chapter 1 also identifies good ways to identify success-critical stakeholders, such as via understanding needs, system scoping, and envisioning opportunities in the ICSM concurrency view, along with developing thorough concepts of operation or value chains.

3. *Underdefined Plans and Requirements.* Often, creating one serious risk will set off others. A good example was the remotely piloted vehicle (RPV) failure story described in Chapter 3, whose initial stakeholders' conspiracy of optimism provided a development budget of $1 billion. Even if it had allocated 30% of its budget or $300 million for systems engineering (as recommended in Figure 4-4), the $300 million was only 10% of the eventual $3 billion cost of the system, leaving the system engineers with inadequate resources to develop both the rainy-day and sunny-day use cases, and to develop adequate evidence of the system architecture's feasibility, resulting in major shortfalls in the system's architecture and risk resolution, and major sources of rework. The concurrent engineering, competitive prototyping approach used in the RPV success story was able to incrementally evaluate more options and perform much more early evidence-based risk identification, and to generate plans, requirements, and architectures that eliminated the major sources of rework.

4. *Architecture/Reuse/Non-Developmental Item Conflicts.* Staying competitive in rapidly evolving marketplaces generally means that much of your system's capability will be provided by commercial products and

services. These are generally opaque and defined only by their interfaces, making it difficult to determine whether their internal assumptions are compatible. Particularly on large projects, different teams may evaluate the NDI components available to support their needs and choose the best-of-breed components for their situation, without realizing that other teams are choosing best-of-breed NDI components with incompatible internal assumptions. This incompatibility may not be recognized as an architecture-breaker problem until integration begins, when it will be very expensive to fix. Such risks are generally identified and resolved early via NDI-interoperability prototyping—that is, buying information to reduce risk. Other NDI-related risks include synchronizing COTS upgrades (typically they are upgraded to a new release every 10 months, and become unsupported after three newer releases; some systems have more than 100 COTS products to synchronize) and making the upgrades synchronous (severe problems may arise with systems of systems having different component systems running versions 3.3, 3.4, and 3.5 of the "same" COTS product). Cloud services present even more of such challenges; for example, Amazon.com was undergoing upgrades every 11 seconds in recent times.

5. *Personnel Shortfalls.* Cost estimation models for knowledge work such as systems engineering (COSYSMO) [7] and software engineering (COCOMO II, SEER, SLIM, True S) identify differences in personnel (capability, experience, and continuity) and team capability (compatibility, continuity) as the largest single contributor (besides size) to differences in cost and productivity. In highly dynamic skilled labor marketplaces, surveys of organizations' top source of risk have identified it to be personnel turnover. From a risk management standpoint, reducing personnel turnover risk involves ways of reducing the probability of loss (building team spirit, career path development, annual or project-completion bonuses) and reducing the size of loss (capturing explicit project information via models, tools, and documentation; spreading tacit knowledge via technical interchange meetings or daily standup meetings; pair or team development; and collective ownership, so that others are able to pick up the work of departed team members).

6. *Immature or Obsolete Processes; Unbridled Requirements Volatility.* Like certain products, some processes are too mature. Sequential, reductionist processes matured for stable and predictable technology and marketplaces have become increasingly risky to use in the increasingly dynamic environments within which most organizations find themselves. But for many traditional organizations and cultures, making instant shifts to highly agile processes will be at least as risky, and more incremental and evolutionary changes such as those suggested at the end of the Introduction will be better. Dynamic environments make requirements volatility inevitable, but the type of unbridled volatility that was a major cause of the U.S. Federal Aviation Administration's Advanced Automation Systems

$3 billion overrun and cancellation needs to be avoided [8]. The ICSM Stage II three-team approach described in Chapter 6 provides a way to stabilize change by having an agile systems engineering team operate in parallel to analyze change requests and perform triage regarding which need to be handled right away, which can be addressed in a future increment, and which can be shelved for future consideration.

7. *Human–System Integration Shortfalls.* As noted with the risk associated with a lack of end-user involvement in system engineering and development, many systems are unnecessarily hard to use or easy to misuse due to minimal involvement of human factors expertise during the early system design stages. Section 3.4 on concurrent hardware, software, and human factors engineering contains guidance on the use of operational concepts, scenarios, and prototypes to address human factors early in the life cycle.

8. *Legacy Asset Incompatibilities.* Fewer and fewer systems have the luxury of being designed as a greenfield system on a clean sheet of paper or whiteboard. In many cases, economic concerns, or the need to provide continuity of service from a brownfield legacy system, require that the design conserve familiarity with the current legacy-system configuration. The ICSM brownfield common case described in Chapter 7 and a more detailed brownfield paper on the ICSM website [9] summarize approaches for reengineering the legacy system to enable incremental transition from the brownfield system to the new system.

9. *Unbalanced Nonfunctional Requirements or -ilities.* The -ilities differ from functional requirements in that they are system-wide properties that specify *how well* the system should perform, as compared to functions that specify *what* the system should perform. Adding a functional requirement to a system's specification tends to have an incremental, additive effect on the system's cost and schedule. Adding an -ility requirement to a system's specification tends to have a system-wide, multiplicative effect on the system's cost and schedule. Also, -ilities are more challenging to specify and evaluate, as their values vary with variations in the system's environment and operational scenarios. Further, the satisfaction of their specifications is much more difficult to verify; it involves much more than placing an X in a functional traceability matrix, as the verification requires considerable effort in analysis across a range of environments and operational scenarios. Such shortfalls in evidence lead to major risks of overruns, as with the Chapter 4 Unaffordable Requirement failure story, where changing the response-time -ility level from 4 seconds to 1 second changed the cost of development from $30 million to $100 million.

10. *Immature Technology.* Technology maturity is often measured by a Technology Readiness Level (TRL), a concept originally developed at NASA in the 1980s [10]. Its scale runs from TRL 1 (basic research) through technology demonstration (TRL 5–6), to technology proven for

use (TRL 7–9). As with -ilities, TRL levels may vary by environment:
a device that is at TRL 9 for use on Earth may be at TRL 3 for use on a
space satellite. Again, the best approach for dealing with these technology
maturity risks is to generate evidence of their operational feasibility in the
environments in which they will be used. For example, suppose that some
of the MedFRS devices under consideration such as the integrated cardiac
monitor, blood pressure monitor, defibrillator, and pulse oximeter and
candidate retinal-scan identification devices have been found to be at TRL
7 in the hospital environments in which they have been initially used, but
that the TRL levels of their performance, interoperability, and fault tolerance
in outdoor catastrophe environments characterized by bad weather,
pollution, and communications outages have not been well established. The
ICSM evidence generation process in Chapter 9 would enable the MedFRS
project team to perform prototyping and interoperability analysis activities
in such environments to determine the candidate equipment versions' TRL
levels in representative catastrophe environments.

15.2.2 Risk Control: Risk Mitigation Planning, Risk Mitigation, Risk Monitoring and Corrective Action

Risk mitigation planning produces plans for addressing each risk (e.g., via avoid-
ance/assurance, transfer, reduction/encouragement, or buying information),
including the coordination of the individual plans with each other and with the
overall project plan. As with risk prioritization, it is important to address situations
where a risk mitigation effort threatens a project's critical path—a particularly
frequent scenario with highly interactive risks that are pushing the technology
frontiers in several directions at once. In such cases, it is often best to defer some
of the capabilities, or if several are needed for success, to reflect this in the project's
schedule. This was the case with the CCPDS-R project described in Chapter 4, which
deferred its Preliminary Design Review from the traditional month 6 to month 14,
by which time all of the risks had been mitigated.

Typical techniques for risk mitigation planning include checklists of resolution
techniques, cost–benefit analysis, and standard risk management plan outlines,
forms, and elements. In many cases, though, the standard forms may be overkill;
a lean alternative is provided later in this chapter.

Risk mitigation produces a situation in which the risks are eliminated or
otherwise resolved (e.g., risk avoidance via relaxation of requirements). Typical
techniques include prototypes, simulations, benchmarks, mission analyses, key-
personnel agreements, design-to-cost approaches, and incremental development
for risk avoidance. Opportunity assurance analysis may use technology trend
analyses, multicorporate agreements, acquisition analyses, and political activities.

The five primary methods of risk mitigation are buying information, risk avoidance, risk transfer, risk reduction, risk acceptance. They are explained by example later in this section.

Risk monitoring and corrective action involves tracking the project's progress toward resolving its risk exposure and taking corrective action where appropriate. Typical techniques include risk management plan milestone tracking and a "top 10 risk event" list whose progress is reviewed and acknowledged at each weekly, monthly, or milestone project review.

A framework/checklist of goals, critical success factors, and questions for risk monitoring at decision points is provided in Appendix A, and a spreadsheet tool for its use is provided on the book's website. Another useful continuous risk monitoring framework is INCOSE's *System Engineering Leading Indicators Guide* [11].

Five fundamental strategies can be used to mitigate a risk: buying information, risk avoidance, risk transfer, risk reduction, and risk acceptance. Like the decision tree, these approaches are equally useful in investigating opportunities.

- *Buying Information.* Sometimes, the best way of mitigating a risk is to gain more insight into the problem. Often prototyping to learn more about requirements or a specific COTS product can reduce or eliminate risks.

- *Risk Avoidance.* Avoiding a risk means taking actions that remove the risk from the critical path or the project. For example, negotiating with the customer to support a reduced performance should certain risks occur effectively mitigate the risk.

- *Risk Transfer.* Transferring risk involves an action that moves the risk from one party to another, or shares the risk exposure between several parties such that no single party is overly burdened.

- *Risk Reduction.* Actions can be taken that reduce the risk exposure by lowering the probability or the magnitude of loss.

- *Risk Acceptance.* This is a decision that the risk exposure is low enough that the project can succeed even if the risk occurs.

Let's consider how each of these strategies would be used for the MedFRS project's COTS selection activity. Suppose that during the MedFRS Valuation phase, there is an opportunity to choose either a higher-performance COTS product B or a comparably priced but lower-performance COTS product C. Without further evidence about the relative merits of COTS products B and C, the project would choose B. However, in this case, the MedFRS project has identified concerns that product B has serious architectural mismatches with another project-essential COTS product A. This will cause the project to overrun by 3 months and $300,000.

The risk management plan in this case could use one or more of the main risk mitigation strategies, In general, the best one to try first is buying information, which will provide more insight on which of the other strategies to employ.

- *Buying Information.* The project decides to spend $30,000 on prototyping the integration of COTS packages B and C with COTS package A. It finds the architectural mismatches between A and B, and the likely resulting costs and schedules needed to resolve them, and also finds that COTS package C would integrate easily with A, albeit with a 10% performance loss. This information enables the stakeholders to better evaluate the other risk mitigation strategies.

- *Risk Avoidance.* This option would be best if the key Ensayo stakeholders agree that the reduction in performance is preferable to the prospect of late delivery, and agree to go with COTS product C rather than product B.

- *Risk Transfer.* If the stakeholders decide that the increase in performance is worth the extra time and money, they should establish a risk reserve of 3 months and $300,000 to be used to the extent that it will be needed during integration, but with award fees for the developer to the extent that less resources are actually needed.

- *Risk Reduction.* To eliminate the schedule risk, the developer and the stakeholders agree to perform a parallel integration of A and B early in the project with the added cost but with no delay in delivery schedule.

- *Risk Acceptance.* The developer decides that having a proprietary solution to integrate products A and B will provide the organization with a competitive edge on future projects, and decides to fund and patent the solution, while giving Ensayo a royalty-free license to use it. From a risk/opportunity standpoint, the business case for having a proprietary solution for integrating A and B would have given the developer a sufficiently high payoff to generate a positive opportunity exposure for taking this option.

Usually, some combination of the risk mitigation strategies will prove mutually acceptable to all of the stakeholders. Nevertheless, in some situations, irreconcilable differences among the stakeholders may leave the project with no feasible options. In this case, it is best to have found this fact out early rather than at the end of the project. Based on Principle 1, the ICSM decision at the milestone review in such a scenario is to discontinue the project with no further expenditure of stakeholders' resources, or to redefine the project scope in such a way that is mutually satisfactory to the stakeholders.

15.3 Risk Management within ICSM

As described in the introduction to this chapter, the ICSM provides a sound foundation for risk entrepreneurship by placing risk and opportunity at the center of the decision process. To support these decisions, evidence-based reviews provide sound data about technical progress, risks, and opportunities.

Many risks stem from stakeholder concerns, misunderstandings, and inconstancy. The incremental commitment and win-win approaches are a significant

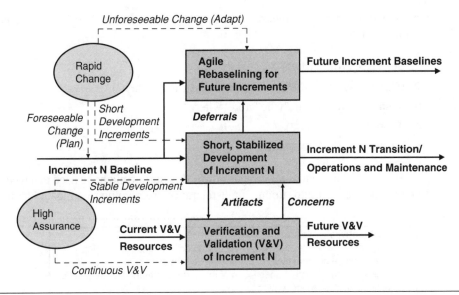

Unforeseeable Change (Adapt)

Rapid
Change

Agile
Rebaselining for
Future Increments

Future Increment Baselines

*Foreseeable
Change
(Plan)*

*Short
Development
Increments*

Deferrals

Increment N Baseline

Short, Stabilized
Development
of Increment N

**Increment N Transition/
Operations and Maintenance**

*Stable Development
Increments*

Artifacts   *Concerns*

High
Assurance

**Current V&V
Resources**

Verification and
Validation (V&V)
of Increment N

**Future V&V
Resources**

Continuous V&V

FIGURE 15-1 ICSM Evolutionary View

mitigation for these risks, and provide a means for discussing business and technical risks before they become problems.

ICSM's incremental development and deployment approach enables feedback and supports adaptability. Providing value early to the customer and users provides for early discovery and fixing of unsatisfactory requirements, supports fine-tuning of capabilities or functions to meet changing needs, and offers the chance to respond to risks that materialize late in the project or unforeseen issues that may arise.

The team structure inherent in the model's *evolutionary view* (Figure 15-1) provides a virtual "crow's nest" for scanning the project horizon. As described, this approach establishes a separate engineering team specifically tracking sources of unforeseeable change or possible opportunities, and adjusting later increments' specifications and plans accordingly. This focused, continuous environmental surveillance provides an ideal tool for risk entrepreneurship at the development level.

15.4 Risk and Opportunity Management Tools

A number of useful tools can be applied within the ICSM framework.

15.4.1 Lean Risk Management Plans

The word "plan" often conjures up a heavyweight document full of boilerplate and hard-to-remember sections. Risk management plans should be particularly lean and risk-driven, as illustrated in the following Lean Risk Management Plan Outline [12]:

1. Objectives (the "why")
2. Deliverables and milestones (the "what" and "when")
3. Responsibilities (the "who" and "where")
4. Approach (the "how")
5. Resources (the "how much")

Figure 15-2 provides an example of how this outline might be used to develop a risk management plan to conduct fault-tolerance prototyping to mitigate identified

---

1. Objectives
Determine, reduce level of risk of the fault tolerance features causing unacceptable performance (e.g., throughput, response time, power consumption). Create a description of and a development plan for a set of low-risk fault tolerance features.

2. Deliverables and Milestones
By week 3: Evaluation of fault tolerance option, assessment of reusable components, draft workload characterization, evaluation plan for prototype exercise, and description of prototype.
By week 7: Operational prototype with key fault tolerance features; work-load simulation; instrumentation and data reduction capabilities; and draft description, plan for fault tolerance features.
By week 10: Evaluation and iteration of prototype; revised description, plan for fault tolerance features.

3. Responsibilities
- System Engineer: G. Rodriguez—Tasks 1, 3, 4, 9, 11; support of tasks 5, 10
- Lead Programmer: C. Lee—Tasks 5, 6, 7, 10; support of tasks 1, 3
- Programmer: J. Wilson—Tasks 2, 8; support of tasks 5, 6, 7, 10

4. Approach
Design-to-Schedule prototyping effort; driven by hypotheses about fault tolerance-performance effects; using multicore processor, real-time OS, add prototype fault tolerance features. Evaluate performance with respect to representative workload. Refine Prototype based on results observed.

5. Resources
$60K	Full-time system engineer, lead programmer, programmer (10 weeks)*(3 staff)*($2K/staff-week)
$0K	3 Dedicated workstations (from project pool)
$0K	2 Target processors (from project pool)
$0K	1 Test co-processor (from project pool)
$10K	Contingencies
$70K	Total

FIGURE 15-2 Sample Lean Risk Management Plan [13]

MedFRS risks that proposed fault-tolerance features might seriously compromise performance aspects such as throughput and real-time deadline satisfaction. It also shows examples of the types of information to be provided for responsibilities, the risk management approach, and the needed funding resources. Note that much of this risk plan information can be provided in a resource-loaded network tool.

15.4.2 Electronic Process Guide

The Electronic Process Guide (EPG) provided on the ICSM website includes templates for top 10 lists and lean risk management plans. It also includes risk in the Commitment Point milestone descriptions and documentation.

15.4.3 Top Ten Critical Risks List

The top 10 critical risks list is a mainstay of many risk management approaches. In essence, the project maintains a current list of the most critical risks along with their associated risk management plans. The status of the risks and the mitigation activities are reviewed at least monthly. The risks on the list will evolve, of course. Some will not occur and become moot. Others will stop being uncertain risks and become problems, in which case they will be taken off the list and added to the project work. Other risks will be added as they are identified, or as their probability increases due to their relation to the project status or for other reasons. The types of risks that are identified vary by ICSM phase. For the MedFRS example project, Chapter 5 identifies the primary risks and pitfalls in its discussion of ICSM Stage I phases.

15.5 Using Risk to Determine How Much Evidence Is Enough

As discussed at the end of Chapter 4, determining how much feasibility evidence is enough is one of the decisions covered by the ICSM *Meta-Principle of Balance: Balancing the risk of doing too little and the risk of doing too much will generally find a middle course sweet spot that is about the best you can do.*

References

[1] Charette, Robert N. "The Competitive Edge of Risk Entrepreneurs." *IEEE IT Professional.* July/August 1999:67–71. See also Charette, Robert N. "On Becoming a Risk Entrepreneur." *American Programmer.* March 1995:10–15.

[2] Pyster, A., et al. Guide to the Systems Engineering Body of Knowledge. *Risk Management.* http://sebokwiki.org/1.1.1/index.php?title=Risk_Management. Accessed July 16, 2013.

[3] Canada, J. R. *Intermediate Economic Analysis for Management and Engineering.* 1971.

[4] Kahneman, D., & Tversky, A. "Prospect Theory: An Analysis of Decision under Risk." *Econometrica.* 1979;47(2):263–292.

[5] Conrow, E. *Effective Risk Management: Some Keys to Success,* 2nd ed. AIAA, 2003.

[6] Arnuphaptrairong, T. "Top Ten Lists of Software Project Risks: Evidence from the Literature Survey." *Proceedings, IMECS 2011.* Hong Kong: March 2011.

[7] Valerdi, R. *The Constructive Systems Engineering Cost Model (COSYSMO).* VDM Verlag, 2008.

[8] Glass, R., & Britcher, Robert N. *The Limits of Software: People, Projects, and Perspectives.* Reading, MA: Addison-Wesley Professional, 1999.

[9] Boehm, B. "Applying the Incremental Commitment Model to Brownfield System Development." *Proceedings, CSER 2009,* April 2009.

[10] Mankins, J. *Technology Readiness Levels: A White Paper.* NASA, Office of Space Access and Technology, Advanced Concepts Office, April 6, 1995.

[11] Roedler, G., Rhodes, D., Schimmoller, H., & Jones, C. (Eds.). *INCOSE System Engineering Leading Indicators Guide, Version 2.0.* INCOSE, February 5, 2010.

[12] Boehm, 2009.

[13] Boehm, B. *Software Engineering Economics.* Englewood Cliffs, NJ: Prentice Hall, 1981:182–285.

Afterword

"There is no law of progress. Our future is in our own hands, to make or to mar. It will be an uphill fight to the end, and would we have it otherwise? Let no one suppose that evolution will ever exempt us from struggles. 'You forget,' said the Devil, with a chuckle, 'that I have been evolving too.'"

—William Ralph Inge, English author and Anglican prelate (1860–1954)

The ICSM has been under development in one way or another since Barry's original 1988 paper. This book is certainly not the final installment in that story. We are relatively certain that the precepts upon which the ICSM is built will remain stable for the next decade and perhaps beyond. However, the implementation of those principles, and the means by which they are achieved and maintained, can change rapidly.

To ensure that the ICSM continues to evolve and sustain relevance to systems development, USC will maintain an active web community around this book: http://csse.usc.edu/ICSM. Supported by the website, it will provide tools, white papers, companion books, and other associated publications. It will also provide discussion forums, FAQs, and other means to encourage the use, consideration, and growth of the ICSM community. Most materials will be free, but there may be occasional items that can be purchased for a nominal fee. Support from Addison Wesley Professional and InformIT will make such purchases easy, as well as provide access to related books in the Addison Wesley Pearson catalog.

Additionally, we hope that other social media outlets (e.g., LinkedIn, Yahoo, Google) will provide users with other ways to interact through groups, circles, or similar collaborative venues.

ICSM Evolution

Our intent is to continue to refine the ICSM. We have no doubt that, in accordance with Mr. Inge's exhortation in the epigraph, the devilish problems facing systems development are evolving at least as quickly as our solutions. We intend to use the ICSM's own principles to guide its improvement—to indeed "practice what we preach." Let's take these principles one by one.

Stakeholder Value-Based Guidance

You, the reader, and your managers or your staff members, are key stakeholders in this work. We have drawn extensively from the insight of those acknowledged in the Preface, and will continue to seek out information on how the ICSM applies (or doesn't) to people's work. Please use the website to share your knowledge and stories, ask questions, suggest new products and tools, or build new products and tools and share them.

Incremental Commitment and Accountability

We had to establish a timebox for the publication of this book, and have been only moderately successful in achieving our goals. We will continue to add material to the website in a variety of forms, and this work will proceed incrementally. Several chapters of this book that were not mature enough for the current edition should appear shortly after publication.

Concurrent Multidisciplinary Engineering

The principle of concurrent multidisciplinary engineering is the key to maintaining the usefulness of the ICSM across the many disciplines we hope it can support. We are particularly interested in hearing from and working with the human factors, cognitive science, complexity theory, and other systems-related areas of study not normally included with the engineering disciplines. We agree with a retired NASA executive who told us that at its best, systems engineering as part of development is making sure decisions are made by getting the right people, with the right skills, talking about the right information, at the right time.

Evidence- and Risk-Based Decisions

We are all four empiricists at heart, so evidence in the form of data would be greatly appreciated. USC, through the COCOMO forum, has been a leader in gathering sanitized information from industry and putting it to use for the entire community. The website provides the means to contact us and to upload stories and data about the principles and practices associated with the ICSM. We hope you will all contribute to that knowledge base. We also hope that the academic community will take advantage of the new field of research provided by the ICSM and its application.

On the Horizon

As we were finishing this book, several organizations continued to both inform the ICSM and challenge it to continue evolving. The following organizations provide a wealth of information that supports system development at all levels, from ultra-large scale to individually created.

Systems Engineering Research Center (SERC) (http://www.sercuarc.org)

SERC is a U.S. Department of Defense university-affiliated research center incorporating more than 20 colleges and universities across the United States. Led by Stevens Institute of Technology and the University of Southern California, the SERC is chartered to demonstrably improve the development, integration, testing, and sustainability of complex systems, services, and enterprises through better systems engineering. Its research includes four mutually supportive thematic areas:

- **Enterprise Systems and Systems of Systems:** The evolving need of very large-scale systems composed of smaller systems, which may be technical, sociotechnical, or even natural systems.
- **Trusted Systems:** The need for ways to conceive, develop, deploy, and sustain safe, secure, dependable, and survivable systems.
- **Systems Engineering and Systems Management Transformation:** The need for ways to acquire complex systems with rapidly changing requirements and technology, which are being deployed into evolving legacy environments.
- **Human Capital Development:** The need to respond to the retirement of the baby boomer generation, the reduced numbers of U.S. citizens entering the technical workforce, and the new systems challenges facing technical staff.

Systems Engineering Body of Knowledge (SEBOK) Wiki (http://www.sebokwiki.org)

A team of systems engineers in a SERC project led by Stevens Institute and the Naval Post Graduate School and supported by INCOSE and IEEE created the SEBOK wiki. It has provided a whole new approach to the collection and dissemination of systems engineering theory and practice. The Guide to the SEBOK is a public, web-based portal. The information in the guide is codified in an easily accessible form, and the larger systems community has the opportunity to engage in discussing, contradicting, contributing to, and evolving the body of knowledge. We believe that this is a significant step in improving systems development across many disciplines.

USC Center for Systems and Software Engineering (CSSE) (http://csse.usc.edu)

The USC Center for Software Engineering keeps current with technology, applications, and economic trends with the help of our 42 industry and government affiliates, through their participation in our annual workshops and collaborative projects. These cover such areas as value-based spiral model extensions, COCOMO cost–schedule–quality estimation model extensions, UML-xADL architecture specification extensions, COTS-based system development, and agile methods.

Software Engineering Method and Theory (SEMAT) (http://semat.org)

SEMAT is an action-oriented group of software engineers and computer scientists who are engaged in improving the state of software engineering. Their goal is a reestablishment of software engineering "based on a solid theory, proven principles, and best practices that include a kernel of widely-agreed elements, extensible for specific uses, address both technology and people issues, are supported by industry, academia, researchers and users, and support extension in the face of changing requirements and technology."

Scaled Agile Framework (SAFe) (http://scaledagileframework.com)

SAFe is an open-source framework for applying widely accepted agile and lean practices across large systems and enterprises. Dean Leffingwell and a group of agile and lean software engineering professionals have assembled a significant amount of materials that have begun to see wider adoption across the software development and IT community.

Appendix A

Evidence Evaluation Framework

Goal 1: Concurrent Definition of System Requirements and Solutions

Critical Success Factors and Questions

CSF 1.1 Understanding of stakeholder needs: capabilities, operational concept, key performance parameters, enterprise fit (legacy)

   a. At the FCR, have the key performance parameters (KPPs) been identified in clear, comprehensive, concise terms that are understandable to the users of the system?

   b. Has a concept of operations (CONOPS) been developed showing that the system can be operated to handle both nominal and off-nominal workloads and meet response time requirements?

   c. Has the ability of the system to meet mission effectiveness goals been verified through the use of modeling and simulation?

   d. Have the success-critical stakeholders been identified and their roles and responsibilities negotiated?

   e. Have questions about the fit of the system into the stakeholders' context—acquirers, end users, administrators, interoperators, maintainers, and so on—been adequately explored?

CSF 1.2 Concurrent exploration of solution opportunities; analysis of alternatives (AoAs) for cost-effectiveness and risk (measures of effectiveness)

   a. Have at least two alternative approaches been explored and evaluated?

b. At the DCR, has the customer structured the program plan to ensure that the contractor addresses the allocation of capabilities to hardware, software, and human elements sufficiently early in the development program?

c. Has the claimed degree of reuse been validated?

d. Have the claimed quality of service guarantees been validated?

e. Have proposed commercial off-the-shelf (COTS) and third-party solutions been validated for maturity, compatibility, supportability, suitability, and effectiveness, throughout the expected system lifetime?

CSF 1.3 System scoping and requirements definition (external interfaces; memoranda of agreement [MoA])

a. Have external interface complexities been identified and addressed via MoA or their equivalent? Is there a plan to mitigate their risks?

b. At the DCR, are the major system-level requirements (including all KPPs) defined sufficiently to provide a stable basis for the development through initial operational capability (IOC)?

c. By the FCR, is there a plan to have information exchange protocols established for the whole system and its segments by the DCR?

d. Have the key stakeholders agreed on the system boundary and assumptions about its environment?

CSF 1.4 Prioritization of requirements and allocation to increments

a. Can an initial capability be achieved within the time that the key program leaders are expected to remain engaged in their current jobs (normally less than 5 years or so after the DCR)? If this is not possible for a complex major development program, can critical subsystems, or at least a key subset of them, be demonstrated within that time frame?

b. At the DCR, do the requirements and proposed solutions take into account likely future mission growth over the program life cycle?

c. Have appropriate early evaluation phases, such as competitive prototyping, been considered or executed for high-risk/low-maturity components of the system?

d. Have stakeholders agreed on prioritization of system features and their allocation to development increments?

Goal 2: System Life-Cycle Organization, Planning, and Staffing

Critical Success Factors and Questions

CSF 2.1 Establishment of stakeholder life-cycle responsibilities, authorities, and accountabilities (RAAs) (for system definition and system development)

a. Are the stakeholders who have been identified as critical to the success of the project represented by highly qualified personnel—those who are collaborative, representative, empowered, committed, and knowledgeable?

b. At the FCR, are there validated plans, budgets, and schedules defining how the pre-DCR activity will be done, and by whom?

c. Has the government attempted to align the duration of the program manager's assignment with key deliverables and milestones in the program?

d. Have the key stakeholders agreed to the proposed assignments of system roles, responsibilities, and authorities?

CSF 2.2 Establishment of integrated product team (IPT) RAAs, cross-IPT coordination needs

a. Does the project make effective use of IPTs throughout the supplier hierarchy?

b. Are the IPTs staffed by highly qualified personnel, as in 2.1 (a)?

c. For IPTs addressing strongly coupled objectives, are there super-IPTs for resolving conflicts among the objectives?

CSF 2.3 Establishment of necessary plans and resources for meeting objectives

a. Have decisions about the use of one-shot, incremental, or evolutionary development been validated for appropriateness and feasibility, and accepted by the key stakeholders?

b. Have system definition, development, testing, and evolution plans, budgets, and schedules been validated for appropriateness and feasibility, and accepted by the key stakeholders?

c. Is there a valid business case for the system, relating the life-cycle system benefits to the system total cost of ownership?

CSF 2.4 Establishment of appropriate source selection, contracting, and incentive structures

a. Has the competitive prototyping option been addressed, and the decision accepted by the key stakeholders?

b. If doing competitive prototyping, have adequate plans and preparations been made for exercising and evaluating the prototypes, and for sustaining core competitive teams during evaluation and downselecting?

c. Is the status of the candidate performer's business and team "healthy," both in terms of business indicators and within the industrial base for the program area? Is the program aligned with the core business of the unit, and staffed adequately and appropriately?

d. Has the acquiring organization successfully completed projects similar to this one in the past?

e. Has the candidate performing organization successfully completed projects similar to this one in the past?

f. Is the program governance process, and in particular the system engineering plan, well articulated and compatible with the goals of the program?

CSF 2.5 Establishment of necessary personnel competencies

a. Does the customer have access over the life of the program to the talent required to manage the program? Does it have a strategy over the life of the program for using the best external experts available?

b. At the DCR, have sufficiently talented and experienced program and systems engineering managers been identified? Have they been empowered to tailor processes and to enforce development stability from the DCR through the Development phase?

c. Has the customer attempted to align the duration of the program manager's assignment with key deliverables and milestones in the program?

d. Is the quantity of developer systems engineering personnel assigned, their skill and seniority mix, and the time phasing of their application throughout the program life cycle appropriate?

Goal 3: Technology Maturing and Architecting

Critical Success Factors and Questions

CSF 3.1 COTS/non-development item (NDI)/services evaluation, selection, validation for maturity and compatibility

a. Have COTS/NDI/services opportunities been evaluated prior to baselining requirements?

    b. Have COTS/NDI/services scalability, compatibility, quality of service, and life-cycle support risks been thoroughly addressed?

    c. Has a COTS/NDI/services life-cycle refreshment strategy been developed and validated?

CSF 3.2 Life-cycle architecture definition and validation

    a. Has the system been partitioned to define segments that can be independently developed and tested to the greatest degree possible?

    b. By the FCR, is there a plan to have internal and external information exchange protocols established and validated for the whole system and its segments by the DCR?

    c. Does the project have adequate processes in place to define the verification, testing and validation, and acceptance of systems and system elements at all phases of definition and development?

    d. Is there a clear, consistent, and traceable relationship between system requirements and architectural elements? Have potential off-nominal architecture-breakers been addressed?

    e. Does the architecture adequately reconcile functional hardware part-of hierarchies with layered software served-by hierarchies?

    f. Has a work breakdown structure (WBS) been developed with the active participation of all relevant stakeholders, which accurately reflects both the hardware and the software product structure?

CSF 3.3 Use of prototypes, exercises, models, and simulations to determine technological solution maturity

    a. Will risky new technology mature before the DCR? Is there a risk mitigation plan?

    b. Have the key nontechnical risk drivers been identified and covered by risk mitigation plans?

    c. Is there a sufficient collection of models and appropriate simulation and exercise environments to validate the selected concept and the CONOPS against the KPPs?

    d. Has the claimed degree of reuse been validated?

CSF 3.4 Validated system engineering, development, manufacturing, operations, and maintenance budgets and schedules

    a. Are the major known cost and schedule drivers and risks explicitly identified, and is there a plan to track and reduce uncertainty?

b. Have the cost confidence levels been developed and accepted by the key system stakeholders?

c. Is there a top-to-bottom plan for how the total system will be integrated and tested? Does it adequately consider integration facilities development and earlier integration testing?

d. If timeboxing or time-determined development is used to stabilize schedules, have features been prioritized and the system architected for ease of adding or dropping borderline features?

e. Are there strategies and plans for evolving the architecture while stabilizing development and providing continuity of service?

Goal 4: Evidence-Based Progress Monitoring and Commitment Reviews

Critical Success Factors and Questions

CSF 4.1 Monitoring of system definition, development, and test progress versus plans

a. Are the levels and formality of plans, metrics, evaluation criteria, and associated mechanisms (e.g., integrated master plan, work breakdown structure) commensurate with the level of project requirements emergence and stability? (Too little is risky for prespecifiable and stable requirements; too much is risky for emergent and unstable requirements.)

b. Are the project's staffing plans and buildup for progress monitoring adequate with respect to required levels of expertise?

c. Have most of the planned project personnel billets been filled with staff possessing at least the required qualification level?

d. Is the project adequately identifying and managing its risks?

e. Have the processes for conducting reviews been evaluated for feasibility, reasonableness, completeness, and assurance of independence?

f. Has compliance with legal, policy, regulatory, standards, and security requirements been clearly demonstrated?

CSF 4.2 Monitoring of feasibility evidence development progress versus plans

a. Has the project identified the highest-risk areas on which to focus feasibility analysis?

b. Has the project analyzed alternative methods of evaluating feasibility (e.g., models, simulations, benchmarks, prototypes, reference checking, past performance) and prepared the infrastructure for using the most cost-effective choices?

c. Has the project identified a full set of representative operational scenarios across which to evaluate feasibility?

d. Has the project prepared milestone plans and earned value targets for measuring progress in developing feasibility evidence?

e. Is the project successfully monitoring progress and applying corrective action where necessary?

CSF 4.3 Monitoring, assessment, and replanning for changes in needs, opportunities, and resources

a. Does the project have an effective strategy for performing triage (accept, defer, reject) on proposed changes, which does not destabilize ongoing development?

b. Does the project have an adequate capability for performing change impact analysis and involving appropriate stakeholders in addressing and prioritizing changes?

c. Is the project adequately verifying and validating proposed changes for feasibility and cost-effectiveness?

CSF 4.4 Use of milestone reviews to ensure stakeholder commitment to proceed

a. Are milestone review dates based on availability of feasibility evidence versus on availability of artifacts or on planned review dates?

b. Are artifacts and evidence of feasibility evaluated and risky shortfalls identified by key stakeholders and independent experts prior to review events?

c. Are developer responses to identified risks prepared prior to review events?

d. Do reviews achieve risk-based concurrence of key stakeholders on whether to proceed into the next phase (proceed; skip a phase; revisit the current phase; terminate or rescope the project)?

Appendix B

Mapping between ICSM and Other Standards

Appendix B shows the relationship between the ICSM and the following standards:

- ISO/IEC 15288: System Engineering Standard
- ISO/IEC 12207: Systems and Software Engineering—Software Life Cycle Processes
- CMMI 1.3: Capability Maturity Model Integration for Development
- SEBOK 1.2: The Systems Engineering Body of Knowledge, version 1.2
- SWEBOK 3.0: The Software Engineering Body of Knowledge, version 3.0
- PMBOK 4.0: The Project Management Body of Knowledge, version 4.0
- ITIL: Information Technology Infrastructure Library, 2011 edition

TABLE B-1 Mapping Between the ICSM and ISO/IEC 15288

Processes/Chapters	Stakeholder VB System	Incremental Commitment	Concurrent Development	Evidence and Risk	Stage I	Stage II	Patterns and Common Cases	ICSM and Your Organization	Evidence-Based Management	Cost and Schedule	Risk	Evidence Evaluation	Value-Based Theory	EPG
	1	2	3	4	5	6	7	8	9	10	11	A	C	D
6.1 Agreement Process														
6.1.1 Acquisition Process	✓	✓	✓	✓	✓	✓	✓	✓	✓	✓	✓	✓	✓	
6.1.2 Supply Process	✓	✓	✓	✓	✓	✓	✓	✓	✓	✓	✓			
6.2 Organizational Project-Enabling Processes														
6.2.1 Life-Cycle Model Management Process		✓	✓		✓	✓	✓	✓						
6.2.2 Infrastructure Management Process			✓		✓	✓								
6.2.3 Project Portfolio Management Process					✓	✓	✓	✓						
6.2.4 Human Resources Management Process	✓	✓			✓	✓								
6.2.5 Quality Management Process		✓	✓	✓	✓	✓			✓	✓	✓	✓	✓	
6.3 Project Processes														
6.3.1 Project Planning Process		✓	✓	✓	✓	✓	✓	✓	✓	✓	✓			
6.3.2 Project Assessment and Control Process		✓	✓	✓	✓	✓	✓	✓	✓	✓	✓	✓		
6.3.3 Decision Management Process		✓		✓	✓	✓	✓	✓	✓	✓	✓			
6.3.4 Risk Management Process			✓	✓	✓			✓	✓	✓	✓			
6.3.5 Configuration Management Process			✓		✓	✓			✓		✓			
6.3.6 Information Management Process	✓	✓	✓	✓	✓	✓	✓		✓	✓	✓	✓	✓	
6.3.7 Measurement Process		✓	✓	✓	✓	✓			✓	✓	✓	✓		

TABLE B-1 Mapping Between the ICSM and ISO/IEC 15288 (*Continued*)

Processes/Chapters	Stakeholder VB System	Incremental Commitment	Concurrent Development	Evidence and Risk	Stage I	Stage II	Patterns and Common Cases	ICSM and Your Organization	Evidence-Based Management	Cost and Schedule	Risk	Evidence Evaluation	Value-Based Theory	EPG
	1	2	3	4	5	6	7	8	9	10	11	A	C	D
6.4 Technical Process														
6.4.1 Stakeholder Requirements Definition Process	✓	✓			✓		✓	✓	✓	✓			✓	
6.4.2 Requirements Analysis Process	✓			✓	✓	✓			✓	✓	✓		✓	
6.4.3 Architectural Design Process		✓	✓	✓	✓		✓		✓		✓	✓		
6.4.4 Implementation Process		✓	✓	✓	✓	✓	✓		✓		✓	✓		
6.4.5 Integration Process			✓	✓		✓			✓		✓	✓		
6.4.6 Verification Process			✓	✓		✓			✓		✓	✓		
6.4.7 Transition Process				✓		✓			✓		✓			
6.4.8 Validation Process	✓	✓		✓		✓								
6.4.9 Operation Process		✓				✓			✓			✓		
6.4.10 Maintenance Process		✓				✓								
6.4.11 Disposal Process		✓				✓			✓			✓		

TABLE B-2 Mapping Between the ICSM and ISO/IEC 12207

Processes/Chapters	Stakeholder VB System	Incremental Commitment	Concurrent Development	Evidence and Risk	Stage I	Stage II	Patterns and Common Cases	ICSM and Your Organization	Evidence-Based Management	Cost and Schedule	Risk	Evidence Evaluation Framework	Value-Based Theory	EPG
	1	2	3	4	5	6	7	8	9	10	11	A	C	D
6.1 Agreement Processes														
6.1.1 Acquisition Process	✓	✓	✓	✓	✓	✓	✓	✓	✓	✓	✓	✓	✓	
6.1.2 Supply Process	✓	✓	✓	✓	✓	✓	✓	✓	✓	✓	✓			
6.2 Organizational Project-Enabling Process														
6.2.1 Life-Cycle Model Management Process		✓	✓		✓	✓	✓	✓						
6.2.2 Infrastructure Management Process			✓		✓	✓								
6.2.3 Project Portfolio Management Process					✓	✓	✓	✓						
6.2.4 Human Resources Management Process	✓	✓			✓	✓								
6.2.5 Quality Management Process		✓	✓	✓	✓	✓			✓	✓	✓	✓	✓	
6.3 Project Processes														
6.3.1 Project Planning Process		✓	✓	✓	✓	✓	✓	✓	✓	✓	✓			
6.3.2 Project Assessment and Control Process		✓	✓	✓	✓	✓	✓	✓	✓	✓	✓	✓		
6.3.3 Decision Management Process		✓		✓	✓	✓	✓	✓	✓	✓	✓			
6.3.4 Risk Management Process			✓	✓	✓			✓	✓	✓	✓	✓		
6.3.5 Configuration Management Process			✓		✓	✓			✓		✓			

TABLE B-2 Mapping Between the ICSM and ISO/IEC 12207 (*Continued*)

Processes/Chapters	Stakeholder VB System	Incremental Commitment	Concurrent Development	Evidence and Risk	Stage I	Stage II	Patterns and Common Cases	ICSM and Your Organization	Evidence-Based Management	Cost and Schedule	Risk	Evidence Evaluation Framework	Value-Based Theory	EPG
	1	2	3	4	5	6	7	8	9	10	11	A	C	D
6.3.6 Information Management Process	✓	✓	✓	✓	✓	✓	✓		✓	✓	✓	✓	✓	
6.3.7 Measurement Process		✓	✓	✓	✓	✓			✓	✓	✓	✓		
6.4 Technical Processes														
6.4.1 Stakeholder Requirements Definition Process	✓	✓			✓		✓	✓	✓	✓			✓	
6.4.2 System Requirements Analysis Process	✓		✓	✓	✓				✓	✓	✓		✓	
6.4.3 System Architectural Design Process		✓	✓	✓	✓		✓		✓		✓	✓		
6.4.4 Implementation Process		✓	✓	✓	✓	✓	✓		✓		✓	✓		
6.4.5 System Integration Process			✓	✓		✓			✓		✓	✓		
6.4.6 System Qualification Testing Process			✓	✓		✓			✓		✓	✓		
6.4.7 Software Installation Process			✓		✓				✓		✓			
6.4.8 Software Acceptance Support Process	✓	✓		✓	✓									
6.4.9 Software Operation Process		✓			✓				✓			✓		
6.4.10 Software Maintenance Process		✓			✓									
6.4.11 Software Disposal Process		✓			✓				✓			✓		

(*Continues*)

TABLE B-2 Mapping Between the ICSM and ISO/IEC 12207 (*Continued*)

Processes/Chapters	Stakeholder VB System (1)	Incremental Commitment (2)	Concurrent Development (3)	Evidence and Risk (4)	Stage I (5)	Stage II (6)	Patterns and Common Cases (7)	ICSM and Your Organization (8)	Evidence-Based Management (9)	Cost and Schedule (10)	Risk (11)	Evidence Evaluation Framework (A)	Value-Based Theory (C)	EPG (D)
7. Software-Specific Processes														
7.1 Software Implementation Processes														
7.1.1 Software Implementation Process		✓	✓	✓	✓	✓	✓		✓			✓		
7.1.2 Software Requirements Analysis Process	✓	✓	✓	✓	✓	✓	✓		✓	✓	✓	✓	✓	
7.1.3 Software Architectural Design Process		✓	✓	✓	✓		✓		✓		✓	✓		
7.1.4 Software Detailed Design Process		✓	✓	✓	✓		✓		✓		✓	✓		
7.1.5 Software Construction Process			✓	✓		✓	✓		✓		✓	✓		
7.1.6 Software Integration Process			✓	✓		✓	✓		✓		✓	✓		
7.1.7 Software Qualification Testing Process		✓	✓	✓	✓	✓			✓		✓	✓		
7.2 Software Support Processes														
7.2.1 Software Documentation Management Process			✓	✓	✓	✓			✓	✓	✓	✓		
7.2.2 Software Configuration Management Process			✓		✓	✓								
7.2.3 Software Quality Assurance Process			✓	✓	✓	✓			✓		✓	✓		
7.2.4 Software Verification Process			✓	✓	✓	✓			✓	✓	✓	✓		
7.2.5 Software Validation Process			✓	✓	✓	✓			✓	✓	✓	✓		
7.2.6 Software Review Process			✓	✓	✓	✓			✓	✓	✓	✓		

TABLE B-2 Mapping Between the ICSM and ISO/IEC 12207 (*Continued*)

Processes/Chapters	Stakeholder VB System	Incremental Commitment	Concurrent Development	Evidence and Risk	Stage I	Stage II	Patterns and Common Cases	ICSM and Your Organization	Evidence-Based Management	Cost and Schedule	Risk	Evidence Evaluation Framework	Value-Based Theory	EPG
	1	2	3	4	5	6	7	8	9	10	11	A	C	D
7.2.7 Software Audit Process			✓	✓	✓	✓			✓	✓	✓	✓		
7.2.8 Software Problem Resolution Process	✓			✓	✓	✓			✓	✓	✓	✓	✓	
7.3 Software Reuse Processes														
7.3.1 Domain Engineering Process				✓	✓		✓	✓						
7.3.2 Reuse Asset Management Process			✓	✓	✓	✓	✓		✓	✓	✓	✓		
7.3.3 Reuse Program Management Process			✓	✓	✓	✓	✓		✓	✓	✓	✓		

TABLE B-3 Mapping Between the ICSM and CMMI 1.3

Process Areas/Chapters	Stakeholder VB System	Incremental Commitment	Concurrent Development	Evidence and Risk	Stage I	Stage II	Patterns and Common Cases	ICSM and Your Organization	Evidence-Based Management	Cost and Schedule	Risk	Evidence Evaluation Framework	Value-Based Theory	EPG
	1	2	3	4	5	6	7	8	9	10	11	A	C	D
Project Monitoring and Control (PMC)	✓	✓	✓	✓	✓	✓	✓		✓		✓	✓	✓	
Project Planning (PP)		✓	✓	✓	✓	✓	✓	✓		✓	✓		✓	
Supplier Agreement Management (SAM)	✓		✓	✓	✓	✓	✓		✓	✓	✓			
Configuration Management (CM)			✓	✓	✓	✓			✓		✓	✓		
Measurement and Analysis (MA)				✓	✓	✓			✓	✓	✓	✓		
Process and Product Quality Assurance (PPQA)				✓	✓	✓			✓	✓	✓	✓		
Technical Solution (TS)		✓	✓	✓	✓	✓	✓			✓	✓			
Validation (VAL)			✓	✓	✓	✓			✓	✓	✓	✓		
Verification (VER)			✓	✓	✓	✓			✓	✓	✓	✓		
Product Integration (PI)		✓	✓	✓		✓			✓			✓		
Requirements Development (RD)	✓	✓	✓	✓	✓	✓	✓		✓					
Organizational Process Definition (OPD)		✓		✓				✓					✓	
Organizational Process Focus (OPF)		✓						✓						
Organizational Training (OT)			✓						✓					
Integrated Project Management (IPM)		✓		✓	✓				✓		✓			
Risk Management (RSKM)			✓	✓	✓	✓	✓	✓			✓			
Decision Analysis and Resolution (DAR)	✓				✓	✓			✓		✓	✓		
Organizational Process Performance (OPP)								✓						
Quantitative Project Management (QPM)			✓								✓			

TABLE B-3 Mapping Between the ICSM and CMMI 1.3 (*Continued*)

Process Areas/Chapters	Stakeholder VB System	Incremental Commitment	Concurrent Development	Evidence and Risk	Stage I	Stage II	Patterns and Common Cases	ICSM and Your Organization	Evidence-Based Management	Cost and Schedule	Risk	Evidence Evaluation Framework	Value-Based Theory	EPG
	1	2	3	4	5	6	7	8	9	10	11	A	C	D
Organizational Performance Management (OPM)								✓						
Causal Analysis and Resolution (CAR)				✓							✓			

TABLE B-4 Mapping Between the ICSM and SEBOK

Knowledge Areas/Chapters	Stakeholder VB System	Incremental Commitment	Concurrent Development	Evidence and Risk	Stage I	Stage II	Patterns and Common Cases	ICSM and Your Organization	Evidence-Based Management	Cost and Schedule	Risk	Evidence Evaluation Framework	Value-Based Theory	EPG
	1	2	3	4	5	6	7	8	9	10	11	A	C	D
3.1 Life-Cycle Models														
3.1.1 Life-Cycle Characteristics							✓	✓						✓
3.1.2 Life-Cycle Process Drivers and Choices					✓		✓	✓			✓			✓
3.1.3 Life-Cycle Process Models: Vee														✓
3.1.4 Life-Cycle Process Models: Iterative					✓	✓	✓	✓						✓
3.1.5 Integration of Process					✓	✓		✓						✓

(*Continues*)

TABLE B-4 Mapping Between the ICSM and SEBOK (*Continued*)

Knowledge Areas/Chapters	Stakeholder VB System	Incremental Commitment	Concurrent Development	Evidence and Risk	Stage I	Stage II	Patterns and Common Cases	ICSM and Your Organization	Evidence-Based Management	Cost and Schedule	Risk	Evidence Evaluation Framework	Value-Based Theory	EPG
	1	2	3	4	5	6	7	8	9	10	11	A	C	D
3.1.6 Lean Engineering							✓	✓						✓
3.2 Concept Definition														
3.2.1 Mission Analysis	✓				✓		✓	✓	✓		✓	✓	✓	
3.2.2 Stakeholder Needs and Requirements	✓	✓		✓	✓				✓		✓	✓	✓	
3.3 System Definition														
3.3.1 System Requirements	✓	✓		✓	✓		✓	✓		✓	✓	✓	✓	
3.3.2 Logical Architecture Design		✓	✓	✓	✓		✓		✓			✓		
3.3.3 Physical Architecture Design		✓	✓	✓	✓		✓		✓			✓		
3.3.4 System Analysis	✓	✓	✓	✓	✓		✓		✓	✓	✓	✓	✓	
3.4 System Realization														
3.4.1 System Implementation		✓	✓	✓		✓	✓		✓			✓		
3.4.2 System Integration		✓	✓			✓	✓		✓			✓		
3.4.3 System Verification		✓	✓	✓	✓				✓			✓		
3.4.4 System Validation		✓	✓	✓	✓				✓			✓		
3.5 System Deployment and Use														
3.5.1 System Deployment		✓	✓		✓	✓	✓			✓				
3.5.2 Operation of the System					✓	✓	✓							
3.5.3 System Maintenance			✓				✓							
3.5.4 Logistics						✓								
3.6 Systems Engineering Management														
3.6.1 Planning	✓	✓	✓	✓	✓	✓	✓	✓	✓	✓	✓		✓	
3.6.2 Assessment and Control	✓	✓	✓	✓	✓	✓			✓	✓	✓	✓		
3.6.3 Risk Management			✓	✓	✓	✓	✓	✓	✓		✓	✓		

TABLE B-4 Mapping Between the ICSM and SEBOK (*Continued*)

Knowledge Areas/Chapters	Stakeholder VB System	Incremental Commitment	Concurrent Development	Evidence and Risk	Stage I	Stage II	Patterns and Common Cases	ICSM and Your Organization	Evidence-Based Management	Cost and Schedule	Risk	Evidence Evaluation Framework	Value-Based Theory	EPG
	1	2	3	4	5	6	7	8	9	10	11	A	C	D
3.6.4 Measurement		✓	✓	✓	✓	✓			✓	✓	✓	✓		
3.6.5 Decision Management	✓	✓		✓	✓	✓	✓		✓	✓	✓	✓		
3.6.6 Configuration Management			✓	✓	✓	✓			✓			✓		
3.6.7 Information Management	✓	✓	✓	✓	✓	✓	✓		✓	✓	✓	✓	✓	
3.6.8 Quality Management			✓	✓	✓	✓			✓	✓	✓	✓	✓	
3.7 Product and Service Life Management														
3.7.1 Service Life Extension		✓			✓				✓	✓				
3.7.2 Updates, Upgrades, and Modernization		✓		✓	✓				✓	✓				
3.7.3 Disposal and Retirement	✓				✓				✓	✓				
3.8 Systems Engineering Standards														
3.8.1 Relevant Standards								✓						✓
3.8.2 Alignment and Comparison								✓						✓
3.8.3 Application of Systems Engineering Standards								✓						✓

TABLE B-5 Mapping Between the ICSM and SWEBOK

Knowledge Areas/ Chapters	Stakeholder VB System	Incremental Commitment	Concurrent Development	Evidence and Risk	Stage I	Stage II	Patterns and Common Cases	ICSM and Your Organization	Evidence-Based Management	Cost and Schedule	Risk	Evidence Evaluation Framework	Mappings ICSM and Standards	Value-Based Theory	EPG
	1	2	3	4	5	6	7	8	9	10	11	A	B	C	D
1. Software Requirements	✓	✓	✓	✓	✓	✓	✓		✓	✓	✓	✓		✓	✓
2. Software Design	✓	✓	✓	✓	✓	✓	✓		✓	✓	✓	✓		✓	✓
3. Software Construction	✓	✓	✓	✓	✓	✓	✓		✓		✓	✓			✓
4. Software Testing	✓	✓	✓	✓	✓	✓	✓		✓		✓	✓			✓
5. Software Maintenance	✓	✓	✓	✓		✓	✓				✓				✓
6. Software Configuration Management	✓	✓	✓	✓	✓	✓	✓		✓		✓	✓			✓
7. Software Engineering Management	✓	✓	✓	✓	✓	✓	✓	✓	✓	✓	✓	✓		✓	✓
8. Software Engineering Models and Methods	✓	✓	✓	✓	✓	✓	✓	✓	✓						✓
9. Software Engineering Process	✓	✓	✓	✓	✓	✓	✓	✓	✓	✓	✓	✓		✓	✓
10. Software Quality	✓	✓	✓	✓	✓	✓	✓	✓	✓		✓	✓		✓	✓
11. Mathematical Foundations			✓	✓						✓	✓			✓	
12. Computing Foundations	✓														
13. Engineering Foundations	✓		✓	✓	✓				✓						
14. Software Engineering Economics		✓		✓	✓	✓				✓	✓			✓	✓
15. Software Engineering Professional Practice													✓		

TABLE B-6 Mapping Between the ICSM and PMBOK

Knowledge Areas/ Chapters	Stakeholder VB System	Incremental Commitment	Concurrent Development	Evidence and Risk	Stage I	Stage II	Patterns and Common Cases	ICSM and Your Organization	Evidence-Based Management	Cost and Schedule	Risk	Evidence Evaluation Framework	Value-Based Theory	EPG
	1	2	3	4	5	6	7	8	9	10	11	A	C	D
Project Integration Management		✓	✓	✓	✓	✓	✓		✓		✓	✓		
Project Scope Management	✓			✓	✓	✓	✓	✓	✓	✓	✓		✓	
Project Time Management		✓	✓	✓	✓	✓	✓		✓	✓	✓			
Project Cost Management			✓	✓	✓	✓	✓		✓	✓				
Project Quality Management	✓		✓	✓	✓	✓	✓		✓	✓	✓	✓		
Project Human Resources Management	✓	✓	✓	✓	✓	✓	✓	✓	✓	✓				
Project Communications Management	✓	✓	✓	✓	✓	✓	✓	✓	✓		✓		✓	
Project Risk Management			✓	✓	✓						✓	✓		
Project Procurement Management	✓	✓	✓	✓	✓		✓		✓	✓	✓	✓	✓	

TABLE B-7 Mapping Between the ICSM and ITIL

Volumes/Chapters	Stakeholder VB System	Incremental Commitment	Concurrent Development	Evidence and Risk	Stage I	Stage II	Patterns and Common Cases	ICSM and Your Organization	Evidence-Based Management	Cost and Schedule	Risk	Framework	Value-Based Theory	EPG
	1	2	3	4	5	6	7	8	9	10	11	A	C	D
1. Service Strategy														
1.1 IT Service Management	✓				✓					✓	✓			
1.2 Service Portfolio Management	✓	✓	✓	✓	✓	✓				✓	✓		✓	
1.3 Financial Management for IT Services				✓	✓	✓				✓				
1.4 Demand Management	✓	✓	✓	✓	✓	✓	✓		✓	✓	✓		✓	
1.5 Business Relationship Management	✓	✓		✓	✓	✓	✓	✓	✓	✓	✓		✓	
2. Service Design														
2.1 Design Coordination		✓	✓	✓	✓	✓	✓	✓	✓		✓	✓		
2.2 Service Catalogue	✓	✓			✓	✓				✓	✓	✓		
2.3 Service Level Management	✓	✓		✓	✓	✓			✓	✓	✓			
2.4 Availability Management		✓	✓	✓	✓	✓				✓	✓			
2.5 Capacity Management		✓	✓	✓	✓	✓				✓	✓			
2.6 IT Service Continuity Management		✓		✓		✓			✓	✓	✓			
2.7 Information Security Management System		✓		✓	✓	✓			✓	✓	✓			
2.8 Supplier Management	✓	✓	✓	✓	✓	✓	✓	✓	✓	✓	✓	✓	✓	
3. Service Transition														
3.1 Transition Planning and Support	✓	✓	✓	✓		✓	✓		✓	✓	✓	✓		
3.2 Change Management	✓	✓	✓	✓	✓	✓	✓	✓	✓	✓	✓	✓		

TABLE B-7 Mapping Between the ICSM and ITIL (*Continued*)

Volumes/Chapters	Stakeholder VB System	Incremental Commitment	Concurrent Development	Evidence and Risk	Stage I	Stage II	Patterns and Common Cases	ICSM and Your Organization	Evidence-Based Management	Cost and Schedule	Risk	Framework	Value-Based Theory	EPG
	1	2	3	4	5	6	7	8	9	10	11	A	C	D
3.3 Service Asset and Configuration Management		✓	✓	✓	✓	✓					✓	✓		
3.4 Release and Deployment Management		✓	✓			✓	✓			✓	✓			
3.5 Service Validation and Testing		✓	✓	✓	✓	✓	✓	✓	✓	✓	✓	✓		
3.6 Change Evaluation	✓	✓	✓	✓	✓	✓	✓	✓	✓	✓	✓	✓		
3.7 Knowledge Management	✓	✓	✓	✓	✓	✓			✓					
4. Service Operation														
4.1 Event Management	✓	✓	✓	✓	✓	✓	✓	✓	✓	✓	✓			
4.2 Incident Management	✓	✓	✓	✓	✓	✓	✓	✓	✓	✓	✓	✓		
4.3 Request Fulfillment	✓	✓	✓	✓	✓	✓	✓	✓	✓	✓	✓	✓		
4.4 Problem Management	✓	✓	✓	✓	✓	✓	✓	✓	✓	✓	✓	✓		
4.5 Identity Management	✓	✓		✓	✓	✓		✓	✓	✓	✓			
5. Continual Service Improvement														
5.1 The 7 Step Improvement Process	✓	✓	✓	✓	✓	✓					✓			

Appendix C

A Value-Based Theory of Systems Engineering

The INCOSE definition of "systems engineering" is "an interdisciplinary approach and means to enable the realization of successful systems." The value-based theory of systems engineering presents necessary and sufficient conditions for realizing a successful system and elaborates them into an executable process. The theory and process are illustrated on a supply-chain system example, and evaluated with respect to criteria for a good theory.

Introduction

A good deal of discussion around the development of the INCOSE Technical Vision [1] has been concerned with the following questions:

- What is the distinguishing intellectual content of systems engineering as compared to other engineering disciplines?
- What is a theoretical basis for systems engineering? What is its content and structure? How does it satisfy the criteria for a good theory? How does it address emerging challenges such as sociotechnical systems, emergent requirements, rapid change, and complex systems of systems? How can it be used in the practice of systems engineering? The practice of systems engineering?

A good place to start is with the *INCOSE definition* of systems engineering: *an interdisciplinary approach and means to enable the realization of successful systems*. A good set of objectives for a theory of systems engineering would therefore be to characterize the nature of "successful systems" and the means for realizing them.

The theory outlined in this appendix presents a set of necessary and sufficient conditions for a system to be successful, and a set of necessary steps for realizing a successful system. Its results depend largely on dealing with the value propositions of the system's success-critical stakeholders. It thereby advances the proposition that the ability to deal with value considerations is a key factor in the distinguishing intellectual content of systems engineering. (Another is the ability to deal with combinations of heterogeneous components and humans.)

The intellectual content of most engineering disciplines is component oriented and value neutral. Ohm's law, Hooke's law, and Newton's laws are excellent means of determining how various physical components perform, but they do not address the contributions of this performance to the value of a system involving various possible combinations of heterogeneous physical components and humans.

A Value-Based Theory of Systems Engineering (VBTSE)

Figure C-1 summarizes the "4+1" structure of the VBTSE. The engine in the center is the success-critical stakeholder (SCS) win-win Theory W [Boehm and Ross, 1989], which addresses the questions of "Which values are important?" and "How is success assured?" for a given systems engineering enterprise. The four additional theories that it draws upon are dependency theory (How do dependencies affect value realization? On which stakeholders does success depend?), utility theory (How important are the values?), decision theory (How do stakeholders'

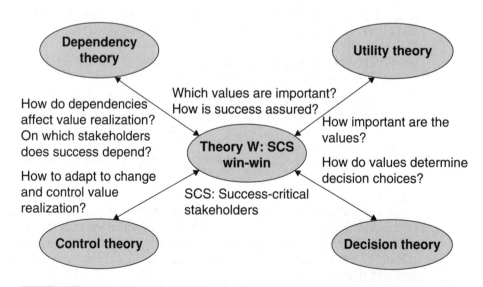

FIGURE C-1 The "4+1" Structure of VBTSE

values determine decisions?), and control theory (How do we adapt to change and control value realization?).

The Central Engine: Theory W

The core of Theory W is the *Fundamental System Success Theorem*: A system will succeed if and only if it makes winners of its success-critical stakeholders.

An informal proof follows. It should be noted that value-based theorems and proofs are less formal than those in such areas as mathematics and physics.

Proof of "if":

1. Everyone significant is a winner.
2. Nobody significant is left to complain.

Proof of "only if":

1. Nobody wants to lose.
2. Prospective losers will refuse to participate, or will counterattack.
3. The usual result is lose-lose.

The proof of "if" is reasonably clear. The proof of "only if" may not be so clear, so we illustrate it in three frequently occurring examples of the primary stakeholders in an enterprise involving a customer contracting with a developer for a software system that will benefit a community of users, as shown in Table C-1.

In Case 1, the customer and the developer attempt to win at the expense of the user by skimping on effort and quality. When presented with the product, the user refuses to use it, leaving everyone a loser with respect to their expectations.

In Case 2, the developer and the user attempt to win at the expense of the customer (usually on a cost-plus contract) by adding numerous low-value "bells and whistles" to the product. When the customer's budget is exhausted without a resulting value-adding product, again everyone is a loser with respect to their expectations.

In Case 3, the user and the customer compile an ambitious set of features to be developed and pressure competing developers to bid low or lose the competition. Once on contract, the surviving bidder will usually counterattack by

TABLE C-1 Win-Lose Generally Becomes Lose-Lose

Proposed Solution	"Winner"	Loser
Quick, cheap, sloppy product	Developer and customer	User
Lots of "bells and whistles"	Developer and user	Customer
Driving too hard a bargain	Customer and user	Developer

colluding with the user or the customer to convert the project into Case 2 (adding user bells and whistles with funded engineering change proposals) or Case 1 (saying, for example, "The contract specifies user-friendly error messages. For my programmers, a memory dump is a user-friendly error message and thus is a contractually compliant deliverable."). Again, everyone is a loser with respect to their expectations.

The Fundamental System Success Theorem does not tell us how to realize and maintain a win-win state. This requires the *System Success Realization Theorem*: Making winners of your success-critical stakeholders requires:

1. Identifying all of the success-critical stakeholders (SCSs).

2. Understanding how the SCSs want to win.

3. Having the SCSs negotiate a win-win set of product and process plans.

4. Controlling progress toward SCS win-win realization, including adaptation to change.

Identifying All of the SCSs: Dependency Theory

Identifying all of the SCSs is in the province of dependency theory (How do dependencies affect value realization?). Dependency theory covers much of the traditional theory of physical systems engineering such as in [2], along with its extensions into "soft systems engineering" such as in [3] and [4].

One aspect of dependency theory addresses theories about stakeholder interdependencies such as sociology and organization theories [5, 6, 7, 8, 9]; theories about human systems integration, particularly the integration of macro-ergonomic and microergonomic concerns [4]; and theories about how people and initiatives combine to realize successful systems, such as in value chains [10] and results chains [11]. Results chains and their extensions are good approaches for identifying a system's success-critical stakeholders, as illustrated in Figure C-3 later in this appendix.

Other aspects of dependencies cover product interdependencies such as physics, electrical engineering, aerospace engineering, civil engineering, computer science, and architectural theories [12, 13, 14]; and process interdependencies such as PERT/Critical Path Methods [15], system dynamics [16], and network flow theory [17]. Dependency theory also covers general interdependencies among products, processes, and stakeholders from such viewpoints as constraint theory [18,19, 20]; optimization theory [21, 22, 23]; engineering economics [24, 25, 26]; operations research [27]; management theory [28, 29, 30, 31]; and general systems engineering text books and handbooks. *The Handbook of Systems Engineering and Management* [32] is a good source of recent coverage of stakeholder interdependencies (Chapters 16–21), product interdependencies (Chapters 8, 12, 13, 23, and 25), process interdependencies (Chapters 1, 2, 14, 15, and 29), and general interdependencies.

Understanding How the SCSs Want to Win: Utility Theory

Understanding how the SCSs want to win (the second predicate in the System Success Realization Theorem) is in the province of utility theory (How important are the values?) [33, 34, 35]. Misunderstanding SCS utility functions does not guarantee failure if an enterprise happens to get lucky. But again, understanding how the SCSs want to win is essentially a necessary condition for win-win achievement. Utility theory also has several branches such as the satisficing theory of bounded rationality [36], multiattribute utility theory [37], and its situation-dependent aspects such as Maslow's hierarchy of needs [38], which states that lower-level needs (food and drink; safety and security) have dominant utilities when unsatisfied and negligible utilities when satisfied.

Having the SCSs Negotiate Win-Win Plans: Decision Theory

Having the SCSs negotiate win-win plans is in the province of decision theory (How do stakeholders' values determine decisions?). Decision theory also has many aspects such as negotiation theory [39, 40], game theory [41, 42], multiattribute decision theory [37], statistical decision theory and the buying of information to reduce risk [43], real options theory [44], and the Theory of Justice [45].

Navigating through all of these decision options can be rather complex. One aid in the stakeholder win-win negotiation context is the win-win equilibrium theory in [46] and [47]. The win-win negotiation model begins with the success-critical stakeholders identifying their win conditions (or value propositions) about the system to be developed and evolved. The SCSs can include considerably more classes than users, customers, and developers. Additional SCS classes can include maintainers, administrators, interoperators of co-dependent systems, testers, marketers, venture capitalists, and, as in [45], representatives of the least-advantaged people whose health, lives, or quality of life may be affected by the system.

Besides win conditions (a synonym for stakeholder value propositions or utility functions), the win-win negotiation model involves agreements (in which all the SCSs agree to adopt a win condition or an option), issues (in which SCSs can identify a conflict between their and others' win conditions), and options (proposals for resolving issues by expanding the option space). Agreements can also be reached by having the SCSs agree to adopt an option to resolve an issue.

A win-win equilibrium state holds when all the win conditions are covered by agreements and there are no outstanding issues. At the beginning of a negotiation, this is true by default. As soon as a stakeholder enters a win condition, the other stakeholders can all accept it via an agreement, in which case the win-win equilibrium state still holds, or some stakeholder enters an issue and an associated conflicting win condition. The negotiation then leaves the win-win equilibrium state, and the stakeholders attempt to formulate options to resolve the issue. The negotiation proceeds until all of the stakeholders' win conditions are entered and the win-win equilibrium state is achieved, or until the stakeholders agree that the project should be disbanded because some issues are irresolvable. In such situations, it is much preferable to determine this before, rather than after, developing the system. In terms of the System Success Realization Theorem, this also makes negotiating win-win plans a necessary condition for win-win achievement.

Controlling Progress toward SCS Win-Win Realization: Control Theory

Controlling progress toward SCS win-win realization (the fourth and final predicate in the System Success Realization Theorem) is in the province of control theory (how to adapt to change and control value realization). As summarized in [48], the necessary conditions for successful enterprise control are observability (the ability to observe the current enterprise state), predictability (the ability to predict whether the enterprise is heading toward an unacceptable state), controllability (the ability to redirect the enterprise toward an acceptable near-term state and a successful end state), and stability (the avoidance of positive feedback cycles that cause control systems to overcompensate and become unstable).

Particularly for VBTSE, it is more important to apply control theory principles to the expected value being realized by the project rather than just to project progress with respect to plans. Traditional "earned value" systems have their uses, but they need to be complemented by business-value and mission-value achievement monitoring and control systems as discussed in [49]. The latter systems involve the use of risk management; adaptive control functions such as market watch and plan renegotiation; and multi-criteria control mechanisms such as BTOPP [50, 11] and balanced scorecards [51]. Particularly in an era of increasing rates of change, this makes both traditional and adaptive control [52] necessary conditions for system success in terms of the System Success Realization Theorem.

Using and Testing the VBTSE: Process Framework and Example

Figure C-2 presents a seven-step process-oriented expansion of the VBTSE framework shown in Figure C-1. In this section, we will apply this version in a step-by-step manner to a supply-chain management system development example. In the next section, we will use the results to evaluate how well it addresses a set of criteria for a good theory.

Step 1: Protagonist Goals

Step 1 of the process starts with a protagonist or change agent who provides the motivating force to get a new project, initiative, or enterprise started. As examples, protagonists can be organization leaders with goals, authority, and resources; entrepreneurs with goals and resources; inventors with goals and ideas; or consortia with shared goals and distributed leadership and resources. (For further process details in a software context, see [53].)

Each class of protagonist will take a somewhat different approach in visiting the seven main steps in Figure C-2 to create and sustain a win-win combination of SCSs to achieve their goals. In this section, we will trace the approach taken by a leader whose goals involve a combination of opportunities and problems, who has the authority and resources to address the goals, and who is open to different ideas for addressing them. She is Susan Swanson, an experienced MBA-holding executive, former bicycling champion, and newly hired CEO of Sierra Mountainbikes, Inc. (a fictitious company representative of two similar companies with less successful projects).

Sierra Mountainbikes Opportunities and Problems

Susan began by convening her management and technology leaders, along with a couple of external consultants, to develop a constructive shared vision of Sierra Mountainbikes' primary opportunities and problems. The results determined a

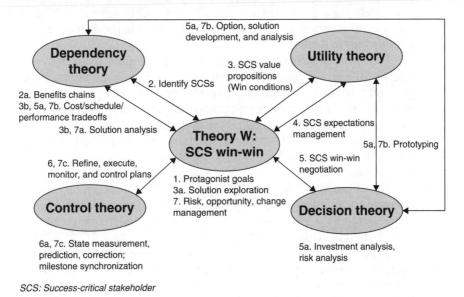

SCS: Success-critical stakeholder

FIGURE C-2 Process-Oriented Expansion of 4+1 VBTSE Framework significant opportunity for growth, as Sierra's bicycles were considered top quality and competitively priced. The major problem area was in Sierra's old manual order processing system. Distributors, retailers, and customers were very frustrated with the high rates of late or wrong deliveries; poor synchronization between order entry, confirmation, and fulfillment; and disorganized responses to problem situations. As sales volumes increased, the problems and overhead expenses continued to escalate.

In considering solution options, Susan and her Sierra team concluded that since their primary core competence was in bicycles rather than software, their best strategy would be to outsource the development of a new order-processing system, but to do it in a way that gave the external developers a share in the system's success. As a result, to address these problems, Sierra entered into a strategic partnership with eServices Inc. for joint development of a new order-processing and fulfillment system. eServices was a growing innovator in the development of supply-chain management systems (an inventor with ideas looking for protagonist leaders with compatible goals and resources to apply their ideas).

Step 2: Identifying the Success-Critical Stakeholders

Step 2 in the process version of the VBTSE shown in Figure C-2 involves identifying all of the success-critical stakeholders involved in achieving a project's goals. As seen in Figure C-3, the Step 2a benefits chain was jointly determined by Sierra and eServices; it includes not only the sales personnel, distributors, retailers, and customers involved in order processing, but also the suppliers involved in timely delivery of Sierra's bicycle components (our benefits chain extension to the Thorp/DMR results chain includes identifying SCSs in parallelograms and unifying assumptions in a table).

The Benefits Chain includes initiatives to integrate the new system with an upgrade of Sierra's supplier, financial, production, and human resources management information systems. The Sierra–eServices strategic partnership is organized around both the system's benefits chain and business case, so that both parties share in the responsibilities and rewards of realizing the system's benefits. Thus, both parties share a motivation to understand and accommodate each other's value propositions or win conditions and to use value-based feedback control to manage the program of initiatives.

This illustrates the "only if" part of the Fundamental System Success Theorem. If Susan had been a traditional cost-cutting, short-horizon executive, Sierra would have contracted for a lowest-bidder order-processing system using Case 3 in Table C-1, and would have ended up with a buggy, unmaintainable stovepipe order-processing system and many downstream order-fulfillment and supplier problems to plague its future. In terms of the VBTSE process in Figure C-2, however, Sierra and eServices used the benefits chain form of dependency theory to identify additional SCSs (sales personnel, distributors, retailers, customers, suppliers) who also need to be brought into the SCS win-win equilibrium state.

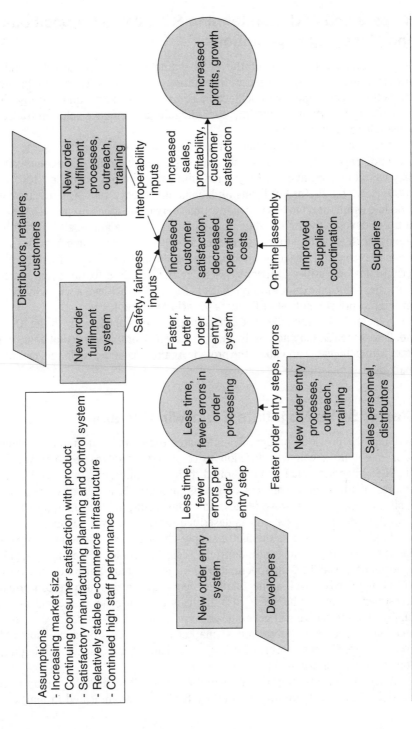

FIGURE C-3 Benefits Chain for Sierra Supply-Chain Management

Steps 3 and 4: Understanding SCS Value Propositions and Managing Expectations

Step 3 (understanding all of the SCSs' value propositions or win conditions) primarily involves utility theory. In addition, it involves Theory W in reconciling SCS win conditions with achievable solutions (Step 3a), and various forms of dependency theory in conducting cost/schedule/performance solution tradeoff and sensitivity analyses (Step 3b).

For example, the suppliers and distributors may identify some complex exception reporting, trend analysis, and customer relations management features they would like to have in the system's initial operational capability (IOC) in early 2005. However, the use of forms of dependency theory such as software cost and schedule estimation models may show that there is too much proposed IOC software to try to develop by the IOC date. In such a case, Sierra and eServices will have to revisit the SCSs' utility functions in Step 4 (expectations management) by showing them the cost and schedule model credentials and results, and asking them to recalibrate their utility functions, prioritize their desired features, and participate in further solution exploration (go back to Step 3a) to achieve a win-win consensus on the top-priority subset of features to include in the IOC.

In some cases, the SCSs' IOC needs might be irreconcilable with the IOC schedule. If so, the SCSs may need to live with a later IOC, or to declare that a SCS win-win state is unachievable and abort the project. Again, it is better to do this earlier rather than later.

Step 5: SCSs Negotiate a Win-Win Decision

Actually, the previous paragraph anticipates the content of Step 5, in which the SCSs negotiate a win-win decision to commit themselves to go forward. Once the SCSs have identified and calibrated their win conditions in Steps 3 and 4, the process of identifying conflicts or issues among win conditions, inventing and exploring options to resolve issues, and converging on agreements to adopt win conditions or options proceeds as described for the win-win negotiation model.

In a situation such as the Sierra supply-chain project, the number of SCSs and the variety of their win conditions (e.g., cost, schedule, personnel, functionality, performance, usability, interoperability) means that multiattribute decision theory will be involved as well as negotiation theory. Susan will also be concerned with investment theory or business case analysis to assure her stakeholders that the supply-chain initiative will generate a strong return on investment. As many of the decisions will involve uncertainties (market trends, COTS product compatibilities, user interface choices), forms of statistical decision theory such as buying information to reduce risk will be involved as well.

User interface prototypes are actually ways of buying information to reduce the risk of misunderstanding SCS utility functions, as indicated in Figure C-2 by the arrow between decision theory and utility theory. The other components of Step 5a in Figure C-2 involve other aspects of dependency theory, such as performance analysis, business case analysis, or critical-path schedule analysis. As also shown in Figure C-2, these analyses will often proceed at increasing levels of detail in supporting Steps 3a, 5a, and 7a as the project proceeds into detailed design, development, integration, and testing.

Table C-2 summarizes the business case analysis for the Sierra project. Dollar values are all in millions of 2004 dollars for simplicity. The analysis compares the expected sales and profits for the current system (columns 4 and 5) and the new system (columns 7 and 8) between 2004 and 2008; the cumulative increase in profits, investment cost, and resulting return on investment (columns 11–13); and expected improvements in other dimensions such as late delivery and customer satisfaction (columns 14–17). The bottom line is a strong 2.97 ROI, plus good expected outcomes in the customer satisfaction dimensions. More detail can be found in [49].

The negotiations converge on a number of win-win agreements, such as involving the suppliers and distributors in reviews, prototype exercising, and beta-testing; having Sierra provide eServices with two of its staff members to work on the software development team; and agreeing on compatible data definitions for product and financial interchange. At one point in the negotiation, an unfortunate go-back is necessary when an agreement on a product definition standard is reversed by the management of one of the distributors, who disclose that they are now committed to an emerging international standard. After some renegotiation, the other SCSs agree to this at some additional cost. But it brings up another necessary condition for successful win-win negotiations (and other collaborative ventures such as agile methods): that the stakeholder representatives be CRACK (collaborative, representative, authorized, committed, and knowledgeable) participants [54]. Some other perspectives on win-win management are found in [55] and [56].

Steps 6 and 7: Planning, Executing, Monitoring, Adapting, and Controlling

As with the dependency analyses, project planning, executing, monitoring, adapting, and controlling proceed incrementally in increasing amounts of detail, generally following a risk-driven spiral process. Questions such as "How much is enough planning, specifying, prototyping, COTS evaluation, business case analysis, architecting, documenting, verifying, validating, etc.?" are best resolved by balancing the risk exposures of doing too little or too much. As Risk Exposure = Probability (Loss) * Value (Loss) is a value-based concept, risk balancing is integral to VBTSE [57].

Value-based planning and control differs most significantly from traditional project planning and control in its emphasis on monitoring progress toward value

TABLE C-2 Expected Benefits and Business Case

Date	Current System				New System Financial								Customers			
	Market Size ($M)	Market Share (%)	Sales	Profits	Market Share (%)	Sales	Profits	Cost Savings	Change in Profits	Cumulative Change in Profits	Cumulative Cost	ROI	Late Delivery (%)	1.1.1 Customer Satisfaction (0-5)	In-Transit Visibility (0-5)	Ease of Use (0-5)
12/31/03	360	20	72	7	20	72	7	0	0	0	0	0	12.4	1.7	1.0	1.8
12/31/04	400	20	80	8	20	80	8	0	0	0	4	-1	11.4	3.0	2.5	3.0
12/31/05	440	20	88	9	22	97	10	2.2	3.2	3.2	6	-.47	7.0	4.0	3.5	4.0
12/31/06	480	20	96	10	25	120	13	3.2	6.2	9.4	6.5	.45	4.0	4.3	4.0	4.3
12/31/07	520	20	104	11	28	146	16	4.0	9.0	18.4	7	1.63	3.0	4.5	4.3	4.5
12/31/08	560	20	112	12	30	168	19	4.4	11.4	29.8	7.5	2.97	2.5	4.6	4.6	4.6

realization rather than toward project completion. Particularly in an era of increasing rates of change in market, technology, organizational, and environmental conditions, there is an increasing probability that managing to a fixed initial set of plans and specifications will produce systems that are out of step and noncompetitive with projects managing adaptively toward evolving value realization.

Perhaps the most provocative example is the traditional technique of "earned value management." It assigns "value" to the completion of project tasks and helps track progress with respect to planned budgets and schedules, but has no way of telling whether completing these tasks will add to or subtract from the business value or mission value of the enterprise. Example failure modes from this approach are systems that had to be 95% redeveloped on delivery because they failed to track evolving requirements [58], and start-up companies that fail to track closure of market windows.

If an organization has used Steps 1–5 to identify SCSs, determine their value propositions, and develop business cases, it has developed the framework to monitor expected value realization, adjust plans, and control progress toward real SCS value achievement. Table C-2 shows how this is done for the Sierra project, based on the initial budgets, schedules, and business case. Value-based monitoring and control for Sierra requires additional effort in terms of technology watch and market watch activities, but these help Sierra to discover early that its in-transit-visibility (ITV) COTS vendor was changing direction away from Sierra's needs. This enabled Sierra to adapt by producing a timely fallback plan, and to proactively identify and approach other likely ITV COTS vendors. The result, as shown in the ITV column and explained in the Risks/Opportunities column of Table C-3, was an initial dip in achieved ITV rating relative to plans, but a recovery to close to the originally planned value. The Risks/Opportunities column also shows a "new hardware competitor" opportunity found by market watch activities that results in a $200,000 hardware cost savings that mostly compensates for the added software costs of the ITV fallback. The use of prioritized requirements to drive value-based Pareto- and risk-based inspection and testing, as discussed in [59] and [60], is another source of software cost savings.

The bottom-line results are a good example of multiattribute quantitative/qualitative balanced-scorecard methods of value-based monitoring, adaptation, and control. They are also a good example of use of the necessary conditions for value-based control based on control theory. A traditional value-neutral "earned value" management system would fail on the criteria of business-value observability, predictability, and controllability, because its plans, measurements, and controls deal only with internal-project progress and not with external business-value observable and controllable factors. They also show the value of adaptive control in changing plans to address new risks and opportunities, along with the associated go-backs to revisit previous analyses and revise previous plans in Steps 7a, 7b, and 7c.

TABLE C-3 Value-Based Expected/Actual Outcome Tracking

Milestone	Schedule	Cost ($K)	Opportunity Cost Savings	Market Share (%)	Annual Sales ($M)	Annual Profits ($M)	Cumulative Profits	ROI	Late Delivery (%)	Customer Satisfaction	ITV	Ease of Use	Risks/Opportunities
Life-Cycle Architecture	3/31/04	400		20	72	7.0			12.4	1.7	1.0	1.8	(1)
	3/31/04	427		20	72	7.0			12.4	1.7	1.0	1.8	
Core Capability Demonstration (CCD)	7/31/04	1050											
	7/20/04	1096								2.4*	1.0*	2.7*	(2)
Software Initial Operational Capability (IOC)	9/30/04	1400											
	9/30/04	1532								2.7*	1.4*	2.8*	
Hardware IOC	9/30/04	3500											(3)
	10/11/04	3432											
Deployed IOC	12/31/04	4000		20	80	8.0	0.0	–1.0	11.4	3.0	2.5	3.0	(4)
	12/20/04	4041		22	88	8.6	0.6	–.85	10.8	2.8	1.6	3.2	
Responsive IOC	3/31/05	4500	300						9.0	3.5	3.0	3.5	
	3/30/05	4604	324						7.4	3.3	1.6	3.8	
Full Operational Capability CCD	7/31/05	5200	1000							3.5*	2.5*	3.8*	(5)
	7/28/05	5328	946										

Full Operational Capability Beta-Testing	9/30/05	5600	1700								3.8*	3.1*	4.1*
	9/30/05	5689	1851										
Full Operational Capability Deployed	12/31/05	6000	2200	22	106	12.2	3.2	–.47	7.0	4.0	3.5	4.0
	12/20/05	5977	2483	24	115	13.5	5.1	–.15	4.8	4.1	3.3	4.2
Release 2.1	6/30/06	6250										

(1) Increased COTS ITV risk, fallback identified.
(2) Using COTS ITV fallback; new HW competitor; renegotiating HW.
(3) $200,000 savings from renegotiated HW.
(4) New COTS ITV source identified, being prototyped.
(5) New COTS ITV source initially integrated.
* Interim ratings based on trial use.

VBSE Theory Evaluation with Respect to Goodness Criteria

The Sierra example in the previous section provides an opportunity to evaluate the VBTSE theory with respect to a set of criteria for a good theory discussed further in [53].

Utility: Addressing Critical Success Factors. The results chain method in Step 2 identified missing success-critical initiatives and stakeholders that were the downfall of supply-chain initiatives at Hershey's and Toys "R" Us [61]. The risk-driven inspection and test approaches in Step 6 avoid wasting inspection and test time on trivial-value aspects of the system.

Generality: Covering procedural, technical, economic, and human concerns; covering small and large systems. The seven-step process and its ability to accommodate parallel activities and go-backs were sufficient to cover the Sierra project's procedural needs. Technical and economic concerns are addressed in the use of dependency theory for cost, schedule, performance, and business case analyses in Steps 3a, 5a, and 7b. Human concerns are the essence of Theory W and utility theory, and of the SCS negotiations in Step 5. The steps in the VBTSE have worked well for several mid-sized supply-chain and customer-relations management systems similar to Sierra, for more than 100 small real-client e-services projects at USC, and as a framework for addressing very large systems of systems in such areas as defense and air traffic control.

Practicality: Supporting practical needs for prediction, diagnosis, solution synthesis, good-practice generation, and explanation. The theory draws on a wide variety of dependency models (e.g., cost, schedule, performance, quality) to predict outcomes. In a stable, well-understood environment, managing to the predictions usually produces a self-fulfilling prophecy. In less stable and less familiar situations such as the Sierra case study, dependency theory is able to diagnose risks such as missing stakeholders in Step 2, Theory W is able to support synthesis of SCS win-win solutions in Steps 3–5, and adaptive control theory is able to generate good value-achievement monitoring practices to support in-process diagnosis and re-synthesis in Steps 6 and 7. The control theory necessary conditions of observability, predictability, and controllability are able to explain why traditional earned value systems would not have addressed and resolved these value-domain problems.

Preciseness: Providing situation-specific and accurate guidance. The theory is no more (and no less) accurate than its constituent theories in predicting outcomes of unprecedented situations, but it is able to provide situation-specific guidance, as shown in its application to the Sierra supply-chain project. Also, several examples were provided in the Sierra process discussion of how the theory would have generated different guidance in different situations, such as with the distributor management's reversal of a win-win agreement on a product definition standard in Step 5, and with the ITV COTS vendor's change of direction in Steps 6 and 7.

Parsimony: Avoiding excess complexity; ease of learning and application. The theory's use of risk management to determine "how much is enough" for planning, specifying, testing, and other steps helps avoid excess complexity and makes "everything as simple as possible, but no simpler" (Einstein, 1879–1955). Its ease of learning and use has been tested mainly on USC's more than 100 e-services projects. These are developed by teams of five to six MS-level students who learn the technologies as they go, and have a 92% success rate of on-time, satisfied-customer delivery [62].

Falsifiability: Ability to be empirically refuted. The case study identified a particular situation in which application of the theory could not produce a win-win solution, which would lead to a timely decision to cancel the project. This involved incompatible and non-negotiable SCS win conditions about IOC content and schedule in Steps 3 and 4. A similar outcome could have resulted from the distributor management change of direction in Step 5.

Actually, there are several other classes of situations in which our experience has shown that the win-win approach may not succeed. One is that *people may disguise their true win conditions*. In one situation, a stakeholder rejected a COTS product for being too expensive. When the price was lowered, the stakeholder said that some essential features were missing. When the vendor offered to supply the features at no extra cost, the true reason came out: the stakeholder had experienced bad dealings with the COTS vendor in the past.

Another situation in which the win-win approach may fail is when *some people like to win by making others lose*. It is best to seek other partners when you encounter such people. Another is that *you can't make omelets without breaking eggs*. Many large-scale dams that benefited millions of people had to drown some other people's homes and villages. Generous payments can reduce the loss, but generally not completely eliminate it. Finally, *some situations have only one winner*. A good example involves political elections, in which political parties are motivated to discredit and demonize the candidates and platforms of other parties.

However, many apparent only-one-winner or zero-sum-game situations can be turned into win-win situations by expanding the option space. A good example is provided in *Getting to Yes* [40], in which a boundary-line location stalemate on ownership of the Sinai Desert between Egypt and Israel was resolved by creating a new option: the land was given back to Egypt, satisfying its territorial win condition, but it was turned into a demilitarized zone, satisfying Israel's security win condition. Other examples are provided in [63].

Conclusions and Areas for Further Research

The VBTSE has been shown to apply well to a reasonably complex supply chain application. In other situations, versions of the theory have been successfully applied to more than 100 small e-services applications, and to the initial stages of some very large systems of systems. The VBSTE satisfies the main criteria for a good theory (utility, generality, practicality, preciseness, parsimony, and falsifiability) reasonably well, particularly when compared to other theories involving explanations of human behavior.

The theory identifies several fruitful areas for further research. Some of these areas involve elaborations of aspects of utility theory, decision theory, and dependency theory to address particular VBTSE issues. Others are extensions of the theory to cover such areas as manufacturing, lean and agile methods, quality assurance, COTS-based applications, life-cycle support, and combinations of these and the other areas covered. Finally, as with all theories, the initial VBSE theory needs many more tests. The easiest tests to start with address its ability to explain differences between success and failure on completed projects. Other tests that can be done right away examine its ability to generate good systems and software engineering practices; an early example is found in [63].

Further analyses can be performed on the VBSTE's consistency with other theories, such as the chaos-type theories underlying agile and adaptive software development [52] or the theories underlying formal software development [64] and generative programming approaches [65], and mathematical systems engineering theories [2]. Tests of utility, generality, practicality, preciseness, and parsimony basically involve trying to apply the theory in different situations, observing its successes and shortfalls, and generating improvements in the theory that improve its capability in different situations or uncover unstated assumptions that should be made explicit to limit its domain of dependable applicability. We hope that this initial presentation of the theory will be sufficiently attractive for people to give this option a try.

Acknowledgments

The research described in this appendix has been supported by a National Science Foundation grant "Value Based Science of Design," and by the affiliates of the USC Center for Software Engineering.

References

[1] Crisp, H., et al. *INCOSE Technical Vision*, Version 1.3. INCOSE, September 2005.

[2] Wymore, A. Wayne. *A Mathematical Theory of Systems Engineering: The Elements*. New York: Wiley, 1967.

[3] Checkland, P. *Systems Thinking, Systems Practice*. Wiley, 1981.

[4] Booher, H. (Ed.). *Handbook of Human–Systems Integration*. Wiley, 2003.

[5] Argyris, C. *Organizational Learning*. Reading, MA: Addison-Wesley Professional, 1978.

[6] Daft, R. *Organization Theory and Design* (8th ed.). South-Western College Publishing, 2003.

[7] March, J., and Simon, H. *Organizations*. Wiley, 1958.

[8] Parsons, T. *Social Systems and the Evolution of Action Theory*. Free Press, 1977.

[9] Rifkin, S. *The Parsons Game: The First Simulation of Talcott Parsons' Theory of Action*. PhD dissertation, George Washington University, 2004.

[10] Baldwin, C., Clark, K., Magretta, J., Dyer, J., Fisher, M., and Fites, D. *Managing the Value Chain*. Harvard Business School Press, 2000.

[11] Thorp, J., and DMR's Center for Strategic Leadership. *The Information Paradox: Realizing the Benefits of Information Technology*. McGraw-Hill, 1998.

[12] Alexander, C. *The Timeless Way of Building*. Oxford University Press, 1979.

[13] Rechtin, E. *Systems Architecting: Creating and Building Complex Systems*. Upper Saddle River, NJ: Prentice Hall, 1991.

[14] Shaw, M., and Garlan, David. *Software Architecture: Perspectives on an Emerging Discipline*. Upper Saddle River, NJ: Prentice Hall, 1996.

[15] Wiest, J. D., and Levy, F. K. *Management Guide to PERT/CPM*. Upper Saddle River, NJ: Prentice Hall, 1970.

[16] Forrester, J. *Industrial Dynamics*. MIT Press, 1961.

[17] Ford, L., and Fulkerson, D. R. *Flows in Networks*. Princeton University Press, 1962.

[18] Friedman, G. "Constraint Theory." *International Journal of Systems Science*. 1976.

[19] Friedman, G. *Constraint Theory: Multidimensional Mathematical Model Management*. Springer, 2005.

[20] Goldratt, E. *The Goal*. North River Press, 1984.

[21] Bellman, R. *Dynamic Programming*. Princeton University Press, 1957.

[22] Dantzig, G. *Linear Programming and Extensions*. Princeton University Press, 1963.

[23] Intriligator, M. *Mathematical Optimization and Economic Theory*. SIAM Press, 2002.

[24] Boehm, B. *Software Engineering Economics*. Upper Saddle River, NJ: Prentice Hall, 1981.

[25] Marschak, J., and Radner, R. *Economic Theory of Teams*. Yale University Press, 1972.

[26] Newnan, D., Eschenbach, T., and Lavelle, J. *Engineering Economic Analysis, Ninth Edition*. Oxford University Press, 2004.

[27] Churchman, C. West, Ackoff, Russell L., and Arnoff, E. Leonard. *Introduction to Operations Research*. New York: Wiley, 1957.

[28] Cyert, R., and March, James G. *A Behavioral Theory of the Firm*. Upper Saddle River, NJ: Prentice Hall, 1964.

[29] Koskela, L., and Howell, G. "The Underlying Theory of Project Management Is Obsolete." *Proceedings, AMI Research Conference*. 2002:293–302.

[30] Simon, H. *The Science of the Artificial*. MIT Press, 1969.

[31] Womack, J., and Jones, D. *Lean Thinking*. Simon and Schuster, 1996.

[32] Sage, A., and Rouse, W. *Handbook of Systems Engineering and Management*. Wiley, 1999.

[33] Debreu, G. *Theory of Value*. Wiley, 1959.

[34] Dupuit, J. "On the Measurement of the Utility of Public Works," translated by R. H. Barback. *International Economic Papers*, 1844(1952);2:83–110.

[35] Fishburn, P. C. *The Foundations of Expected Utility*. Dordrecht, 1982.

[36] Simon, H. *Models of Man*. Wiley, 1957.

[37] Keeney, R. L., and Raiffa, H. *Decisions with Multiple Objectives: Preferences and Value Tradeoffs*. Cambridge University Press, 1976.

[38] Maslow, A. *Motivation and Personality*. Harper, 1954.

[39] Raiffa, H. *The Art and Science of Negotiation*. Belknap/Harvard University Press, 1982.

[40] Fisher, R., and Ury, W. *Getting to Yes: Negotiating Agreement without Giving in*. Houghton Mifflin, 1981.

[41] Luce, R. D., and Raiffa, H. *Games and Decisions*. John Wiley, 1957.

[42] von Neumann, J., and Morgenstern, O. *Theory of Games and Economic Behavior*. Princeton University Press, 1944.

[43] Blackwell, D., and Girshick, M. *Theory of Games and Statistical Decisions*. Wiley, 1954.

[44] Luehrman, T. A. "Investment Opportunities as Real Options: Getting Started on the Numbers." *Harvard Business Review*. July/August 1998:51–67.

[45] Rawls, J. *Theory of Justice*. Belknap/Harvard University Press, 1971, 1999.

[46] Boehm, B., and Bose, P. "A Collaborative Spiral Software Process Model Based on Theory W." *Proceedings, ICSP 3, IEEE*, October 1994.

[47] Lee, M. J. *Foundations of the WinWin Requirements Negotiation System*. PhD dissertation, University of Southern California, 1996.

[48] Brogan, W. *Modern Control Theory*. Upper Saddle River, NJ: Prentice Hall, 1974 (3rd ed., 1991).

[49] Boehm, B., and Huang, L. "Value-Based Software Engineering: A Case Study." *IEEE Computer*. March 2003:21–29.

[50] Scott Morton, M. *The Corporation of the 1990s: Information Technology and Organization Transformation*. Oxford University Press, 1991.

[51] Kaplan, R., and Norton, D. *The Balanced Scorecard: Translating Strategy into Action*. Harvard Business School Press, 1996.

[52] Highsmith, J. *Adaptive Software Development*. Dorset House, 2000.

[53] Boehm B., and Jain, A. "An Initial Theory of Value-Based Software Engineering." In S. Biffl, A. Aurum, B. Boehm, H. Erdogmus, and P. Gruenbacher (Eds.), *Value-Based Software Engineering*. Springer Verlag, 2005:15–37.

[54] Boehm, B., and Turner, Richard. *Balancing Agility and Discipline: A Guide for the Perplexed*. Boston, MA: Addison-Wesley Professional, 2004.

[55] Waitley, D. *The Double Win*. Berkeley, 1985.

[56] Covey, S. *The Seven Habits of Highly Successful People*. Fireside/Simon & Schuster, 1989.

[57] Boehm, B. "VBSE: Seven Key Elements and Ethical Considerations." In S. Biffl, A. Aurum, B. Boehm, H. Erdogmus, and P. Gruenbacher (Eds.), *Value-Based Software Engineering*. Springer Verlag, 2005.

[58] Boehm, B. "Software and Its Impact: A Quantitative Assessment." *Datamation*. May 1973:48–59.

[59] Gerrard, P., and Thompson, N. *Risk-Based E-Business Testing*. Artech House, 2002.

[60] Lee, K., and Boehm, B. "Empirical Results from an Experiment on Value-Based Review (VBR) Processed." *International Symposium on Empirical Software Engineering*. 2005.

[61] Carr, D. "Sweet Victory." *Baseline*. December 2002.

[62] Boehm, B., Egyed, A., Kwan, J., Port, D., Shah, A., and Madachy, R. "Using the WinWin Spiral Model: A Case Study." *IEEE Computer*. July 1998:33–44.

[63] Boehm, B., and Ross, R. "Theory-W Software Project Management: Principles and Examples." *IEEE Trans. SW Engineering*. July 1989:902–916.

[64] Jones, C. B. *Software Development: A Rigorous Approach*. Upper Saddle River, NJ: Prentice Hall, 1980.

[65] Czarnecki, K., and Eisenecker, Ulrich. *Generative Programming: Methods, Tools, and Applications*. Boston, MA: Addison-Wesley Professional, 2000.

Index

Safari
Books Online

FREE
Online Edition

Your purchase of *The Incremental Commitment Spiral Model* includes access to a free online edition for 45 days through the **Safari Books Online** subscription service. Nearly every Addison-Wesley Professional book is available online through **Safari Books Online**, along with thousands of books and videos from publishers such as Cisco Press, Exam Cram, IBM Press, O'Reilly Media, Prentice Hall, Que, Sams, and VMware Press.

Safari Books Online is a digital library providing searchable, on-demand access to thousands of technology, digital media, and professional development books and videos from leading publishers. With one monthly or yearly subscription price, you get unlimited access to learning tools and information on topics including mobile app and software development, tips and tricks on using your favorite gadgets, networking, project management, graphic design, and much more.

Activate your FREE Online Edition at
informit.com/safarifree

STEP 1:   Enter the coupon code: ASXKWWA.

STEP 2:   New Safari users, complete the brief registration form.
Safari subscribers, just log in.

If you have difficulty registering on Safari or accessing the online edition,
please e-mail customer-service@safaribooksonline.com

ICSM Concurrency View

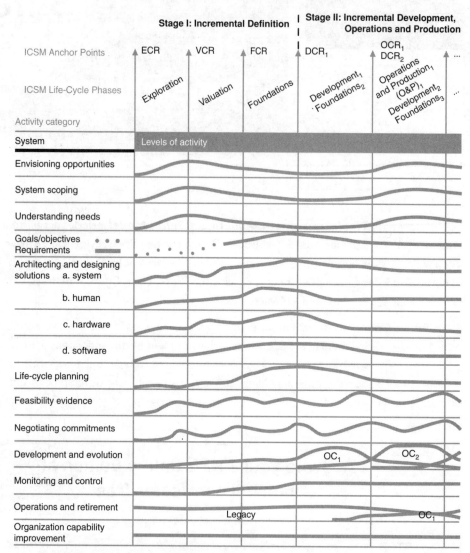

	Stage I: Incremental Definition	Stage II: Incremental Development, Operations and Production

ICSM Anchor Points: ECR · VCR · FCR | DCR_1 | OCR_1 DCR_2 · ...

ICSM Life-Cycle Phases: Exploration · Valuation · Foundations | $Development_1$ $Foundations_2$ | $Operations$ and $Production_1$ $(O\&P)_1$ $Development_2$ $Foundations_3$ · ...

Activity category

- System — Levels of activity
- Envisioning opportunities
- System scoping
- Understanding needs
- Goals/objectives · · ·
- Requirements ▬▬▬
- Architecting and designing solutions a. system
- b. human
- c. hardware
- d. software
- Life-cycle planning
- Feasibility evidence
- Negotiating commitments
- Development and evolution OC_1 OC_2
- Monitoring and control
- Operations and retirement Legacy OC_1
- Organization capability improvement

OC = Operational Capability   ECR = Exploration Commitment Review   VCR = Valuation Commitment Review
FCR = Foundations Commitment DCR_n = Development Commitment Review$_n$ OCR_n = Operations Commitment Review$_n$

Reprinted with permission from *Human-System Integration in the System Development Process*, 2007 by the National Academy of Sciences, Courtesy of the National Academies Press, Washington, D.C.